To Improve Health and Health Care, 1998–1999

Stephen L. Isaacs and
James R. Knickman, Editors

Foreword by Steven A. Schroeder

To Improve Health and Health Care, 1998–1999

The Robert Wood Johnson Foundation Anthology

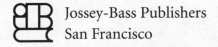 Jossey-Bass Publishers
San Francisco

Jossey-Bass books and products are available through most bookstores. To contact Jossey-Bass directly, call (888) 378-2537, fax to (800) 605-2665, or visit our website at www.josseybass.com.

Substantial discounts on bulk quantities of Jossey-Bass books are available to corporations, professional associations, and other organizations. For details and discount information, contact the special sales department at Jossey-Bass.

For sales outside the United States, please contact your local Simon & Schuster International Office.

 Manufactured in the United States of America on Lyons Falls Turin Book. This paper is acid-free and 100 percent totally chlorine-free.

Library of Congress Cataloging-in-Publication Data

To improve health and health care, 1998–1999 : the Robert Wood Johnson Foundation anthology / Stephen L. Isaacs and James R. Knickman, editors ; foreword by Stephen A. Schroeder. — 1st ed.
    p.   cm.
  Includes bibliographical references and index.
  ISBN 0-7879-4391-6 (cloth : acid-free paper)
  1. Robert Wood Johnson Foundation.   2. Public health—Research grants—United States.   3. Public health—United States—Endowments. 4. Medicine—Research grants—United States.   I. Isaacs, Stephen L. II. Knickman, James.   III. Robert Wood Johnson Foundation.
  RA440.87.U6 T6 1998
  610'.79'73—ddc21
                                                                                          98-25526
                                                                                          CIP

FIRST EDITION
PB Printing   10 9 8 7 6 5 4 3 2 1

~ Contents

—⁓— Introduction

As we approach the last year of the twentieth century, market forces increasingly dictate the way in which health services are delivered; government can no longer be counted on to provide services for its neediest citizens; and an aging population, with its attendant chronic conditions, threatens to strain a health care system attuned to treating acute illnesses. Moreover, as addictions and unhealthy behaviors cut short the lives of too many Americans, the need to confront directly the behavioral factors that influence health becomes increasingly clear. These are monumental challenges—the kinds that The Robert Wood Johnson Foundation has been addressing since 1972 through its program investments.

These investments reflect the Foundation's mission of improving the health and health care of all Americans. Through the demonstration, research, training, and communications programs it funds, it attempts to advance one or more of its three goals: to improve access to basic health care for Americans of all ages; to improve services for people with chronic illnesses; and to reduce the harm caused by substance abuse. Both the goals and the investments are substantial. In 1997 alone, the Foundation awarded $331 million to carry out more than one thousand grants.

This book, the second in The Robert Wood Johnson Foundation *Anthology* series, has three purposes. First, to demystify the world of philanthropy—at least as seen from the Foundation's vantage point. Second, to provide a public accounting of the Foundation's program investments. Third and finally, to offer useful lessons gained from more than a quarter century of grant making.

To accomplish these purposes, we invited the authors—some of whom work for the Foundation, others of whom come from institutions that manage or evaluate Foundation-funded programs, and two of whom are professional journalists—to discuss as candidly as possible why programs were launched, what happened under them, and what lessons were gained from them. We selected programs that were mature, had the potential to provide important lessons, and represented a range of the Foundation's interests.

FOREWORD

Programs do not appear in a vacuum—either politically, economically, or philosophically. In the Foreword, Steven Schroeder, president of The Robert Wood Johnson Foundation, articulates the core values that frame the Foundation's investment choices and shape its culture. Adapted from a presentation he made to the board of trustees in July 1997, Dr. Schroeder's message seeks to identify the fundamental principles that characterize the Foundation.

COMBATING SUBSTANCE ABUSE

In 1991, the Foundation broke new ground by adopting a new goal: to reduce the harm caused by substance abuse. In the first chapter, Robert Hughes, a Foundation vice president, discusses why and how the organization became involved in substance abuse in the first place. Looking at both the people involved and the institutional processes, he reflects on the significance of goal setting for philanthropy and offers an insider's guide to the workings of a major foundation.

Once the Foundation embraced the substance abuse goal, it then developed a number of strategies to reach it. One of them was to seed the new field of tobacco policy research. In Chapter Two, Marjorie Gutman, David Altman, and Robert Rabin—each of whom has played a key part in developing this new field—write about two national tobacco policy research initiatives launched by the Foundation and the significance of the research they produced. The chapter demonstrates the potentially important role that such research can play in transforming public policy.

Chapter Three describes a very different approach to combating substance abuse. The chapter focuses on the single-minded effort of one committed individual to affect change through a particularly American subculture—baseball. Sportswriter Leonard Koppett captures the passion and personality of Joe Garagiola, a former major league star turned activist in his quest to combat the use of spit tobacco. It is the story of his campaign and the creation (told almost parenthetically) of the National Spit Tobacco Education Program that

he helped establish with Foundation support. It is a powerful reminder of the impact one committed individual, with philanthropic
support, can have.

The landscape changes from the ballpark to the office park in
Chapter Four. Thomas Mangione, Jonathan Howland, and Marianne
Lee, three Boston-based researchers, report the results of their survey
on drinking and the workplace. After studying seven Fortune 500
companies and surveying nearly fourteen thousand managers, they
find that corporate drinking policies are misdirected. By targeting
problem drinkers, who are relatively few in number, company policies
ignore moderate-to-light drinkers, who, by dint of their far larger
numbers in the workplace, cause many more job-related performance
problems. The authors reveal a number of myths that, if recognized
and acted upon, could change the way American corporations address
alcohol and the workplace.

INCREASING ACCESS TO CARE

Since it became a national philanthropy in 1972, the Foundation has
had a goal of increasing people's access to health care services. Chapters Five and Six discuss two of the approaches the Foundation has
used to reach that goal. The first tries to improve medical education, in
the expectation that appropriately trained physicians will be more
responsive to people's needs; the second approach tries to improve the
nursing profession, so that patients will receive better care.

In Chapter Five, Lewis Sandy, the Foundation's executive vice president, and Richard Reynolds, his predecessor in the position, write
about the Foundation's long relationship with those huge medical conglomerates known as academic health centers. Beginning in the 1970s,
when academic health centers were viewed as "the center of the health
and health care universe," and concluding in the 1990s, when academic
health centers' place at the center of power had eroded, they trace the
Foundation's efforts to open these institutions to new ideas, particularly the idea of training more generalist physicians.

In Chapter Six, Thomas Rundall, David Starkweather, and Barbara
Norrish—from the School of Public Health of the University of Cal-
ifornia, Berkeley—report on their evaluation of the Strengthening
Hospital Nursing program. A joint endeavor of the Pew Charitable
Trusts and The Robert Wood Johnson Foundation, it was a large
demonstration project whose purpose was to improve patient care by

restructuring hospital services around nursing. The struggle to reorganize hospital services in the midst of the massive changes occurring throughout the entire health care system permeates the chapter. Although overtaken by managed care and the subsequent *weakening* of hospital nursing, the authors find that the Strengthening Hospital Nursing Program did make some lasting improvements in patient care in the sites they studied.

IMPROVING SERVICES FOR PEOPLE WITH CHRONIC ILLNESS

To a great extent, patient care has moved from the hospital to the community. This shift is due largely to the greater number of people with chronic conditions that do not necessarily require hospitalization and to the economics of managed care. As the chapter on Springfield, Massachusetts, in last year's *Anthology* revealed, community and home-based services for the chronically ill tend to be disorganized, underfunded, and inadequate. Three chapters in this year's *Anthology* examine Foundation-funded programs aimed at improving services for chronically ill individuals.

The Faith in Action program, like the Reach Out program reported in last year's *Anthology,* attempts to tap the spring of voluntarism—in this case by funding coalitions of religious organizations whose members volunteer to serve the homebound and other chronically ill individuals. In Chapter Seven, Paul Jellinek, Terri Gibbs Appel, and Terrance Keenan—current and former staff members who played key roles in the program's development—offer an inside perspective on the thinking behind the program, the people who made it happen, and its potential influence in an era when more and more social services are expected to be provided by volunteers.

In Chapter Eight, Lisa Lopez, a journalist who specializes in health issues, goes to the heart of services for the chronically ill: how they are provided in health maintenance organizations, or HMOs, and how they are organized in the community. She reports on two demonstration programs that test new approaches to improving services. The first provides funds to HMOs that restructure the way care is given to chronically ill individuals, and the second attempts to coordinate services offered in the community by nursing homes, physicians, home health organizations, and social services agencies.

In Chapter Nine, Leonard Saxe and Theodore Cross, professors in the Family and Children's Policy Center at the Heller School at Brandeis University, report on the Mental Health Services Program for Youth, which supported the coordination of community-based services for children with severe mental disabilities. They found that this approach offered the children more access to care and permitted them to live outside of mental institutions. The limited scope of the evaluation did not, however, enable them to determine whether the program improved the mental health of the young people it served.

COMMUNICATIONS

Many people know of The Robert Wood Johnson Foundation by hearing the name mentioned on National Public Radio. What they may not realize is that the Foundation's support of public radio, brought about by a recognition of the public's need for reliable information, is part of a much broader communications strategy. The Foundation was one of the early philanthropic supporters of public broadcasting on health care issues and, since then, it has greatly expanded its work with the media. In Chapter Ten, Victoria Weisfeld, a senior communications officer at the Foundation, discusses how decisions about funding radio and television projects are made and chronicles the hits, misses, and near-misses of the Foundation's work with these media.

A LOOK BACK

Although it is not widely known, in the 1970s the Foundation played a pivotal role in establishing physician assistants and nurse practitioners as viable health professions. In the final chapter, Terrance Keenan, one of the Foundation's first staff members, offers a personal and evocative memoir of this work. His recollections include physicians who flew their own planes to supervise nurse practitioners in remote areas of Utah and nurse practitioners riding the circuit in rural Alabama in a van outfitted as a mobile medical office. It's a time and history that should not be lost.

Princeton, New Jersey   STEPHEN L. ISAACS
May 1998   JAMES R. KNICKMAN

Core Values of
The Robert Wood Johnson
Foundation

In 1994, Stanford University professors J. C. Collins and J. I. Porras published *Built to Last*,[1] which described the successful habits of visionary companies. Their book explored the life span of eighteen successful, visionary companies—and an equal number of less visionary ones—to derive key performance characteristics that distinguished the best institutions from the lesser ones. Although many of their observations are relevant to philanthropy, one appears particularly pertinent: "Visionary companies preserve core purposes and values but also continuously strive for progress."

CORE PURPOSES AND VALUES

The idea is that successful companies resolutely adhere to their core—defined by the authors as consisting of both purpose and values—yet at the same time are extremely flexible in searching for ways to express that core. How does this apply to The Robert Wood Johnson Foundation? What are our core purpose and values? Do our daily actions reflect our core?

It is easy to identify our core purpose because it is the same as our mission—to improve health and health care for all Americans. Our purpose

---

This chapter is adapted from the president's message at the July 1997 meeting of The Robert Wood Johnson Foundation's board of trustees.

is clear and concise, and it is shared by trustees and staff. Core values refer to "the organization's essential and enduring tenets—a small set of timeless guiding principles that require no external justification; they have *intrinsic* value and importance to those inside the organization." Core values permeate the actions of an organization, are enduring, and can be changed only slowly and with great effort.

Our core values are not as obvious as our core purpose. We are a relatively young organization, and our values are still being formed. Nevertheless, I would like to identify a few values that I think do characterize us:

- *We pursue goals that are important to the health of the American public.*

This may seem like a self-evident statement that flows from our mission, but it is a helpful guide in our grant making. By keeping our focus on the health of the *entire* population, we can emphasize issues—such as access to health care—that are more germane to vulnerable subgroups. Underlying the value of improving the health of the public is a sense of egalitarianism, because it is the less fortunate members of our society whose health is most in jeopardy. We can also address problems such as substance abuse that affect everyone, including the more economically fortunate. This focus also assures that we value our assets as a public trust for which our actions should be accountable. To make good on this core value, it becomes necessary to be eclectic in whom we choose as partners and in the variety of solutions that we explore. Thus, we have cast a broad net for potential grantees, seeking them in all sectors of the American landscape—both public and private—rather than focusing our support on a particular sector such as hospitals or medical schools.

Fidelity to this value also mandates that all those who might use the knowledge and the wisdom gathered through our grants to advance these goals should have unfettered access to this information. This focus on openness translates into the way we operate our research programs, the content of our in-house publications, and our efforts to help grantees communicate their experiences and findings.

- *The integrity of our data and our monitoring processes are paramount.*

This value is embedded in our early and continuing commitment to evaluation and to rigorous fiscal monitoring. It guides us when our agendas and our findings conflict. For example, we are currently involved in a campaign to decrease the number of uninsured children. The larger the number, the more compelling is the argument for programs to expand coverage. For the past year, the figure "ten million uninsured children" has been widely reported and commonly accepted in the national debate surrounding this issue. Recently, Paul Ginsburg and his colleagues in the Health Tracking project, which is funded by the Foundation, conducted a study that reveals the number may be closer to eight and a half million. In this instance, it is clear that our value of fidelity to the integrity of data will trump our desire to advance a particular issue. We will defend the number that we think is correct, even at the expense of weakening the programmatic argument.

- *We speak through and about our grantees and do not seek a high institutional profile.*

Some foundations seek to advance their causes by elevating their public profiles, thereby adding gravity and credibility to their actions and statements. Given that foundations have limited grant money to achieve ambitious goals, this seems to me a defensible strategy as long as it avoids unseemly perquisites. We have chosen a different path, and in general it serves us well. One manifestation of this core value is our relatively large investments in training programs that develop young professionals—a strategy that is relatively expensive and has a long and often important payoff, but will not generate media coverage or public recognition. Another expression of this core value is our newsletter, ADVANCES, which exemplifies how we use our communications program to promote the accomplishments of our grantees and of the issues that we support.

A challenge posed by this core value is that it makes it more difficult to improve and influence the policy process. There are two broad pathways to accomplish that—one direct and one indirect. The direct path entails establishing the Foundation itself as active in the policy process. This strategy would influence how we select our staff, as well as how much of a presence the Foundation would establish in Washington. The indirect path—which, in general, is the one we have chosen—is to help position our grantees engaged in health policy research to make the appropriate connections. To accomplish this, we have invested in specific training for our grantees, and have provided technical assistance to link grantees with the media and with policy makers. Because it is difficult to navigate the indirect path, we pay a price in the potential attenuation of policy leverage.

> • *We seek to employ and develop a staff that is distinguished by its professionalism and competence.*

This might seem paradoxical in an organization that values working through its grantees, but I believe it is an authentic part of our culture. We seek intelligent, motivated, highly ethical staff members who care passionately about our mission. We work them hard, help them develop, and value them highly even after they leave us. We see our professional staff as agents for change while they are with us and in their subsequent positions. We strive to maximize their growth and potential while they are here, and even afterward. For our support staff, many of whom make long-term commitments to us, we try to provide a nurturing, dignified atmosphere that is respectful of their contributions, helps them to grow, and encourages them to be creative in their work.

STRIVING FOR PROGRESS

In my view, we do very well at preserving our core purpose, and are still in the process of developing a set of core values. How well do we do in continuously striving for progress? That question leads to two other characteristics of visionary companies.

One characteristic is that visionary companies "try a lot of stuff and keep what works." Collins and Porras found that outstanding companies engaged in a restless search for innovation, which they characterize by phrases such as "stirring the pot," "avoiding routinization," and "tolerating failures." Working in such an environment can be both exhilarating and anxiety-provoking. It is a rare philanthropy that fits such a description, and I cannot honestly say that it describes us. There are strong forces within philanthropies to define characteristic ways of doing things, and then to avoid deviating from those norms. I do think that we are relatively flexible, and that we are improving in our experimentation with different forms of grant making, monitoring, and dissemination. But we can be even more flexible, and should try to be so.

Another characteristic of visionary companies is that they set "big, hairy, audacious goals," or BHAGs. Sony set out to elevate Japanese culture and national status. Henry Ford had the dream of democratizing the automobile. At the time, these aspirations seemed mere wishful thinking to outsiders. But inside the companies, they helped to catalyze new ideas and a fierce determination to accomplish these goals.

How applicable are BHAGs to philanthropy? I'm not sure how to answer that question. I used to think that our access and substance abuse goals were pretty audacious. After all, saying that we will "assure access to basic health care services for all Americans" is mighty big talk for a $300-million-a-year foundation operating in a trillion-dollar industry. And trying to reduce harm from substance abuse is also pretty big game. Yet translating audacious goals into effective grant making turns out to be difficult. And I sometimes cringe when I hear us oversell the potential impact of a good grant that can't possibly achieve all that its proponents claim.

As I think about the idea of BHAGs, I find myself torn between wanting our reach to exceed our grasp, but also wishing to fashion grants whose goals are achievable. I want to see the Foundation find the balance between stretching as much as possible while still holding to realistic performance standards for which we can be held accountable.

FINAL THOUGHTS

If a study were to be published on philanthropies, would we be classified as visionary? The only previous such work, *The Golden Donors,* written by Waldemar Nielsen in 1985,[2] rated The Robert Wood Johnson Foundation as the best of the large philanthropies. That was a wonderful legacy for me to inherit in 1990, but I question whether it really applied to us then—or does today. We are still a very young foundation, and it is not clear whether others would share Nielsen's criteria or verdict.

What does seem clear to me is that many of the qualities that distinguish visionary companies are ones we should aspire to. These include preserving core values while continuously searching for improvement, focusing on how to strengthen the organization, putting a high priority on staff development, and setting audacious goals. It would be interesting to come back in twenty-five years and see whether our successors and—more important—others would be able to call us a visionary foundation.

Princeton, New Jersey   STEVEN A. SCHROEDER
May 1998   President
                                    The Robert Wood Johnson Foundation

Notes

1. J. C. Collins and J. I. Porras, *Built to Last: Successful Habits of Visionary Companies,* HarperBusiness, New York, 1994.
2. W. Nielsen, *The Golden Donors: A New Anatomy of the Great Foundations,* E. P. Dutton, New York, 1985.

⟿ Acknowledgments

Producing *To Improve Health and Health Care, 1998–1999* has been a communal effort, and we would like to acknowledge the contributions of other members of this community.

The idea of the *Anthology* originated, in part, with Frank Karel, vice president for communications of The Robert Wood Johnson Foundation. The first person we turn to for guidance, he has been a source of creativity, editorial judgment, and political wisdom. C. P. Crow, executive editor of the *Anthology* series, is an editor whose eye for meaning and ear for language improved every chapter. Molly McKaughan also served as a copy editor. Her understanding of the Foundation and her touch as a writer combined to strengthen the book. Margaret Trejo, president of Trejo Productions, is responsible for the clarity of the graphics.

To make sure that the *Anthology* is as unbiased and objective as possible, we called upon a committee of outside reviewers. Richard Morrill, a senior fellow with MathTech; Patricia Patrizi, a consultant with the Consortium for Policy Research in Education; and Jonathan Showstack, an adjunct professor at the University of California at San Francisco, comprised the outside review committee. They were thoughtful, careful, and tough in their review. The final product has benefited from their clear thinking and strong analytical skills.

Within the Foundation, a number of people worked to assure the success of the *Anthology*. Richard Toth was an ever-reliable source of information on the Foundation's programs and grant making. Deborah Malloy and Sherry Georgianna arranged meetings, set up conference calls, and coordinated the work of the two editors. Linda Potts handled contractual matters between the Foundation and the Center for Health and Social Policy with aplomb and efficiency. Jeanne Weber and Hope Woodhead developed mailing lists and served as liaison with Jossey-Bass on distribution matters.

At Jossey-Bass, Andy Pasternack, editor of the health series, brought vision and order to this unique collaborative venture between a publisher and a foundation.

Finally, we owe special gratitude to Barbara Stearns, the research and editorial assistant for the *Anthology*. Her dedication and good sense improved the book in more ways than it is possible to recount. From strengthening language of the text and catching errors the rest of us had missed to coordinating with authors and overseeing the entire production of the book, she handled her assignments with tact, humor, and a high degree of professionalism.

S.L.I.

J.R.K.

To Improve Health and Health Care, 1998–1999

Combating
Substance Abuse

CHAPTER ONE

~~ Adopting the Substance Abuse Goal

A Story of Philanthropic Decision Making

Robert G. Hughes

Editors' Introduction

A question frequently asked of anybody who works at a foundation is, How do you decide how to spend the money? The challenge of picking and choosing from among so many potentially worthy initiatives is ever present in philanthropy, and obviously of great interest to potential grantees. This chapter offers a candid look at how The Robert Wood Johnson Foundation went about deciding to devote a substantial part of its annual grant making budget to the problem of substance abuse.

The decision to make grants that would attempt to "reduce the harm caused by tobacco, alcohol, and illegal drugs" was a significant departure for the Foundation. For its first fifteen years, the Foundation focused more on improving health *care* (particularly access to medical services) than on tackling determinants of health. Adoption of the substance abuse goal was a first step toward addressing both the *health* and *health care* aspects of the Foundation's mission.

The chapter describes the staff and board processes that led to shaping and adopting the substance abuse goal, and assesses the consequences over the next six years of adopting that goal. The author, Robert Hughes, who is currently a vice president of the Foundation, was actively involved in the planning process that took place in 1990 and 1991. He continues to do grant making in the area of substance abuse.

—◆◇◆—

In 1991, the Robert Wood Johnson Foundation adopted three goals that would guide its grant making through the last decade of the twentieth century: to assure that Americans of all ages have access to basic health care, to improve the way services are organized and provided to people with chronic health conditions, and to promote health and prevent disease by reducing harm caused by substance abuse.

The substance abuse goal constituted the biggest departure from past Foundation goals and grant-making activities. Before 1991, substance abuse had been subsumed under the priority of reducing destructive behavior, one of ten Foundation priorities in the late 1980s. Substance abuse was not on the agenda at all before 1987. The emergence of substance abuse as one of three goals signaled a significant new direction for the Foundation. Early in 1997, it had become the single largest area targeted for Foundation investment, amounting to more than a fourth of the Foundation's $900 million in commitments (grants and programs authorized to be paid in the future). The magnitude of this investment reflects the impact of adopting a goal on subsequent Foundation grants.

THE IMPORTANCE OF ORGANIZATIONAL GOALS

A goal is important for a foundation because it sets boundaries, for both the philanthropy and the public, delimiting what the foundation's grant making will include or exclude. It is, fundamentally, a statement of organizational values—a judgment that the adopted goal is more important than competing goals, and that this judgment will be used in future funding discussions. It makes a claim about the worth of investing in a specified area and, moreover, delineates what will *not* be within the scope of consideration for funding. The more specific and narrow a goal, the greater the possible influence philanthropic investments may have, but the smaller the range of interests that can be accommodated under it. The broader a goal, the less focused are the philanthropic investments, but the greater range of interests that can be accommodated. This tension between focus and breadth is a central issue for foundations.

Compared with many other types of organizations, a philanthropy is unusually flexible in its ability to adopt goals. It does not confront the market discipline imposed by the need to attract new resources, and does not worry about selling a product to consumers. It does not have a responsibility to any public agency. A philanthropy is also unusually flexible in its ability to change once goals have been adopted. Most organizations are constrained from changing what they do because they have to perform a specific function—educate students, say, or produce a product—and they have staff expertise and investments in equipment or technology to facilitate that work. The work that philanthropies do—allocating resources, mainly through grants—can be refocused on different purposes. Indeed, although the influence of goals on behavior is probably overrated for most types of organizations, for philanthropies that influence may be underrated. Philanthropies are more insulated from outside influence, and the work of the organization itself can be changed with comparatively little disruption. But a foundation will still be influenced strongly by its own history, as was the case with The Robert Wood Johnson Foundation and its adoption of the substance abuse goal.

FOUNDATION GOALS
IN HISTORICAL CONTEXT

The Robert Wood Johnson Foundation's mission, "to improve the health and health care of all Americans," has remained unchanged since it became a national philanthropy in 1972. The mission set the broad, long-term direction for the Foundation, but focused goals were needed to help potential grantees and the Foundation trustees and staff understand how that mission would be accomplished. In 1973, the Foundation decided on three areas that would guide grant making: the need for ready access to personal health care, the need to improve the performance of the health care system in order to ensure quality care, and the need to develop mechanisms for the objective analysis of public policies in health.

Over the next decade, the first of these areas—access to care—became a hallmark issue for the Foundation and accounted for 77 percent of all grants. The two other areas, though less visible and attracting less grant funding, helped shape the Foundation during its formative years. The focus on health care systems and trying to make improvements by first understanding how systems function and then devising ways to make them better has provided the conceptual underpinnings for many Foundation programs. Similarly, the value placed on objective analyses became firmly embedded in Foundation culture, reflected not only in support of projects that carried out analyses of public policies, but also in the practice of commissioning independent evaluations of the Foundation's own programs.

Between 1972 and 1991, the Foundation twice changed its goals. A review and revision of goals in 1981 was prompted by the changes in the health system that had occurred in the decade since the original ones were established. In 1987, the Foundation's goals were revised once more because of a change in leadership. That year, Leighton Cluff succeeded David Rogers as president. In the fall of 1989, Dr. Cluff announced his plans to retire, and the stage was set for a review of the Foundation's goals by the new leadership.

ADOPTING NEW GOALS

In 1990, when the Foundation's board of trustees selected Steven Schroeder as the third president and fellow trustee, they understood that one of his first activities would be to review the Foundation's goals. In his interviews with board members, Dr. Schroeder had conveyed an interest in taking the Foundation in the direction of working on substance abuse problems. The board was receptive to this direction, and had taken steps several years before to encourage the staff to address problems of illegal drug use and alcohol problems. As a result, the Foundation was already supporting projects directed at reducing substance abuse, most visibly the Partnership for a Drug-Free America, a national media campaign aimed at deglamorizing drug use, and Fighting Back, a national program that supported community coalitions working to reduce the demand for alcohol and illegal drugs. This program, launched in 1988, was the largest Foundation program to date. However, the Foundation had virtually no other substance abuse programs.

Initially, Schroeder was struck by the disparity between the mission, which included improving *health* and health care, and the programs, which were mainly in health care. This disparity suggested possibilities for new directions that could enhance the Foundation's focus on improving health that did not rely on improving the health care system. This notion fit well with Schroeder's own experience as an internist seeing patients with problems caused by tobacco and alcohol use, and his training in public health and epidemiology. The evidence of the importance and the scale of health problems stemming from substance abuse was overwhelming, and the problem seemed to offer great promise as an area for Foundation work.

Schroeder's first board of trustees meeting after he joined the Foundation as president was in July, 1990. (See Figure 1.1.) At that meeting, he told his fellow board members that during the past few months he had received advice about the Foundation and its goals from perhaps forty people, including health experts, former Foundation officials, and senior officers at other large philanthropies. At this initial meeting, Schroeder indicated his own preferences by listing "substance abuse (cigarettes, alcohol, and cocaine)" first among a preliminary list of possible goal areas suggested to the board. The board agreed that as a next step the staff would develop a strategic plan and present it to the board in early 1991.

STAFF ENGAGEMENT IN
THE PLANNING PROCESS

A consideration of new goals topped the agenda at the weekly program staff meeting (attended by the entire grant-making staff) immediately after the July board of trustees meeting. Richard Reynolds, the Foundation's executive vice president, appointed two thirteen-member committees with the broad charge of identifying areas or goals that the Foundation should consider. The membership of these two committees included the Foundation's entire professional staff from program units, communications, financial monitoring, and research and evaluation. The two committees were to report their findings at the September 25, 1990 program staff meeting.

Both committees produced ten-page reports. Neither gave substance abuse the prominence it eventually achieved. In one report, alcohol and drug abuse was one of five proposed topics; in the other report, substance abuse was subsumed under a goal focusing on prevention. Equally noteworthy was the total absence of tobacco in one report, and only a passing reference to it in the other. In some ways, this was not surprising given the composition of the staff. Many had devoted their professional lives to the issues that access involved, had come to the Foundation specifically to work on them, and were most experienced with the ideas, problems, and organizations associated with access to medical care. So it was understandable that few staff members spontaneously championed a goal largely outside their own work experi-

cJ/P

**Figure 1.1. Chronology of Selected Events Leading to
the Adoption of the Substance Abuse Goal.**

July, 1990	President and board of trustees agree to have the staff initiate strategic planning process, examining Foundation goals.
September, 1990	Two staff reports on potential goals.
October, 1990	Three goals proposal for initial consideration. Substance Abuse emerges as the first goal. Board retreat on future Foundation direction set for February.
November, 1990–January, 1991	Three staff work groups, one for each goal, research areas and prepare materials for Board Retreat.
February, 1991	Board reviews proposed goals, debates merits and risks, adopts goals.

ences. In addition, many staff members faced barriers similar to those the rest of the country still faced—a lack of understanding about the nature and the pervasiveness of substance abuse problems, the stigma associated with addicted people, and a reluctance to come to grips with issues that lie outside the health care system and in the domain of personal behavior, organizational policy, and societal values.

THREE PROPOSED GOALS

The timing of the reports allowed the Foundation's senior management to review the committees' reports and to draft language for goals well in advance of the October 1990 board meeting:

1. Improving access to basic health care by promoting the availability of services and their appropriate allocation.

2. Improving the health of people with complex needs requiring the integration of services in multiple settings.

3. Improving the health of people by reducing the incidence and the prevalence of significant preventable disease and disability. Under this goal, one of the priority areas suggested was reducing the demand for tobacco and illegal drugs and discouraging the irresponsible use of alcohol.

This initial synthesis of the two September 1990 staff reports established that the Foundation would aim to have only three goals, an important step in trying to achieve focus. Moreover, the phrasing of the third goal made important modifications to the language used in the staff reports. Now the priority area specifically included tobacco, listing it before illegal drugs and alcohol. In addition, this language began to wrestle with the differences among tobacco, alcohol, and illegal drugs. The emerging scientific evidence that alcohol was not always harmful, and under some circumstances could be beneficial, made lumping it together with tobacco and illegal drugs problematic in terms of what the ultimate goal should be. For alcohol in particular, the experience of Prohibition provided a reminder of the need to describe carefully what the Foundation hoped to accomplish. The challenge was to develop a coherent idea and a direction for grant making that encompassed three substances with quite different social, historical, cultural, and medical characteristics. And under closer examination, even the three terms—tobacco, alcohol, and illegal drugs—describe remarkably different categories: a plant, a chemical compound, and substances classified by the law. The thorniness of crafting the language is illustrated by the observation that at various times in the twentieth century the category "illegal drugs" included alcohol and excluded heroin, cocaine, and marijuana, and that for children tobacco and alcohol are illegal drugs.

After several weeks of discussion of the three goals proposed in the initial synthesis, senior Foundation officials agreed on new language for the goals that would shape the next phase of staff work and outside review. The three proposed goals were:

1. Reducing the harmful effects and the irresponsible use of tobacco, alcohol, and drugs

2. Assuring that all Americans have access to basic health care

3. Improving the availability and the utilization of services needed by people with complex, chronic health conditions and related conditions

There were three important changes from the earlier draft of goals. First, substance abuse became a specific goal, not a priority within a broader goal. Second, this goal was now listed first instead of third. The new order was based on ideas about how the goals related to one another and to people's health, beginning with a goal that addressed behavior outside the health care system, progressing to a concern that all people get into the system for basic services, and that, once in the system, people with chronic health problems would get the care they needed. Third, the idea of reducing harmful effects provided a common aim across tobacco, alcohol, and illegal drugs that did not require qualification because of differences among the three. This phrasing simplified the goal.

With the refined goals, organizational decision making entered the next phase. The board of trustees reviewed the history of the Foundation's mission and goals at its October meeting, along with the three proposed goals and a work plan for adopting new Foundation directions. The proposed work plan provided the steps for consulting with outside experts, preparing reports, and obtaining periodic comments from board members. These steps would lead to a board of trustees retreat in February of 1991, to be devoted exclusively to future Foundation directions. The board approved the work plan, and staff work groups began to prepare a report on each goal.

The work group on the substance abuse goal prepared a twenty-four-page report that summarized the extent of substance abuse in the country, noted existing activities to address substance abuse, reviewed past Foundation work in the area, and proposed a framework for future Foundation efforts, along with examples of possible programs. This report became part of the briefing book prepared for the board of trustees retreat.

THE FEBRUARY 1991 RETREAT

A substantial portion of the February retreat was devoted to a consideration of the Foundation's future goals. The board members reacted somewhat differently to each proposed goal. That they embraced the access goal quickly and without extensive commentary was not surprising; it reaffirmed a long-standing institutional commitment. The proposed chronic care goal was accepted, but the discussion contained a bit of skepticism, stemming in part from the goal's breadth and complexity. However, the most active board discussions were generated by the proposed goal of reducing the harm caused by tobacco, alcohol, and illegal drugs.

The board members considered important risks as well as rationales for adopting the substance abuse goal. The risks included moving into an area where the Foundation had little experience. Pursuing this goal could embroil the Foundation in controversial issues such as the legalization of substances or issues of personal behavior and cultural values or suggest moving into program areas with which the Foundation had scant familiarity, such as law enforcement. The board carefully considered the potential damage that could be done to the Foundation's reputation if it adopted this goal. The board's experience with and knowledge from the Partnership for a Drug Free America and the Fighting Back program contributed to its understanding of illegal drug and alcohol issues. Including tobacco sharpened the focus of the discussion and highlighted the risk of Foundation-supported antitobacco projects that would attract industry attention and opposition and might embroil the Foundation in a controversy that could overshadow other work it supported. The board members understood well the economic strength of the tobacco industry and how influential the industry could be. In addition, they looked carefully at the decades-long decline in tobacco use and considered what the Foundation could bring to this issue when the trend was already going in the right direction.

Still, the data on tobacco and the harm it caused strongly supported the idea that tobacco should be included in the goal—a point most persuasively made by several former smokers and board members with expertise in clinical medicine. The estimates of deaths due to tobacco use—435,000 a year compared to 100,000 a year for alcohol and 20,000 a year from illegal drugs—made tobacco hard to ignore. Central to the discussion was the assessment of how well this goal fit with the Foundation's mission of improving the health and health care of all Americans. The board members considered the risks and the rationales and concluded that addressing the substance abuse problem in the United States—including tobacco—was, in the words of one trustee, "the right thing to do." They adopted the goal.

EARLY TRANSITIONS AND PROGRAM DEVELOPMENT

A goal is not self-implementing; it simply sets some boundaries and directions for the organization. In the process of reviewing proposals and developing programs, a primary use of the goal itself is being clear about what will not be considered. For both potential applicants and staff members, the main value of a goal is to exclude projects or activities not related to it. A goal is not particularly useful in making choices among the large variety of proposed projects that can make legitimate claims to contribute toward its fulfillment. For unsolicited ad hoc proposals and staff-developed programs, being consistent with a goal is a necessary, but not a sufficient, condition for securing Foundation support.

The boundaries that a goal provides are continuously being negotiated. People with project ideas that may not have addressed substance abuse directly recast their ideas to highlight the effects on substance abuse. Staff members developing program ideas, which undergo the same review and approval process as external proposals, make similar accommodations in their work. Indeed, a major challenge of philanthropic work is interpreting goals so that they remain useful in making decisions about specific projects and in determining how to allocate scarce resources.

Several specific circumstances served to spark the Foundation's early substance abuse programs after the goal was adopted. First was the chance to use the knowledge and the network developed in programs already under way—Fighting Back and the Partnership for a Drug-Free America. These contacts provided valuable ideas for new projects. Second, the board had directed staff members to begin grant making that targeted tobacco use with children's projects, because that area was seen as the one of broadest consensus. This led to staff work with Stop Teenage Addiction to Tobacco (STAT), and STAT received the first large tobacco-related grant given by the Foundation—$1.2 million. Third, the Foundation actively recruited new staff members with expertise in substance abuse. Fourth, Joseph Califano, the former Secretary of Health, Education, and Welfare, visited the Foundation and shared his vision for establishing a multidisciplinary "think/action tank" to focus on addiction in this country. Out of this visit came a planning grant, and eventual Foundation support for a new organization—the National Center on Addiction and Substance Abuse, or CASA, at Columbia University.

All did not fall into place quickly or smoothly, however. For example, the Foundation's senior management decided to form work groups from among the professional staff for each of the three major goals. To determine the membership for these groups, staff members were asked which goal group—access, chronic care, or substance abuse—they would prefer to work in. Twenty-one of thirty staff members selected access, and only four chose substance abuse. After some informal discussions between staff members and leadership about the need for each goal group to have roughly the same number of people, the substance abuse group got under way with eleven staff members.

Within the Foundation, goal groups develop and review program proposals and make initial recommendations for funding (or not). The substance abuse goal group, as it was called, had the challenge of learning about new issues and developing a portfolio of investments in the field. The largest investments are set forth in Exhibit 1.1 at the end of this chapter. They reflect a variety of approaches—from multisite demonstrations to research to communications projects—and address a range of problems—from children smoking to binge drinking to helping communities overcome problems stemming from alcohol and illegal drugs.

1991–1996: GROWTH, CONTROVERSY, AND CHALLENGES

After only half a decade of Foundation grant making in the area of substance abuse, it is too early to judge the ultimate impact of adopting the substance abuse goal. But it is not too early to see how selected aspects of this work have unfolded. First, the development of the substance abuse portfolio occurred at a time of substantial growth in the Foundation's assets. The amount awarded for grants rose from $129 million in 1991 to $267 million in 1996. This means that the investments in substance abuse programs were not made at the expense of more traditional Foundation goals.

Second, this new goal energized the organization. It provided new challenges and substantive issues, and forced substantial organizational learning among staff and board members over just a few years. And the feedback from the Foundation's various public audiences was positive. This feedback and organizational learning were mutually reinforcing, as the entire organization became more confident about the benefits and fit of these issues with the Foundation's mission. In particular, the more the organization understood the depth and pervasiveness of the health problems caused by tobacco, the greater the resolve to reduce tobacco use.

Third, working in substance abuse gave the Foundation greater experience in supporting programs that involved controversy. Of course, what is controversial can be relative. In 1991, the Foundation thought tobacco was a potentially controversial topic. Yet by 1994, when health care reform had risen to the top of the national agenda and strong criticisms were directed at the Foundation for its activities, one trustee asked, "Why can't we do something noncontroversial like go after tobacco?"

Fourth, the type and the mixture of interventions supported to reduce substance abuse, as displayed in Exhibit 1.1, were quite varied. At the February 1991 retreat, the board expressed a willingness to support different types of activities, and encouraged staff members to be creative in working toward the goals. The relatively new substance abuse area provided opportunities, and the new approaches tried in substance abuse have influenced Foundation work in its more traditional grant-making areas.

Fifth, despite the specific focus of the goal, the array of Foundation-sponsored substance abuse projects resists conceptual coherence and programmatic integration. Tobacco, alcohol, and illegal drugs cause different types of harm. Reducing teenage tobacco use requires approaches different from those aimed at reducing binge drinking on college campuses or helping former drug abusers leaving prison get off to a positive start in their home communities. Further, the diversification of programs—responding to the breadth of worthwhile approaches to reducing substance abuse—stretches the capability of any single conceptual framework.

Sixth, the substance abuse goal remains only loosely tied to other Foundation goals. The issues inherent in developing approaches to improve access to health care services and chronic care services intertwine to a certain extent. Substance abuse is less connected to access and chronic care than these two goals are to each other. In part, this reflects the separate status of substance abuse within health and health care historically. From treatment programs to payment systems to insurance coverage to prevention programs, substance abuse has been separate from other health and health care problems. These divisions have dampened the potential links that could have been made across Foundation goals—in access to substance abuse treatment, for instance, or viewing addiction to various substances as chronic illnesses. However, some recent programs such as Addressing Tobacco in Managed Care Organizations, and Screening and Brief Intervention for Alcohol Abuse in Managed Care (see Exhibit 1.1) are beginning to make these links.

Seventh, the Foundation's selection of the substance abuse goal and its investment of substantial resources in support of the goal helped legitimize a field that had received little philanthropic support. Although some other philanthropies do grant making in this area, it remains woefully underfunded.

CONCLUSION

Choosing a new goal can help keep an organization vibrant by infusing new ideas, providing the opportunity to work on new problems, and promoting a receptivity to different perspectives. Yet there is also great value in building on experience and sticking with established goals over time. Achieving the most productive balance—between continuity and change, between established approaches to problems and untested new ones, between a focus on well-understood issues and unfamiliar ones—is among the most important challenges facing a Foundation's leadership.

ℐℐℐ

Exhibit 1.1. Major (over $1 million) Foundation Investments to Reduce Substance Abuse.

Time Period	Funding[1] (in millions)	Project or National Program[2]
1988–2001	$71.2	Fighting Back: Community Initiatives to Reduce Demand for Illegal Drugs and Alcohol
1989–2000	$24.0	Media Campaign to Reduce Demand for Illegal Drugs; Partnership for a Drug-Free America
1990–2000	$ 1.5	National Replication for a Health-Risk Prevention Program for Girls (Best Friends)
1991–1994	$ 1.2	Four-Community Project to Reduce Adolescent Tobacco Use (Stop Teenage Addiction to Tobacco-STAT)
1991–1996	$ 1.1	Study to Identify Modifiable Workplace Factors Affecting Alcohol Abuse
1991–1999	$16.3	Join Together: National Technical Assistance Project for Community Substance Abuse Initiatives
1991–2000	$17.8	The Center on Addiction and Substance Abuse at Columbia University
1991–2000	$13.5	Healthy Nations: Reducing Substance Abuse Among Native Americans
1992–1997	$ 1.2	Elementary School Program to Prevent Substance Abuse and Other Problems
1992–1997	$ 4.6	Tobacco Policy Research and Evaluation Program
1992–1998	$ 1.5	Program to Prevent the Onset of Substance Abuse and Other Problem Behavior
1992–1999	$ 4.7	National Support Center for Community Substance Abuse Coalitions (CADCA)
1992–2001	$ 9.0	Program to Reduce Substance Abuse Among Jail Inmates (Health Link)
1992–2001	$ 5.6	Free to Grow: Head Start Partnerships to Promote Substance-Free Communities
1993–2001	$ 4.9	Smoke-Free Families: Innovations to Stop Smoking During and Beyond Pregnancy
1993–2001	$33.2	SmokeLess States: Statewide Tobacco Prevention and Control Initiatives

ↄℐ℘

Exhibit 1.1. Major (over $1 million) Foundation Investments to Reduce Substance Abuse, *continued.*

Time Period	Funding[1] (in millions)	Project or National Program[2]
1994–2003	$29.0	Substance Abuse Policy Research Program
1994–1996	$ 3.3	Home Box Office Substance Abuse Series
1995–2001	$10.2	Reducing Underage Drinking through Coalitions
1995–2002	$ 8.6	A Matter of Degree: Reducing High-Risk Drinking Among College Students
1996–1998	$ 4.4	Production, Promotion, and Outreach for a Public Television Series on Addiction and Recovery
1996–1998	$ 2.2	Increasing Understanding of Changes in Substance Abuse and Mental Health Care
1996–1999	$ 4.7	National Spit Tobacco Education Program: Major League Baseball Initiative
1996–2000	$ 1.5	Higher Education Center for Alcohol and Other Drug Prevention
1996–2000	$ 3.8	Screening and Brief Intervention for Alcohol Abuse in Managed Care
1996–2001	$20.0	National Center for Tobacco-Free Kids
1996–2003	$ 6.3	Addressing Tobacco within Managed Care Organizations
1996–2004	$ 8.0	Research Network on the Etiology of Tobacco Dependence
1997–2002	$20.5	Surveillance of Youth Alcohol, Tobacco, and Other Drug Use (ATOD)

[1]These amounts do not include technical assistance, and evaluation grants and/or authorizations.
[2]The Foundation provides a number of multi-year, multi-site national programs whose grantees are located throughout the country, administered by an external national program office.

CHAPTER TWO

～ Tobacco Policy Research

Marjorie A. Gutman
David G. Altman
Robert L. Rabin

Editors' Introduction

This chapter looks at one strategy used by the Foundation to help the nation address problems associated with tobacco use: the support of policy-related research. It describes two key research programs—the Tobacco Policy Research and Evaluation Program and its successor, the Substance Abuse Policy Research Program. Although funding research might seem like an indirect way of decreasing tobacco use, the chapter makes a strong case that these programs provided useful information rapidly to those in a position to formulate policies on tobacco use.

These programs shaped a new field of research. In the past, researchers interested in tobacco tended to focus on epidemiological questions—such as patterns of use and cancer rates across different types of users—or assessments of strategies to reduce initiation into tobacco use or to stop people from smoking. The new programs, however, steered researchers into another important area of research: assessments of public and private-sector policies that can affect tobacco use.

These policies might involve regulatory issues, taxes, or different approaches to reducing access to tobacco products by youth.

In addition to the research described in this chapter, the Foundation supports a large effort to develop a surveillance system of tobacco policies directed at young people. It also sponsors evaluations of interventions to change the behavior of smokers, funds surveys of tobacco use, and supports the work of leading researchers trying to understand better why people smoke.

Marjorie Gutman is a former senior program officer at the Foundation. She is currently the director of prevention research at the Treatment Research Institute at the University of Pennsylvania. Robert Rabin, an attorney, is professor of law at Stanford University. David Altman is professor of public health sciences at the Wake Forest University School of Medicine.

I n the late 1990s, it is hard to remember that even a decade ago tobacco policy was not constantly in the headlines. A "tobacco settlement" had not been proposed, or even thinkable. Attorneys representing plaintiffs with tobacco-induced disease had never won a case against the industry. The industry whistle-blowers of the nineties had yet to emerge. States had not initiated lawsuits against tobacco companies to recover Medicaid expenditures attributable to smoking. The Food and Drug Administration had not yet taken steps to regulate tobacco as a drug. States such as California and Massachusetts had not yet passed landmark tobacco excise tax increases. National health care reform, to be funded in part by increases in the federal excise tax on tobacco, had not yet been proposed. The international journal *Tobacco Control* did not exist. Grassroots advocacy organizations were by and large living-room operations run by a handful of dedicated activists. And The Robert Wood Johnson Foundation and other funders were not actively involved in supporting tobacco policy research and programs. Eventually, of course, all these negatives became positives and, as a result, tobacco policy moved front and center.

One could argue that these developments, and the concurrent wave of public and policy maker recognition of the health, economic, ethical, and social costs of smoking, had their roots in the previous three decades. Still, many tobacco-related problems remain. Although more than fifty million Americans have quit smoking since the Surgeon General's report of 1964—a report that jump-started the transformation of societal views toward tobacco—monthly use of tobacco among male high school seniors did not change much from 1980 to 1990, while use among females dropped only slightly.[1-3]

Worse still, smoking among teenagers rose rapidly in the 1990s. Between 1992 and 1995, the percentage of high school seniors who had smoked cigarettes during the past month increased 20 percent— from 28.5 percent to 33.5 percent. Among younger adolescents, the number of smokers rose by an even more dramatic 33–34 percent: the percentage of high school sophomores who had smoked during the past month increased from 20.8 percent in 1992 to 27.9 percent in 1995, and, during the same years, the percentage of eighth-graders who had smoked during the past month rose from 14.3 percent to 19.1 percent.[4,5]

Internationally, tobacco use is on the rise, with a pandemic clearly in sight.[6,7] To meet the growing international demand for tobacco products, the tobacco companies produce nearly six trillion cigarettes a year, or a thousand cigarettes (fifty packs) for everyone on earth. Tobacco company investments in marketing, litigation, and lobbying remain substantial and effective. In Congress, statehouses, and city council chambers around the country, tobacco lobbyists remain highly effective advocates for positions that benefit the industry. Tobacco company profits, despite the considerable negative press the companies have received, continue to rise. Indeed, most analysts predict that if the tobacco companies, the state attorneys general, and Congress agree on a settlement for Medicaid expenses, the stock value of tobacco companies will increase markedly. In essence, then, the tobacco companies have thus far weathered intense criticism, internal bickering, damaging documents and testimony, and negative public opinion and are stronger financially than ever before.

ORIGINS OF THE TOBACCO POLICY RESEARCH PROGRAM

Because of the burden of death and illness attributable to smoking, The Robert Wood Johnson Foundation adopted the prevention of tobacco use as a priority within its goal area of reducing harm from substance abuse in February 1991, and two months later authorized funding for the Tobacco Policy Research and Evaluation Program, or TPREP. Although there was a relative paucity of tobacco policy studies at the time that TPREP was established, available epidemiological data provided persuasive evidence that a Foundation commitment to tobacco policy research could improve the health of many Americans. Since TPREP was launched, public momentum for reducing smoking has surged and tobacco control policy has come of age.[8] Although it is not possible to quantify the specific contributions that TPREP and its successor, the Substance Abuse Policy Research Program, have made to the field and to policy making, the research generated under these two programs and the researchers themselves have been at the forefront of recent tobacco policy discussions.

In the late 1980s, it was estimated that more than four hundred thousand deaths a year were attributable to tobacco use—one-third of all deaths from major chronic diseases.[9] Cigarette smoking during pregnancy accounted for 20 to 30 percent of low-birth-weight infants and about 10 percent of infant deaths; as much as 25 percent of Medicare expenditures was due to diseases related to smoking—heart and lung disease and certain cancers.[10]

Further, the proportion of smokers, especially among young people, did not portend well for the future. Despite the enormous health and fiscal costs of smoking, 1990 data indicated that 29 percent of Americans had smoked during the past month at the time they were interviewed. Although this represented a decline from 40 percent in 1965, it was still much higher than stated public health goals. Approximately two-thirds of all high-school seniors had smoked once or more in their lives, and close to one-third had smoked in the last month before being interviewed.[11] Twenty percent of seniors smoked daily, and 30 percent of them had started smoking by the sixth grade. Of even greater concern, trends in the number of teenagers smoking had leveled off in the beginning of the 1980s after declining during the previous decade. We now know that since 1991 an upturn has occurred in the proportion of teenagers who have smoked. By 1996, about half of American eighth-graders had already used tobacco.[12]

The Foundation's trustees and staff members recognized that there was a clear need to dedicate resources toward reducing tobacco use, but they also recognized that such an effort could be controversial because it pitted Foundation resources against a powerful industry. The challenges taken on by the Foundation were to identify policies that could help reduce tobacco use; assess their feasibility, effectiveness, and likely consequences; and facilitate decision makers' use of the understanding gained through these analyses.

The Foundation's involvement in the tobacco policy arena was made easier by the diligent groundwork that several key organizations laid in the 1980s. Indeed, the initiative built substantially on the work of the National Coordinating Committee for Tobacco-Related Research, or NCCTR. The NCCTR, whose chairman was former Surgeon General Jesse L. Steinfeld, was established in 1982 by the American Cancer Society following a recommendation that emerged from the National Conference on Smoking and Health. The NCCTR had multiple purposes: to provide a means of assessing scientific progress in the field of tobacco and health, to share future research plans among the participating agencies and voluntary organizations, and to recommend priority topics for additional research. As part of carrying out this charge, in 1987 the NCCTR, along with the National Cancer Institute, reviewed and categorized the tobacco-related research funded by the Institute and the National Heart, Lung, and Blood Institute, the two principal government sponsors of tobacco-related research. This review concluded that some areas, such as self-help and physician cessation interventions, had been adequately studied, whereas relatively little work had been done in policy research.

Prompted by this finding and by a report on tobacco policy research prepared for the National Cancer Institute by John Pinney, former director of the Office of Smoking and Health at the Centers for Disease Control and Prevention, or CDC,[13] the NCCTR established a subcommittee on policy research. The NCCTR engaged in a variety of activities, including the formation of study groups to identify and set priorities among policy research questions in the following areas: tobacco tax and pricing policy, smoke-free air policy, access to tobacco products, regulation of tobacco products, tobacco marketing and promotion, and insurance and reimbursement. In short, by the late 1980s a broad spectrum of organizations and health professionals, including those that funded the majority of all tobacco research in the United States, had determined the need for policy research and had identified at least some of the priority policy topics.

The Foundation was also encouraged to enter the area by the low level of support available from other sources. Although it was not possible to assess exactly how much total funding was available for tobacco policy research, it was possible to estimate the approximate resources devoted to such projects by major funders of tobacco research. The National Cancer Institute was the major federal source of funding for research on smoking, and the American Cancer Society was the voluntary health organization with the most interest. Although the Society largely supported biomedical cancer research, it did fund a small amount of policy research through specific projects. However, neither the National Cancer Institute nor the American Cancer Society had an initiative or a research program in this area. The CDC's support of tobacco policy research was also project-specific. Taken together, the Centers for Disease Control, the National Cancer Institute, and the American Cancer Society were allocating about $1 million a year for tobacco policy projects.

In addition, the state of California, with funding derived from a state tax increase instituted in 1991 and administered by the California Tobacco-Related Disease Research Program, had begun providing a small amount of funding for tobacco policy research.[14] Of the roughly $30 million a year awarded in research grants in the first two funding cycles, nine of 289 awards totaling $1 million could be considered policy research. Funding was limited to California researchers.

Yet another incentive for the Foundation to undertake a tobacco policy research initiative was the fact that government funders were less likely than a private foundation to pay for more controversial policy science.

Given these factors, in April 1991 the Foundation's board of trustees authorized $5 million over two years for TPREP. The first Call for Proposals was mailed in September 1992, and the first set of grants was awarded in early 1993. A second round of grants was awarded a year later. Subsequently, in 1994 the board of trustees authorized an expansion of policy research initiatives to include alcohol and illicit drugs as well. As a result, the Substance Abuse Policy Research Program, or SAPRP, came into being. This new program was initially granted $11 million over the years 1994 to 1996, and was renewed in 1997 for three more years and $18 million. Thus, the Foundation has committed $34 million for policy research on tobacco, alcohol, and illicit drugs to be awarded between 1992 and 2000.

TOBACCO POLICY RESEARCH: STRUCTURE AND IMPLEMENTATION

TPREP was an investigator-initiated, peer-reviewed program that supported investigators conducting research on a diverse array of tobacco policy topics. The initiative encouraged researchers from a variety of relevant fields such as medicine, public health, law, sociology, political science, psychology, and health economics to apply their expertise to tobacco. Research projects could address policies at the national, state, local, or organization levels in the public sector, or private-sector policies within companies, associations, or trade groups.

The overall goal of the program was to increase the amount of policy science available to public and private policy makers as they considered new policies to reduce tobacco use. More specifically, the initiative aimed to increase the awareness of policy alternatives and their feasibility and potential consequences.

All the Foundation's research has an applied focus, but particular attention was given in this initiative to active and creative dissemination of findings in order to heighten their use by decision makers.

Along these lines, investigators were required to include a section in their proposals on dissemination plans, and technical assistance was provided to maximize active and creative efforts.

The secondary goal of the program was to "grow the field" of tobacco policy research. When the program was initiated, a highly committed but fairly small number of individuals were engaged in tobacco policy research. The expectation was that the initiative would attract additional researchers from a wide range of relevant disciplines to the study of tobacco policy, in addition to providing an increased and more stable level of support for existing tobacco policy researchers. The Foundation thought that the initiative could also serve as a focal point for sharing findings, methods, and concerns among individuals conducting research in this area. Less tangible but nonetheless important, the Foundation hoped that the program would heighten the visibility and the credibility of tobacco policy research in the health and policy sciences.

Two rounds of competitive proposal review were contemplated, the second round eighteen months after the first. It was anticipated that perhaps twenty projects would ultimately be funded. Individual projects could range up to $350,000, and could last up to three years. A national program office was established at Stanford University under the leadership of Robert Rabin of the Law School, who became program director, and David Altman of the Medical School, who became deputy director. The program office was responsible for publicizing the initiative, overseeing and participating in the competitive review and selection process, monitoring the performance of grantees, providing technical assistance as needed, convening grant recipients at annual meetings, coordinating the dissemination of findings to appropriate audiences, and ensuring that proposed projects complemented rather than duplicated policy research supported by other funders. A pool of peer reviewers and a National Advisory Committee were established to assist the national program office in this process. During the early stages of the program, a national ad hoc advisory group consisting of seven tobacco control experts was convened to provide guidance and advice to program and Foundation staff on program priorities.

Two hundred twenty applicants submitted letters of intent for the first round of grants, from which eleven were selected. The ten second-round grantees were selected from a pool of 114 applicants. A list of the grants awarded under the TPREP appears in Exhibit 2.1 at the end of this chapter.

About 25 percent of the researchers supported under TPREP reported in interviews that they were relatively new to the field of tobacco policy research.[15] Thus, the effort to support and expand research on tobacco policy was able to attract researchers from a wide array of disciplines to investigate a broad spectrum of the current policy issues, including researchers who had not studied tobacco policy previously. At the same time, the program helped to continue, and even accelerate, the work of researchers who were already in the forefront of tobacco policy research.

SAPRP, begun in 1994, was modeled after TPREP. As of June 1998, thirty-five tobacco-related grants had been funded (see Exhibit 2.2 at the end of this chapter). These were selected from a pool of 371 applicants who submitted letters of intent requesting almost $35 million. An innovative new structure for grant making was introduced with the SAPRP program. Applications for grants could be submitted on either of two schedules. Using the more typical process, applications for grants between $100,000 and $350,000 were submitted at one deadline per year and reviewed and awarded in a "batch." However, to provide also for "quick-strike" research capacity, applications for grants under $100,000 could be submitted on a rolling basis, at any date, and grants were awarded accordingly. Using this fast track, research could be fielded rapidly to fit the reality of policy making. For example, baseline information could be collected rapidly before a new policy is put into place.

Across the two initiatives, a broad array of policy studies has been funded. Sixteen grants have focused on the evaluation of multiple tobacco policy interventions (access, media, cessation, and smoke-free buildings). Nine grants have been concerned with economic issues, including taxing and pricing, state Medicaid expenditures attributable to smoking, and the economic impact of progress toward a tobacco-free society. Almost half that number have supported projects characterized by legal or historical analysis, including legal analysis of the constitutionality of banning or limiting billboards, and of whether tobacco products fit the regulatory definition of a drug. A comparable proportion of grants was devoted to other major current policy areas—marketing, youth access, media and marketing, secondhand smoke—and to an analysis of the attitudes of the public and policy makers and evaluations of multiple policy interventions.

In keeping with the goals of the program, investigators from a wide variety of disciplines were awarded grants, including experts in economics, public health, medicine, law, psychology, sociology, communications, and management. Economics was the discipline of approximately 31 percent of the researchers supported under the program, with psychology, law, and behavioral science being the next most well represented disciplines.

THE ROLE OF RESEARCH IN POLICY MAKING

A key goal of TPREP and SAPRP has been to provide credible policy analysis and socioeconomic research findings to assist policy makers and the public in sifting through and assessing the options available to them in making important health policy decisions. What has occurred in the crucial linkage between research and policy? Summary information on studies supported by TPREP is suggestive and encouraging. Most of the studies supported under SAPRP were not completed as this chapter was being written and thus were not included in the discussion of the research-to-policy linkage. As of the end of 1997, the twenty-one studies supported under TPREP had produced thirty-nine articles in peer-reviewed journals and fifty-four presentations at professional conferences.[16] The findings presented in these articles and presentations were cited 203 times in the media, including major newspapers such as the *New York Times, Washington Post,* and *Wall Street Journal,* on television, radio, and the World Wide Web. More directly related to policy making, five presentations were made before federal and state legislative bodies, and on thirty-nine occasions, findings from the studies were cited in legal cases, including depositions, briefs, and other documents. Six studies funded under the program were cited in the commentary accompanying the FDA tobacco regulations. The dissemination of the findings will undoubtedly increase with time, as more information and new papers emerge.

Two case studies help to illustrate how research findings informed policy making. The first describes an analysis of the effect of the price of cigarettes on consumption,[17] and the second an analysis of whether tobacco meets the legal definition of a drug.[18]

Case Study No. 1

Not surprisingly, research on economic issues related to tobacco policy has been of keen interest to policy makers and the public. In the first round of TPREP grants, an award was made to Dr. Frank Chaloupka at the University of Illinois at Chicago to study the impact of cigarette prices on demand among young people. Previous research by Chaloupka and others had shown that an increase in the price of cigarettes reduced not only the probability of smoking but also the amount of cigarette consumption among adult and younger tobacco users.[19] Among adults, it was estimated that a 10 percent increase in the price of cigarettes reduced consumption by 3 to 4 percent. Among younger people, however, the data were less conclusive. Chaloupka proposed to use a larger, more representative dataset to explore the question of how price affects demand and to control for the level of state restrictions on smoking in public places and laws governing how old you must be to buy cigarettes. Partly as a result of additional funding from the CDC, Chaloupka, in collaboration with Dr. Henry Wechsler of Harvard University, was also able to conduct substudies on how sensitive young people were to the price of tobacco products.

One clear finding emerged from Chaloupka's studies: higher cigarette prices had a negative impact on cigarette smoking among teenagers and young adults; that is, increased cigarette prices (which would result from increases in cigarette excise taxes) led to sharp reductions in cigarette smoking among high school and college students. Moreover, these effects were not limited to reductions in the number of cigarettes consumed by smokers. Increases in the price of cigarettes also significantly reduced the number of students who used tobacco. Indeed, every 10 percent increase in the price of cigarettes was estimated to reduce consumption by 11.1 percent among college students and 13.1 percent among high school students. Chaloupka also found that young men were more sensitive to price than young women, and that young black people were nearly three times as sensitive to price as their white counterparts. These findings were published in peer-reviewed journals and widely cited in the press and among policy makers.

Chaloupka testified at the House Ways and Means Committee during the debate on the Clinton Health Care Reform Act, and advised Senator Kennedy's office in 1996 and 1997. He has also provided expert consultation to several states in recent years. For the American Cancer Society project on tobacco tax policy, he helped staff members produce state-level estimates of price effects, and provided advice on this topic for the National Center for Tobacco-Free Kids, a center funded in part by The Robert Wood Johnson Foundation. Most recently, Chaloupka has conferred with staff members of the special congressional committee for the tobacco settlement, and has assisted the American Medical Association in assessing that settlement.

Many of these federal and state efforts couple the increase in cigarette excise tax with the earmarked use of the resulting revenues for a worthy, related cause—tobacco prevention and treatment or providing medical insurance for uninsured children and families. It should be noted that more of these tax increase attempts have failed than have succeeded, and that the tax increases that have been enacted have tended to be small. In addition, in states that have raised the excise tax, the tobacco industry has responded in some instances by lowering prices or increasing marketing. Given the power of the tobacco industry at all levels, however, it is remarkable that so much action has occurred.

Research findings on the price sensitivity of adults and younger people are only one factor, and perhaps not the biggest factor, in the popularity of this policy option. Policy makers and the public are less averse to "sin" taxes than to other taxes, and the fact that an increase in the tobacco tax produces not only reductions in demand and attendant health benefits but also revenue for worthy purposes enhances their appeal.

Case Study No. 2

The second example of the relationship between research and policy impact focuses on an analysis of whether tobacco meets the definition of a drug within the Food & Drug Act—and thus comes under the FDA's authority to regulate it. Dr. John Slade, of St. Peters Medical Center and the University of Medicine and Dentistry of New Jersey, used an unconventional method in making his analysis: he collected extensive information and documents generated by and about the tobacco industry—court documents, patents, scientific papers generated by industry-supported scientists, industry newsletters, and other public documents—and analyzed them for evidence on whether tobacco fits the legal definition of a drug.

Slade's interest in the regulatory role of the FDA arose a decade ago, when he began noticing nicotine delivery products that were occasionally introduced by the tobacco industry. In the late 1980s, for example, the R. J. Reynolds Tobacco Company test-marketed a novel nicotine product called Premier, which looked like a cigarette but did not burn tobacco. It consisted primarily of an apparatus with a charcoal fuel element that focused heat on nicotine and glycerin. The American Medical Association and the American Public Health Association sent petitions to the FDA to regulate this product as a drug. Slade conducted analyses on Premier, communicated with the FDA about it, and later wrote articles about it. After testing Premier for three or four months, Reynolds withdrew the product before the FDA took any action.

From Slade's perspective, these earlier episodes helped to educate staff members at the FDA to the view that tobacco products are similar to pharmaceutical products. The interest of the American Medical Association and the American Heart Association in having the FDA play a central role in regulating tobacco also helped to sensitize staff members at the FDA to the possibility of FDA authority. Other petition drives sponsored by these organizations in the late 1980s, such as the one to regulate cigarettes because of claims for weight reduction made in advertising, helped to move the cause forward. In the late eighties and early nineties, Representative Michael Synar, an Oklahoma Democrat, introduced bills on FDA regulation. Though these bills were not enacted into law, they did raise public awareness of this policy alternative. In January 1993, the American Medical Association held a tobacco workshop to help develop the agenda on tobacco for the newly elected Clinton administration. This further focused attention on the potential role of the FDA.

Thus the idea of the FDA's regulating tobacco as a drug was certainly under discussion in some circles when Slade received a Robert Wood Johnson Foundation grant in 1993 to conduct a detailed policy analysis. As a result of the grant, he was able to accelerate his work and thereby have the time to respond to requests for information from FDA staff members. In one case, he sent information to the FDA on patents issued to tobacco companies. One patent filed by inventors at RJR described nicotine absorption as important to the drug delivery function of cigarettes.

In August 1995, the FDA made its historic decision to propose regulating nicotine as a drug. As a result, Slade used his research to provide a formal commentary on the proposed FDA regulations on behalf of the American Society for Addictive Medicine. The commentary Slade eventually submitted in 1996 was the second most extensive one submitted, exceeded only by that from the tobacco industry. Slade's commentary included a lengthy analysis of whether tobacco fit the legal definition of a drug (he concluded that it did) and several boxes of documents upon which the analysis was based. In the final FDA ruling, published in August 1996, Slade's commentary is cited several times, as are other studies supported under TPREP.[20]

These two case studies illustrate a few key lessons about bringing research findings from TPREP and SAPRP to bear on informing policy making. First, timing is critical. The Robert Wood Johnson Foundation invested resources in tobacco policy research at a time when there was sufficient capacity in the research community to conduct high-quality studies, but the field was not oversaturated with either researchers or other funders. In fact, once the Foundation invested relatively limited resources, it had the dual effect of attracting more researchers to the field and helping funders realize that tobacco policy research was a legitimate place to invest. Fortuitously, substantive developments in tobacco policy—from litigation to whistle-blowers to tax increases—further facilitated the increased relevance of tobacco policy topics among the research community, the public, and policy makers, and produced fertile ground for disseminating results.

Second, the combination of applying stringent review standards for which studies were funded, combined with flexibility in funding studies that might be too risky for other funders to support, led to a funding portfolio that was both methodologically strong and innovative. In addition, the Foundation generally invested both in investigators with known track records in tobacco control or other research fields and in new investigators showing potential for developing into high-quality researchers.

FUTURE DIRECTIONS FOR TOBACCO POLICY RESEARCH

SAPRP will continue funding investigator-initiated tobacco policy research for at least three more years. A number of broad areas are in need of additional research. In the most recent call for proposals, many general topics were identified as being of interest:

- The effects of policies to control the availability and the accessibility of tobacco
- The intended and unintended consequences of changes in policies regulating tobacco

- The effects of societal trends in attitudes and norms on tobacco
- The effects of tobacco treatment policies within organized health care systems
- The effects of harm reduction policies
- Policy studies on tobacco and social class, ethnicity, and gender
- The nature and effects of changes in advertising and media policies
- Changes in how school systems select and monitor or assess tobacco prevention programs
- The interplay between litigation and legislation in developing controls on tobacco
- Legal, ethical, and historical policy analyses of public- and private-sector strategies that influence tobacco use

More specifically, future research should take into account emerging societal and industry trends. For example, changes in information technology are occurring rapidly, both in the United States and abroad, opening up new channels of communication—the Internet and other interactive media. These information technologies will undoubtedly be used by tobacco companies to promote their products, so understanding the impact of the new technologies is critical. Moreover, regulation of tobacco company marketing, either through a settlement or in a more piecemeal fashion, will change the ways in which tobacco companies reach consumers. We need to look no further than the early 1970s, when, despite bans on cigarette advertising on television and radio, the tobacco companies were able to reach consumers more cost-effectively through print and promotional media campaigns. If billboards, certain promotions, and some magazine advertising are banned in the nineties, we must be ready to study the effects of new industry strategies to market tobacco.

There is also a great need for research on new products. Whether or not the FDA is granted the ability to regulate nicotine, there are new nicotine and nonnicotine delivery devices being test-marketed (RJR's Eclipse "low-smoke" cigarette, for example) or in the product development stage. The health impact of these products and how they are regulated is important to examine.

In the mid-nineties, tobacco litigation has emerged as an effective strategy for rectifying many of the problems caused by tobacco use.

Researchers need to study different litigation strategies, documents obtained through the litigation process, and the impact of this approach.

Changes in health care systems brought about by managed care and welfare reform have considerable influence on reimbursement for prevention, cessation, and treatment services available to a large number of current and future tobacco users. The impact of these changes in reimbursement and service delivery on tobacco prevention and cessation needs further study. Also, the availability and the use of nicotine replacement products, both over the counter and through prescription, will require study.

The impact of economic adjustments in the tobacco sector among farm families and communities heavily dependent upon tobacco has emerged in recent years as a topic worthy of much additional research.

The effects of tobacco policies on tobacco use remains a key area for further research. For example, there is still much to learn about the impact on tobacco use of policies that limit tobacco marketing, young people's ability to buy tobacco, and smoking in public settings.

Tobacco use in foreign countries and the role played by American tobacco companies may well be the most important tobacco policy issue of the next century. Although Foundation guidelines currently state that "studies of policies in other countries will be considered only to the extent they may directly inform U.S. policy," other philanthropies are well advised to dedicate resources to this critically important issue. Unfortunately, whatever progress the nation makes is more than offset by a steep increase in worldwide demand for tobacco.

CONCLUSION

In the 1992 annual report of The Robert Wood Johnson Foundation—a report that highlighted the Foundation's commitment to substance abuse—the chairman of the board of trustees, Sidney F. Wentz, wrote, "This country will somehow bring substance abuse under control. . . . There's no sword to cut through this Gordian knot, but we, as a Foundation, are obliged to keep picking at the strands of it with unremitting determination if we are ever to achieve our goal of improved health care for all Americans." In the short period of time that the Foundation has funded tobacco policy research, much has been achieved. Indeed, in the past ten years the field of tobacco policy research has literally blossomed. There is now a critical mass of established researchers. There is a recognition by the larger research community that tobacco-related research must include policy studies. And, largely as a result of investments made by the Foundation, both directly and through its influence on other funders, substantially more resources are available to support tobacco policy research.

Tobacco policy research has made important contributions both to the policy sciences and to policy impact. Indeed, the ability of tobacco policy researchers to contribute to the academic enterprise and to policy making reflects the vitality of the field. The Robert Wood Johnson Foundation, through its investment in tobacco policy research, provided critical support at a critical time to this emerging subdiscipline. By providing this support, the Foundation effectively pursues its mission to improve the health and health care of all Americans. As we look to the future, we see tobacco policy research thriving in a dynamic environment. The continuing harm caused by tobacco use in the United States and abroad necessitates that tobacco policy research remain front and center.

Notes

1. G. A. Giovino, M. W. Schooley, B. P. Zhu, J. H. Chrismon, J. P. Peddicord, R. K. Merritt, C. G. Husten, and M. P. Erickson. "Surveillance for Selected Tobacco-use Behaviors—United States—1990–1994," *MMWR* (1994), 43, 1–43.

2. L. D. Johnston, P. M. O'Malley, and J. G. Bachman, *National Trends in Drug Use and Related Factors among American High School Students and Young Adults, 1975–1993* (Rockville, Md: U.S. Department of Health and Human Services, 1994).

3. U.S. Department of Health and Human Services, *Preventing Tobacco Use Among the Young: A Report of the Surgeon General* (Atlanta, Ga.: Public Health Service, Centers for Disease Control and Prevention, Office on Smoking and Health, 1994).

4. J. M. McGinnis and P. R. Lee, "Healthy People 2000 at Mid Decade," *Journal of the American Medical Association* 273 (1995), 1123–1129.

5. L. D. Johnston, *Cigarette Smoking Continues to Rise Among American Teenagers in 1996* (University of Michigan, 1996).

6. R. Peto and others, *British Medical Bulletin* 52 (1996), 12–21.

7. C.J.L. Murray and A. D. Lopez, *Lancet* 349 (1997), 1498–1504.

8. R. M. Davis, "Tobacco Policy Research Comes of Age," *Tobacco Control* 4 (1995), 6–9.

9. U.S. Department of Health and Human Services, *Reducing the Health Consequences of Smoking—25 Years of Progress: A Report of the Surgeon General* (Vol. DHHS Publication No. CDC89–8411, Rockville, Md.: U.S. Department of Health and Human Services, Office on Smoking and Health, 1989).

10. See note 9.

11. See note 3.

12. See note 5.

13. J. Pinney, *Report on a Study of Tobacco Policy Research and Development* (Prepared for the Smoking, Tobacco, and Cancer Program, National Cancer Institute, Bethesda, Md.: Corporate Health Policies Group, Inc., 1989).

14. J. P. Pierce, D. M. Burns, C. Berry, B. Rosbrook, J. Goodman, E. Gilpin, D. Winn, and D. Bal, "Reducing Tobacco Consumption in California: Proposition 99 Seems to Work." *JAMA* 265 (1991), 1257–1258.

15. The Lewin Group, *Assessment of the Substance Abuse Policy Research Program and Tobacco Policy Research and Evaluation Program* (Fairfax, Va.: The Lewin Group, 1997).

16. See note 15.

17. F. Chaloupka, personal communication, July 29, 1997.

18. J. Slade, personal communication, July 29, 1997.

19. See note 3.

20. Food and Drug Administration, *Regulations Restricting the Sale and Distribution of Cigarettes and Smokeless Tobacco Products to Protect Children and Adolescents; Proposed Rule Analysis Regarding FDA's Jurisdiction over Nicotine-Containing Cigarettes and Smokeless Tobacco Products* (Federal Register 60, No. 155, 21 CFR Part 801, et al.: Department of Health and Human Services, Food and Drug Administration, 1995).

Exhibit 2.1. Tobacco Policy Research and Evaluation Program Grant Titles.

Principal Investigator	Institution	Project Title
Frank Chaloupka, Ph.D.	University of Illinois, Chicago	Price, Policy, and Youth Tobacco Use
Susan Curry, Ph.D.	Group Health Cooperative of Puget Sound	The Impact of Different Coverage Structures on the Utilization and Cost-Effectiveness of Smoking Cessation Services
Ronald Davis, M.D.	Michigan Department of Public Health	Policy-Makers' Support for Community Tobacco Control Policies: The Impact of Local Public Opinion Profiles
June Flora, Ph.D.	Stanford University	Cigarette Advertising and Promotion Code: Adolescent Perceptions of Smoking-Related Cues
Donald Garner, J.D.	Southern Illinois University at Carbondale	Prohibition of Tobacco Billboard Advertising
Adam Goldstein, M.D.	University of North Carolina, Chapel Hill	State Legislators and Tobacco Control Legislation
Kenneth Warner, Ph.D.	University of Michigan	Economic Impact of Progress Toward a Tobacco-Free Society: A Regional Macroeconomic Analysis
Nancy A. Rigotti, M.D.	Massachusetts General Hospital	Does Active Enforcement of Tobacco Sales Laws Reduce Adolescents' Smoking?
Daniel Longo, Sc.D.	University of Missouri-Columbia, School of Medicine	The Effect of Workplace Smoking Policies on Smoking Behavior
Shoshanna Sofaer, Dr.Ph.	George Washington University Medical Center	Factors Influencing Implementation of the Synar Amendment

ॐ

Exhibit 2.1. Tobacco Policy Research and Evaluation Program Grant Titles, *continued.*

Principal Investigator	Institution	Project Title
Glorian Sorensen, Ph.D., M.P.H	Dana-Farber Cancer Institute	Organized Labor and the Diffusion of Worksite Tobacco Control Policies
Lisa Bero, Ph.D.	University of California, San Francisco	Evaluation of the Quality and Sponsorship of Research on Environmental Tobacco Smoke
K. Michael Cummings, Ph.D., M.P.H	Health Research, Inc., Roswell Park Cancer Institute	Environmental and Policy Determinants of Tobacco Use
Richard Daynard, J.D., Ph.D.	Tobacco Control Resource Center, Inc.	Analysis of the Implications of the Americans with Disabilities Act for Environmental Tobacco Smoke Policy
Marc Galanter, J.D.	University of Wisconsin	Assessing the Contribution of Private Law to the Control of Tobacco Risks
Peter Jacobson, J.D.	RAND Corporation	Assessing the Implementation of Tobacco Control Laws
Rick Kropp, M.A.	North Bay Health Resources Center	Study of Compliance Mechanisms to Reduce Tobacco Sales to Minors
Leonard Miller, Ph.D.	University of California, Berkeley	State-by-State Analysis of the Economic Costs of Smoking
John Slade, M.D.	St. Peter's Medical Center	Are Tobacco Products That Contain Nicotine Drugs Under the Food, Drug, and Cosmetic Act?
Peter Arno, Ph.D.	Montefiore Medical Center Albert Einstein College of Medicine	The Potential Social, Political, and Ethical Impacts of Regulating Tobacco as a Drug

cↂↁↂ

Exhibit 2.2. Substance Abuse Policy Research Program: Tobacco-Related Grant Titles.

Principal Investigator	Institution	Project Title
William Hoyt, Ph.D.	University of Kentucky	The Impact of Food Stamps on Marijuana, Tobacco, and Alcohol Use
Theodore Keeler, Ph.D.	University of California, Berkeley	Helping Those Who Help Themselves: Policies to Enhance Individual–Directed Smoking Cessation and Deterrence
Gregory Pope, M.S.	Center for Health Economics Research, Inc.	Smoke-Free Restaurant Ordinances in Massachusetts: A Study of Their Adoption and Economic Impact
Kathryn Montgomery, Ph.D.	Center for Media Education	Virtual Ads Reaching Real Children: The Selling of Alcohol and Tobacco in Cyberspace
Alan Morrison, J.D.	Public Citizen Foundation	Public Citizen: Tobacco Control Project
Lois Biener, Ph.D.	University of Massachusetts at Boston, Center for Survey Research	Tracking Change in Response to the Massachusetts Tobacco Control Program
K. Michael Cummings, Ph.D.	Health Research, Inc., Roswell Park Cancer Institute	Economic and Political Consequences of New York City's Smoke-Free Restaurant Law
Mark Wolfson, Ph.D.	University of Minnesota, School of Public Health	Enforcement of Laws Regulating Youth Access to Tobacco
Daniel Longo, Sc.D.	University of Missouri-Columbia, School of Medicine	Smoking and the Workplace: An Analysis of Relapse
Tim Lynch, Ph.D.	Florida State University	Evaluation of Medicaid Smoking-Related Nursing Home Costs in Florida

Exhibit 2.2. Substance Abuse Policy Research Program: Tobacco-Related Grant Titles, *continued.*

Principal Investigator	Institution	Project Title
Kathleen Kelly, Ph.D.	Colorado State University	The Policy Impact of Restricting Tobacco and Alcohol Advertising
Michael Siegel, M.D., M.P.H.	Boston University School of Public Health	The Influence of Tobacco Marketing and Counter-Advertising on Smoking Initiation Among Youth
William Evans, Ph.D.	University of Maryland at College Park	The Health and Economic Impact of Workplace Smoking Bans
Gregory Falkin, Ph.D.	National Development and Research Institutes, Inc.	Cigarette Smoking Policies in Correctional Institutes: A Study of Bans and Restrictions on Smoking
Richard Daynard, J.D.	Tobacco Control Resource Center	Effective Responses to the Tobacco Industry's Legal Challenges to Local Tobacco Control Efforts: An Empirical Study
Henry Wechsler, Ph.D.	Harvard University, School of Public Health	College Alcohol and Tobacco Policies and Student Use
Vincent Miller, Ph.D.	Miller & Associates	Refinement of a Model to Assess Smoking-Related Medical Care Expenditures
Joseph DiFranza, M.D.	University of Massachusetts Medical Center	An Evaluation of Federal and State Implementation of the Synar Regulations
Sandra Decker, Ph.D.	New York University, Robert F. Wagner Graduate School of Public Service	Interdependence in Cigarette and Alcohol Policies and Consumption
Harold Pollack, Ph.D.	University of Michigan	Substance Abuse Policies and Infant Death
Donald Garner, J.D.	Southern Illinois University at Carbondale, School of Law	Tobacco and Alcohol Advertising Control Policies: Amicus Curiae Briefs

✐

**Exhibit 2.2. Substance Abuse Policy Research Program:
Tobacco-Related Grant Titles,** *continued.*

Principal Investigator	Institution	Project Title
Cindy Pomerleau, Ph.D.	University of Michigan	Fear of Weight Gain as a Barrier to Smoking Cessation in Women
Beth Glover Reed, Ph.D.	University of Michigan, School of Social Work	Federal and State Level Policies and Women: Impact on Services for Alcohol, Tobacco and Other Drugs
A. Thomas McLellan, Ph.D.	Treatment Research Institute	Impact of Managed Care on Substance Abuse Treatment: A Study of Purchasers and Recipients of Services
Barry Lester, Ph.D.	Women and Infants Hospital of Rhode Island	Database of Research on Prenatal Drug Exposure and Child Outcome
Linda Pederson, Ph.D.	Morehouse School of Medicine	Comprehensive Tobacco Control Policies and Smoking Behavior
John Tauras, Ph.D.	University of Illinois at Chicago	Price, Tobacco Control Policies, and Smoking Initiation and Cessation
Glorian Sorensen, Ph.D., M.P.H.	Dana-Farber Cancer Institute	Public Sector Unions and Smoke-Free Policies at the Worksite: A Case Study
David Mendez, Ph.D.	The University of Michigan	The Impact of Smoking Control Policies on Future Smoking Prevalence and Health Status: A System Dynamics Analysis
Marcia Ward, Ph.D.	The University of Iowa	Effectiveness of Clinical Practice Guideline Implementation on Smoking Cessation
James Berman, J.D.	The Center for Social Gerontology, Inc.	Smoking Policies in Elderly Facilities: Assessment of Current Policies and Development of Model Policies

ઝD

Exhibit 2.2. Substance Abuse Policy Research Program: Tobacco-Related Grant Titles, *continued.*

Principal Investigator	Institution	Project Title
Mark Wolfson, Ph.D.	Wake Forest University School of Medicine	Enforcement of Tobacco Age-of-Sale Laws-II
Frank Sloan, Ph.D.	Duke University	Risk Perceptions, Information and Smoking Decisions
William Evans, Ph.D.	University of Maryland, College Park	Research on the Impact of Higher Cigarette Taxes on Maternal Smoking
Kathryn Montgomery, Ph.D.	Center for Media Education	Analysis of the Efficacy of Screening, Blocking and Ratings Technologies for Preventing Youth Access to Alcohol- and Tobacco-Related Websites

CHAPTER THREE

~~~ The National Spit Tobacco Education Program

Leonard Koppett

Editors' Introduction

The 1986 Surgeon General's report on the Health Consequences of Smokeless Tobacco Use focused attention on oral cancer and other diseases caused by "smokeless" or "spit" tobacco. At that time, the smokeless or "chewing" tobacco industry was in the midst of a campaign, begun in the late 1970s, to change attitudes toward its products while ramping up efforts to reach a more youthful audience. The industry, which used celebrity baseball players as models in its advertisements, attempted to convey a message that *smokeless* was synonymous with *harmless*.

The marketing strategy was successful. Sales of moist snuff—commonly referred to as "dip"—rose by 55 percent between 1978 and 1985. Baseball players, particularly, took to spit tobacco. A 1985 survey of male college baseball players found that 40 percent used spit tobacco regularly. A survey taken two years later revealed that over half of professional baseball players had a history of spit tobacco use and that 34 percent were current users.

Staff members at The Robert Wood Johnson Foundation were involved with early efforts—led mainly by the National Cancer Institute—to reverse the trends and decrease the use of spit tobacco. One strategy was to form partnerships with Major League Baseball to break the link between spit tobacco use and the game of baseball. Star players, league officials, and public health leaders were actively engaged in the program, which also had the support of the Major League Teams Physicians Association and the Professional Baseball Athletic Trainers Society.

In 1990, the NCAA banned the use of tobacco in all tournament play. In 1992, Major League Baseball banned spit tobacco for all minor league players in its Rookie and Class A leagues. The Los Angeles Dodgers and the Oakland A's were among the first teams to address the problem of spit tobacco. Los Angeles banned players from carrying snuff or chewing tobacco while in uniform, and Oakland banned tobacco advertising in its program.

In the fall of 1995, The Robert Wood Johnson Foundation held discussions with Oral Health America to develop a program aimed at increasing the level of engagement by major league players. This new program built on the work of Joe Garagiola—former major leaguer, television broadcaster, and recognized ambassador for baseball. Named the National Spit Tobacco Education Program (NSTEP), the initiative involved all twenty-eight major league teams. The Foundation's initial support of $800,000 included community outreach in six major-league cities to build bridges between the team and the local tobacco control and public health community. In its first year the campaign generated more than $30 million worth of media publicity, including national broadcast and print advertising and in-stadium and player promotions. In 1997, support for NSTEP was renewed for three years at a level of $3.5 million in 1997.

The cooperation of Major League Baseball can be attributed largely to the passion and persistence of Joe Garagiola. Garagiola brings a reputation for honesty and integrity within baseball and outside the game. That reputation, combined with his status as a baseball insider, grants him access to many people—from owners and league officials to players, coaches, trainers and to the media and the public. His particular brand of leadership may serve as a lesson for other public health campaigns.

In this chapter, Leonard Koppett, a baseball Hall of Fame sportswriter, chronicles how Joe Garagiola led an effort that changed the way Major League Baseball viewed and responded to the problems of spit tobacco. Joe Marx, a senior communications officer, and Tracy Orleans, a senior scientist, at The Robert Wood Johnson Foundation, reviewed drafts of the chapter. Their comments and suggestions were invaluable.

A s a boy in St. Louis, Joe Garagiola was the second-best baseball player on his block. The best was Larry Berra, also known as Yogi. After World War II, both Joe and Yogi became major league players, and Yogi went on to make it into the Hall of Fame. Yogi's malapropisms, many of them given circulation by Joe, have become a part of the language. "It ain't over till it's over" was one of Berra's maxims, and on another occasion he said, "It was déjà vu all over again." When Garagiola's baseball career ended, his own wit and way with words led him to a second career as a broadcaster and speaker. His work on nationally televised weekly broadcasts and World Series broadcasts gave his style a major showcase, and led to other broadcasting work.

Garagiola became a host on the Today show, wrote a couple of books, and in due course took a leadership position in the Baseball Assistance Team, or BAT, which is devoted to helping former players in need of financial aid and other help, especially those who did not enjoy the benefits of baseball's big-money era. It was through BAT that the scope of the tobacco problem involving ballplayers came to his attention.

"I can't really pinpoint the day that I started with this tobacco thing, any more than I can say that I had a plan to form a national group and do what is being done today," Garagiola said one day in Phoenix, where he now lives. "I'm very grateful for how it has evolved. But I'm not doing a humility act when I tell you that it just happened. I used to do my own little campaign, all by myself, when I was doing the Game of the Week. I'd have my scorebook with me all the time, and I always tried to find a newspaper clipping about oral cancer. I would paste it on the left-hand side of my scorebook so that when I wrote down the lineups it would be there."

Garagiola went on, "Well, you know how ball players are. They're going to come over to see what you're writing. So they would come over and see me writing the lineup—and one or two or more would wind up reading about chewing tobacco. It was always some simple headline, like 'Tobacco Causes Cancer,' and if we talked about it, it was always a one-on-one exchange. I would get on certain guys. One in particular who comes to mind is Bobby Cox. He was managing Toronto. I was sitting on the bench with him, and we talked about it.

'Bobby, that stuff is really bad,' I said. 'And I think you've got a sore in your mouth. You ought to let the trainer look at you.' One day he had the trainer look and found that he had a little sore there. The next time I saw him, he had switched to herbal, the nontobacco thing. I said, 'Bobby, that's great. But are you going to stand at home plate and tell kids who are watching you chew this stuff that it's herbal, that it really is not tobacco? It's just as important to get the message out that you're not using tobacco as it is to stop using it. Don't you see?' And he said, 'Well, what do you want me to do?' I told him, 'Use gum.' The last time I saw him, even before he said hello, he said, 'My jaws are about to fall off from chewing this gum,' and I said, 'Well, you're not going to die from tired jaws.' That's the way it went. I would talk to these guys and kind of get on them, but that didn't do much. It was like trying to hit with a broken bat."

As a writer, I was around all the same people at the same time as Joe Garagiola. One of the first things you learned as a writer was where to put your feet so that the tobacco-chewing players wouldn't ruin your shoes when they spat. Nobody seemed to object to their chewing.

"It was just so prevalent," Garagiola said. "I chewed when I played. I didn't know why. I thought it was part of being a ballplayer. Now I'm convinced guys chew, first of all, out of peer pressure; second, out of boredom; and third, to give off a macho image. I don't lean too much on the macho image part because I think a lot of guys get upset at that, but I do know about boredom. What happens is that you start to play games with the stuff. I spent enough time in the bullpen to know how bored you can get out there.

"In those days, there was none of this dip that you put next to your gums. It was all leaf tobacco, and you put the big chew in your mouth and kept it to one side and did a lot of spitting. So you think of games: who could spit the farthest, who could spit the straightest; hold out your foot, a dollar you can't hit it; there's an ant, let's see who can drown the ant. First guy to drown the ant wins the pot. So it was kind of like a fun thing, and yet it was becoming pretty addictive. That's why I don't minimize it. Guys tell me, 'I only chew when I come to the ball park. I never chew at home. I only chew when I play golf. I only use this stuff when I fish.' But that's not true, because the stuff is addictive. I know I wound up using it at home and thinking nothing of it. So what I was trying to do was simply to tell the other side of the story."

The other side of the story was never mentioned. Writers always write what the people they cover are talking about, and nobody ever talked against chewing. Smoking a cigarette in the dugout became unacceptable at some point, so a player—or the manager—would step down into the passageway to the clubhouse for a smoke. We wrote about that, taking it lightly or not, but that's what we do: reflect what's going on around us.

"The tobacco companies have a word, and the guy who came up with that word should get a huge bonus, because with that one word they really put a whole new spin on this tobacco business, be it chew, be it snuff, be it dip," Garagiola went on. "The word is 'smokeless.' They refer to it as 'smokeless tobacco.' My big battle is to convince people that 'smokeless' is not 'harmless.' Now, 'smokeless' is a nice, fuzzy, protective kind of word, making you think it's a substitute for cigarettes—so go ahead and use it. I don't know how much stronger it is, but I've heard experts say that the nicotine from just one dip is the equivalent of what you can get from four cigarettes. Then how much is one can?

"Well, we did start to carry the message into the clubhouses, and they passed a rule against using tobacco in the minor leagues. There's a fine for doing it, and in the minors any fine is significant. But the policing is supposed to be done by managers and umpires, and they don't do it. They can't. So I don't think we can just ban tobacco use in the minors or the majors. There's no way to police it. That's why education is the key. When you finish a presentation, ballplayers will come up to you and say, 'Man, I really want to quit. What do I do?' Well, up to last year all we could do was give them a '1-800 FOR CANCER' number, and they could call and get some brochures. That was not really the answer."

Garagiola paused, and then said, "So what I was doing was a one-on-one thing. Wherever I went to make a speech, I would manage, somehow, to get the tobacco issue in there. Then a lot of guys would come up and say, 'Man, I'd like to help in your battle.' Well, that sounds good, but nobody was stepping up. Where it really kind of got started was here in Phoenix. I was doing a banquet, and my motivation had just been intensified by two statistics I saw. One was that in 1993, here in Arizona, 9.8 percent of the third- to sixth-graders were users. Now, I'm not a numbers guy, I'm a people guy, but this really got me. I thought, *third- to sixth-graders*? That's scary. Somebody has to say something. So I started talking about that, and people found it very hard to believe.

"Then I read a report that 20 percent of American high school boys, grades nine to twelve, are *current* spit tobacco users. Among white high school boys, it was 25 percent. Well, at this banquet in Phoenix, I was introduced to Don McKenzie, who was on the board of directors of Oral Health America. 'Don may be able to help you fight tobacco.'

"I said, 'If you can, good. But I've been getting nothing but lip service, I want you to know that. So if you're going to help, fine. If not, let's just say hello and I won't waste your time and you won't waste mine.' He looked at me and said, 'I've never been introduced to a guy like that before.' I said, 'Well, if we were just introduced to make friends, I'd be a little friendlier. But I get sick and tired of lip-service people.' He said, 'I think I can help you. I believe we're trying to do something. I'd like to talk to you about it.' So I said, 'Good, let's have a meeting.'"

Garagiola continued, "And he said, 'When can we do that?' I said, 'Any time. You want to do it after the banquet tonight?' He said, 'No, no really, because I have my wife with me and I really can't do it. How about tomorrow?' To myself I thought, I'll find out in a hurry if this guy is for real. 'O.K.,' I said. 'How about seven o'clock?' He said, 'Seven o'clock tomorrow night?' I said, 'No, no, tomorrow morning. I've got a very busy day.'"

"I didn't, but I figured that if this guy would meet me at seven o'clock in the morning, he's serious. Well, he did. We talked. He put me in touch with Oral Health America in Chicago. Their mission is to improve and promote the oral health of Americans. That was the beginning of an important contact."

By that time, Garagiola had collected some powerful real-life examples about tobacco use in baseball. There was the coach in the Cardinal organization known throughout the game for his baseball expertise. He blamed tobacco dip for the fact that a piece of his tongue had to be cut out. "Damn dipping," he said. "My doctor told me I'd better stop, but I had to lose part of my tongue to learn." Unable to speak clearly, he had to learn to speak all over again. Eleven months later, the coach died.

Then there was a young man from Montana who had lost half his face to cancer. Garagiola did a Today show spot with him. He was not a professional, just a guy who loved to play sports. He said that he had started dipping and chewing when he was twelve years old, because everybody else did it. The interview with the young pitcher revealed another aspect of the tragic consequences of tobacco-related disease. The young man talked about his operation, the pain, the inability to raise his arm above his head—and then he told a story about picking up his little boy at school. One day, the boy asked his father to park on the other side of the street. The father thought, He wants to show me how brave he is, that he can walk across the street. But that wasn't it at all. The other kids were teasing his son because of the way his father looked: most of the jaw on the right side of his face had been taken away, and the boy was ashamed of how his father looked.

"Now I'm emceeing the Golden Spikes dinner at the Waldorf in New York, where they honor the college baseball Player of the Year," Garagiola said in Phoenix. "I see all these young faces, and the tobacco thing keeps popping into my mind, and I say to myself, Oh, man, this isn't the spot to do it, but do it. Talk about it. Don't talk about it. I figure they're not paying me, so talking about spit tobacco would be my payday. So I went into my tobacco thing and directed it at these young guys. I gave it my best shot: smokeless is *not* harmless, the whole number. And the reaction from the audience was really good. In fact, it turns out that Alex Rodriquez, now with the Seattle Mariners, was on the dais at the time and heard me. He was one of the first players who wanted to help. He picked up the phone later, I didn't have to call him, and he said, 'What can I do?'

"Anyway, right after the awards dinner was over, Creighton Hale, the head of the Little League, who knew me, came up to me. 'I didn't realize you had such a passion against tobacco,' he said. I let loose.

"Oh, man, I just think we have to do something. We have an oral cancer epidemic on our hands. It's hidden. It's silent. Nobody's doing anything because smoking is getting all the publicity. Secondhand smoke and stop smoking here and no smoking on planes. And the tobacco companies are laughing. They're going to make their money by exporting the cigarettes, and what they will do is target the young people. You see it, the rodeos, the good-old-boys circuit with the Skoal-branded car, the country-western concerts and the rock concerts. And they give these free samples on the college breaks. You can see they're targeting the young people with this stuff and making it sound like a good alternative to cigarettes even though they put on the packages, 'This is not a safe alternative to cigarettes.' Then there's the whole insidious advertising campaign."

Garagiola went on, "I tell him about those little flavor packs, like little tea bags, which sting a little bit but taste like hard candy. That's how you start. And it says on there, 'Try Skoal flavor packs when you can't smoke,' although they don't actually say that. That's how they get you started. After you use that for a while, you want something stronger, and you go to the middle group, and then that buzz is not enough for you and you graduate to the top of the brand. Then they got you.

"At the time, I didn't know it would come out in the tobacco hearings that, yes, that's how they do it. They have a starter product and a graduation product. So Creighton Hale introduced me to Neil Romano. His company does educational programs, and they had done the anti-spit-tobacco campaign for the Little League. We put him in touch with Oral Health America. We got enough money to set up a press conference at the National Press Club in Washington, at which I would have Bill Tuttle tell his story."

Bill Tuttle's story starts with a request to BAT—I had covered him when he played in the major leagues, but had lost touch with him after he retired. He was a first-rate outfielder with Detroit, Kansas City, and Minnesota for eleven years, ending in 1963—when pay scales were low and long before the players had an effective union. In 1993, his wife, Gloria, called BAT because Bill had to go to the hospital and they wouldn't admit him without a $5,000 down payment. She had noticed a big lump on the side of his jaw and thought he was still chewing in the house, but he said he wasn't. They went to a doctor, who took one look and said get him to a hospital immediately. In a thirteen-hour operation, they removed the biggest malignant tumor in the history of the University of Minnesota Hospital.

Gloria was all for going after the tobacco companies because they hadn't told the whole story about spit tobacco. Garagiola asked if they could come to a press conference in Washington. Gloria said sure, as Bill was going around to high schools and talking about it already.

"So Tuttle would be the story," Garagiola said. "But Bill Tuttle or Joe Garagiola was not going to attract a crowd to the National Press Club. So I called Mickey Mantle, asked him what his feelings were, and would he come? And he proceeded to tell me that he was anti-chewing tobacco. That was kind of interesting, because he said that when he came up to the Yankees, Casey Stengel, the manager, asked him if he had to chew that stuff. Mickey said he didn't have to, but he chewed it because he had done it back in Oklahoma. Anyhow, he said, 'Yeah, I'll come.'"

Garagiola went on, "The other player I wanted was Hank Aaron, because I'm a big Aaron fan. We all know what a great ballplayer he was and what he's done. I've always felt that when Henry Aaron has something to say and he believes it, he is going to say it and let the chips fall where they may. So I called Henry and he said, 'Yeah.' He told me a story about a high school kid he had tried to talk out of tobacco, a football player who eventually died. He told me how when he was running the minor league system for the Braves, he wouldn't even put pockets in the back of the players' pants so that they would have no place to put tobacco. Yes, he'd be happy to come.

"With Mickey Mantle and Hank Aaron as my headliners, and then Bill Tuttle and Leonard Coleman"—the president of the National League—"I knew that we would pack the place, because people would show up to at least try to get Mantle's and Aaron's autograph. And that's exactly what happened. It was a very successful press conference—so successful that Senator George Mitchell was having a press conference next door and nobody was showing up, so he came over to our room. So we had a big crowd, lots of cameras, a lot of publicity. Lo and behold, Mantle told a story. Aaron told a story. Coleman told a story, and Tuttle told his story—and Joycelyn Elders, the Surgeon General, was there to hear it. In fact, she even gave facts and figures on what spit tobacco did and was supportive. We got full coverage because the cameras and newspapers were there. That's when we started to develop a plan: we'd go to the major leaguers and tell our story.

"The contact had been made with The Robert Wood Johnson Foundation because they had people who were interested. A proposal was made and they funded our effort, which we called The National Spit Tobacco Education Campaign. We started in the spring of 1996. Until Robert Wood Johnson came along, I was working with a broken bat—now I had a Louisville Slugger.

"When I'd go into a clubhouse, I could see the look on their faces that said, 'Oh, God, here comes another one of those sermons.' They get one from the FBI guy about unsavory characters and betting and all that, and then the insurance people come in. So I tell them right away that baseball did not pay our way. We're here because we believe in it and we thank the ball clubs for giving us the opportunity. But I'm also here to tell you we are going to talk about tobacco, but I'm not saying you should quit. I'm telling you it's a choice. Baseball is a game of choice. I chose to be a catcher. Some of you choose to be pitchers. Some choose to be infielders. I talk choice. You take a curve ball, you choose to hit a fast ball. That's the way it is with tobacco. We want you to make the right choice.

"Then Tuttle tells his story, and when he's finished, I say, 'You know, guys, now I want you to think about your wife or your father or your mother or your sister or brother or loved one, because you heard Bill Tuttle say that the doctor told him his operation was going to take two to two-and-a-half hours—and it took thirteen. Think of your wife or your loved one sitting in that waiting room thinking you're going to come out in two hours, and now it's hour five. It's hour seven.' And then I say, 'But I'm not going to tell you because I didn't live it. Gloria will tell you.'"

Garagiola continued, "And Gloria's even more powerful than Bill, because she doesn't have a script. But she also gets frustrated and angry. One time, she got angry and called me. 'Why don't you just write a letter, just to get it out,' I told her, 'and send it to me.' The letter was so powerful that I called *USA Today* and asked if they would print it. They did. The opening line was 'I'm watching the man I love die.' When I saw it in print, I thought, we have to get this into the hands of the wives. So I called Don Fehr, the head of the Players Association, and with his help we were able to get it to the wives. We got a big reaction from the wives.

"We also had a lot of help from the ballplayers themselves, and most were willing to help. The first players we approached to participate in the campaign were Jeff Bagwell, Frank Thomas, and Hank Aaron. Other players were volunteering to come up and help us. At a typical visit to the ballpark, players would walk up to me and say, 'how's the tobacco thing going? If there's anything I can do, let me know.' Now, because of The Robert Wood Johnson Foundation, we were able to do videos, posters, and all that good stuff. We were able to do things we couldn't do before. So we went to guys like Lenny Dykstra, Mike Piazza, Tino Martinez, Alex Rodriquez, and Paul Molitor, and they agreed to do television spots broadcast during major-league games. We did events in the stadiums and health and antitobacco people brought in kids from the community, and the ballplayers would join us after batting practice—on their own time—to speak to the press and the young people and the Little Leaguers who were in the audience. And we'd hand out a poster featuring a player from every major-league team. Every town we went to, we got newspaper columns, we did interviews in the team's broadcast booth and we did radio and television shows. I also sent a letter and a brochure ('Talking About Spit Tobacco and Baseball with Joe Garagiola') to the networks and the baseball card companies. Fox, NBC, and others tried to keep the cameras away from players who were chewing and spitting. The trading card companies stopped photographing players with a big wad in their cheek. We had our ads in team magazines and other publications. The Seattle Mariners, for one, even made the decision to ban tobacco advertising in all of its publications and in the stadium. And Major League Baseball gave us full-page ads in the World Series and All Star Games programs.

"More help came from Charles Schulz—Sparky—who does the 'Peanuts' comic strip. He not only did a cartoon, he did it on a Sunday, the day before the All-Star Game in 1996. The coverage on that was tremendous. Not only that, he used his own money to do an animation piece for us. It's used by most ball clubs. It's a very powerful one.

"I told my story to President Clinton and urged him not to refer to it as smokeless tobacco but as 'spit tobacco.' I told him why, and he agreed, and he used that in an announcement he made in the East Room of the White House about their effort to keep tobacco away from kids. That was the beginning of getting really big support, because the President talking about not only cigarettes but also spit tobacco brought this subject to the forefront.

"We were doing our spring training tour, and the President wanted to single us out. He called a press conference, and two young women from the Olympic soccer team were to be singled out for their battle against tobacco. Gloria and Bill Tuttle were there with me, and the President singled us out, so that was a sign of approval. Before such a press conference, you get a chance to talk to the President. I asked him if he was going to throw out the first ball at Baltimore—after the strike—and he said yes.

"'If you would just issue another statement,' I said, 'or even have a press conference, which would be great, I think—I'm *sure*—I could get Bud Selig and Don Fehr to be there. That would be the first time that these guys had been together and able to agree on anything, and you would be the guy who brought them together.'"

Bud Selig, owner of the Milwaukee Brewers and the acting commissioner of baseball, and Don Fehr had been the principal opposing figures in the strike that led to cancellation of the 1994 World Series and was settled only after most of the 1995 spring training session had been wiped out. They stood at the opposite poles of the labor war. An earlier attempt by President Clinton to mediate the strike had failed. Garagiola's suggestion had many positive overtones.

Garagiola went on, "The President said, 'I'll talk to my scheduling people.' Well, it worked out. We had the press conference, we went to the ball game with the President, were seen with him, and that really gave us the Good Housekeeping Seal of Approval. Now we were really off and running.

"We got even more funding from The Robert Wood Johnson Foundation in 1997—for three years—to try and get the final piece—cessation programs. We've talked to Major League Baseball and the Players Association and they've agreed to do a cessation program—the job now is to make sure it gets put in place. We can't just do it with brochures. Players have to have experts to help them quit. Guys would walk up to me in the clubhouse after our presentation and say, 'Man, I want to quit.' We want to get to a point where the team doctors and dentists can provide the help. Rather than the players coming up to me for advice . . . that wasn't cuttin' it. I'd feel inadequate giving a brochure. So now the players can get checked regularly for signs of oral cancer at spring training and the cessation specialists will be there to help the players who want to quit.

"We'll start to work on the rural areas with rodeo, 4–H kids, colleges, baseball coaches, and the NCAA. That's how we'll spread the word and get the message out. When I spoke to two thousand coaches of the ABCA (that's the American Baseball Coaches Association) in Dallas, I couldn't believe the number of coaches and managers that were using spit tobacco even though they have a big campaign on: 'If you spit, you sit.' I also spoke at the Little League Congress twice trying to get coaches to spread the word. I want these coaches to be ambassadors. It's like throwing a rock out on the lake and getting the ripple effect. I'm deputizing these guys to go back to their towns and carry out the NSTEP, or National Spit Tobacco Education Program, campaign. But when I did a gig for the Arizona State University baseball team, I asked how strongly it was enforced. 'One of the first things the umpires say,' a coach told me, 'is "look, if you're going to use the stuff, try not to use it in the open, okay?"' So they're not encouraging it, but they certainly are condoning it, because they don't want to be watchdogs.

"On the other hand," Garagiola said, "the trainers have been terrifically supportive—minor league, major league, colleges, all of them.

Supportive from day one had been Fehr and Gene Orza of the Players Association; Len Coleman and Gene Budig, the major league presidents; and Bud Selig. In one sense, baseball gets a bad rap. People say, 'Look at the big leaguers who use it.' But now we're getting kids into the system who use it in high school and college, as if the big leaguers made them do it. Somehow, baseball has got the reputation that tobacco—chew and dip—are part of baseball tradition. Well, as I tell everybody, cancer has never been a tradition.

"More and more prominent players are speaking out for us. Our poster shows one star from every team. Mark McGwire, whose father is a dentist, told a St. Louis audience recently, 'You know how I feel about spit tobacco. It doesn't help you hit. Don't do it. Don't start.' Major league baseball has been most supportive, and many big stars are speaking up for us. And I'll never forget what Mantle and Aaron did for us."

Listening to Garagiola's account, I was struck by two things in particular. One was the possibility suggested by the incident of spreading the word to the wives. Perhaps the best targets for this education campaign are girls and young women. They have the most direct effect on the behavior of boys and men in the same age group. If girls can be persuaded to show boys that they, the girls, find spit tobacco use disgusting, a powerful force against its use might be generated. The other was how much could be accomplished by one determined and talented person who could continue to be motivated through long periods of little visible result.

Of course, Joe had certain advantages that most people don't. The breadth of his contacts and friendships throughout the baseball world, along with his degree of celebrity, gave him access to people who were also notables in this field. It also gave his message credibility. As an ultimate insider, he had an opportunity outsiders can't match. The steps by which Garagiola moved to develop a wider level of support—his persistence and creative use of publicity when the right circumstances presented themselves—can guide all sorts of health education projects.

CHAPTER FOUR

~~ Alcohol and Work

Results from a
Corporate Drinking Study

Thomas W. Mangione
Jonathan Howland
Marianne Lee

Editors' Introduction

Addressing problems associated with alcohol use is the focus of three current Foundation-funded national programs:

- A Matter of Degree, which supports efforts on college communities and surrounding communities to reduce binge drinking
- Reducing Underage Drinking Through Coalitions, which supports state-based citizens' coalitions to develop strategies to address underage drinking
- Screening and Brief Interventions for Alcohol Abuse in Managed Care, which supports new approaches during medical office visits to address alcohol abuse problems

Inappropriate alcohol use is also the focus of a range of other Foundation-funded national initiatives that address problems associated with alcohol, illegal drugs, and tobacco. In addition, the Foundation is currently funding 103 single-site programs that are addressing alcohol abuse.

Despite this substantial Foundation investment, only a handful of efforts have focused on the workplace as a setting to address the problems of alcohol. This chapter presents the findings from a Foundation-funded survey to explore alcohol use and performance problems in the workplace. The authors were part of a team that conducted research for the Worksite Prevention of Alcohol Problems study at the Harvard and Boston University Schools of Public Health, and at the John Snow Inc., or JSI, in Boston, Massachusetts. Thomas Mangione is a senior research scientist at, and Marianne Lee is a consultant with, the JSI Research and Training Institute; Jonathan Howland is a professor at the Boston University School of Public Health.

The effectiveness of corporate efforts to deal with alcohol problems among employees may be limited by misperceptions about who is causing most of the alcohol-related problems and about how alcohol affects work performance. Occasional heavy drinking by otherwise light and moderate drinkers may contribute as much or more to work-performance problems as do the alcohol-dependent drinkers.

Changes concerning society's perspectives on alcohol use have occurred in areas outside the workplace. For instance, a better understanding of the relationship between drunk driving fatalities and alcohol use—that it is not just the alcohol-dependent drinkers who are at risk for traffic crashes, but anyone driving after drinking—has contributed to the change in public policy in recent years. The harm that binge drinking by college students causes other students as well as the drinkers themselves has stimulated debates about alcohol use on campuses across the nation. It may now be time to revisit workplace alcohol policies and practices.

The authors were part of a team that conducted a large study of alcohol use and the workplace.[1] As part of this research we interviewed senior corporate executives and plant managers face to face, conducted over a hundred focus groups with employees, and surveyed nearly 14,000 managers, supervisors, and hourly workers in seven Fortune 500 companies.

Those seven corporations included two conglomerates as well as a paper manufacturing company, an insurance company, a building materials company, a petroleum products company, and a regional utility company. We gathered information about alcohol issues from them through several procedures—we talked extensively with over 150 senior management personnel at each corporate headquarters site and at some selected other worksites; we conducted a survey of 7,255 managers and supervisors in 114 different worksites across the seven corporations; we conducted a survey of 6,540 employees at sixteen selected worksites that represented a range of industries and of management attitudes toward drinking; and we visited to observe the work setting in these selected worksites.

The managerial survey was conducted by mailing questionnaires to the homes of a sample of managers and supervisors in 114 worksites.

We obtained a response rate of 79 percent for a total of 7,255 surveys returned. The employee survey was also conducted by mailing questionnaires to the homes of all employees (supervisors, managers, and hourly workers) in sixteen worksites (at five very large sites we took a sample of employees). We obtained a response rate of 71 percent for a total of 6,540 surveys returned.

For the most part, corporate executives and senior managers were quite willing to talk with us. They were proud of the progress that American industry, and their companies in particular, have made in dealing with alcohol-dependent employees. They have seen the perception of alcohol abuse and dependency shift from being a moral failing to a disease requiring treatment, witnessed the decline of the three-martini lunch in the wake of federal tax reform, and observed the advent of company-supported employee assistance programs, or EAPs, that deal with a range of employee problems but focus primarily on psychological and substance abuse issues. In response to emerging community norms about drunk driving, they have seen attitudes change about the appropriateness of heavy drinking at company-sponsored functions and at lunch. Even with these changes, alcohol consumption is estimated to cost American industry (and hence consumers) about $27 billion annually in lost productivity.[2]

Executives of the seven corporations that participated in the study recognized alcohol as a continuing concern for their industries. The senior managers were confident that they understood the scope of the alcohol problem in their companies and felt that they had put in place reasonable systems to address employee alcohol-dependency problems. They were concerned about the high cost of these substance abuse treatment programs and were interested in other ways that alcohol problems among their employees could be reduced. The findings of the study, however, cast doubt on some fundamental perceptions about workplace drinking, and suggest the true economic costs of alcohol abuse and dependency to business might be greatly underestimated.

The study provides evidence to support two important observations that have not been fully recognized. First, most alcohol-related work-performance problems are caused by employees who would not be considered alcohol dependent; second, drinking patterns away from the worksite can affect work performance and hence both worker safety and the company's bottom line. Furthermore, the study identifies the potential for changing employee drinking practices through new worksite intervention strategies.

In the study, we encountered six beliefs widely held by corporate executives and senior managers concerning alcohol issues in their companies that were challenged by the managerial and employee surveys. The findings suggest new directions that American industry might take to better respond to and prevent employee alcohol-related problems.

MYTH ONE
Alcohol-Related Work-Performance Problems Are Mostly Caused by a Few Alcohol-Dependent Employees

From our interviews of senior executives of the seven companies, it is clear that they have come to understand that alcohol-dependent employees are at risk for coming to work inebriated or drinking on the job. They also believe that working under the influence of alcohol could compromise work performance and present a safety risk to the drinking employee and other workers.

Accordingly, supervisors try to identify workers exhibiting work-performance problems and refer them for treatment if these problems are alcohol related. One corporate executive responsible for developing and implementing alcohol policies in his company said, "Every company I know has a few bad apples. Our job is to identify these individuals, get them help if they will take it, and let them go if they won't. This is the way we solve our alcohol problems. Our company is probably pretty average. Less than 10 percent of our workers have problems with alcohol. When a job performance problem surfaces, we get treatment services for that worker." The results of the survey of employees at sixteen worksites reveal a different picture. The majority of alcohol-related work-performance problems are manifested by workers who are not alcohol dependent. This is a result of two factors: first, the number of alcohol-dependent employees at the workplace is much smaller than the number of non-dependent drinkers (23 percent dependent versus 77 percent nondependent); and second, even though the rate of work-related problems is less among nondependent drinkers than alcohol-dependent employees, *there are so many more nondependent drinkers that their alcohol-related work problems in aggregate exceed those of the dependent employees.*

We sorted workers into three categories by their drinking behaviors, including whether they currently drank and their responses to the

CAGE measure, an alcohol-dependency screening instrument.[3] CAGE is a four-item screening scale for alcohol dependency that includes the following questions: Have you ever felt the need to Cut down on your drinking? Have people ever Annoyed you by criticizing your drinking? Have you ever felt badly or Guilty about your drinking? Have you ever had a drink first thing in the morning (an Eye opener)?

One category was "alcohol dependent." Employees who scored two or more on CAGE were categorized as alcohol dependent even if they were not currently drinking. A second category was nondependent drinkers, which included all drinkers who scored less than two on the CAGE scale. The third was abstainers: lifetime abstainers and those who reported they were no longer drinking and also scored less than two on the CAGE. In our sample, 19 percent were classified as alcohol dependent, 61 percent as nondependent drinkers, and 20 percent as abstainers. These proportions are similar to those reported by other investigators.[4]

We measured work-performance problems by asking employees how many times they experienced five types of performance issues in the past year—absenteeism, arriving to work late or leaving early, doing poor quality work, doing less work, and having arguments with coworkers.[5] These types of questions have been used by other researchers[6,7] as indicators of poor work functioning.[8]

Obviously, there are many reasons someone might be absent or late to work that have nothing to do with drinking, such as traffic problems or sick children. In order to estimate the proportion of work-performance problems reported to us that could be attributed to alcohol use, we first calculated the average number of problems reported by abstainers (4.2 per year); see Figure 4.1.

We then assumed that abstainer-level problems represented the average number of work-performance problems that had nothing to do with drinking. We considered any number of problems over the abstainers' level to be alcohol related for both the nondependent and the alcohol-dependent employees.

Alcohol-dependent employees in the study averaged a total of 6.9 incidents; by subtracting the abstainer levels, we calculated that 2.7 of these incidents (6.9 minus 4.2) could be considered alcohol related. Nondependent drinkers averaged a total of 5.4 incidents; of these, 1.2 could be considered alcohol related—again by comparison with the abstainer level.

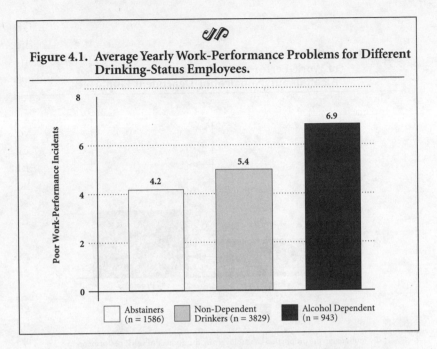

Figure 4.1. Average Yearly Work-Performance Problems for Different Drinking-Status Employees.

As one would expect, alcohol-dependent employees reported more alcohol-related poor work-performance incidents than nondependent drinkers (2.7 versus 1.2 incidents). However, as nondependent drinkers were three times as numerous as alcohol-dependent employees, their contribution as a group to the total number of alcohol-related problems reported turns out to be greater (59 percent versus 41 percent), as illustrated in Figure 4.2.

If corporate managers direct their intervention efforts primarily toward alcohol-dependent employees, they are missing the source of a substantial number of alcohol-related problems. In addition to assisting alcohol-dependent employees, corporations would benefit by trying to affect the drinking behaviors that create work-performance problems among nondependent drinkers.

MYTH TWO

Employees Who Don't Drink on the Job Will Not Have Their Work Performance Affected by Alcohol

Corporate drinking policies have both a humanitarian and a practical justification: to provide assistance to the troubled worker and to

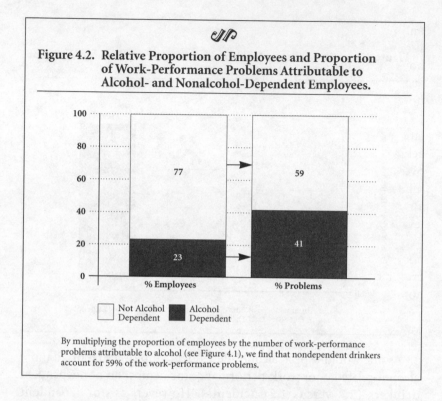

Figure 4.2. Relative Proportion of Employees and Proportion
of Work-Performance Problems Attributable to
Alcohol- and Nonalcohol-Dependent Employees.

By multiplying the proportion of employees by the number of work-performance
problems attributable to alcohol (see Figure 4.1), we find that nondependent drinkers
account for 59% of the work-performance problems.

prevent work-performance problems due to intoxicated personnel.[9]
Most alcohol-related performance problems probably do not result
from being intoxicated but rather from light drinking at lunch or from
the residual effects of heavy drinking the night before. Low blood
alcohol concentrations (BACs) can increase the likelihood of impaired
performance even when an employee is not, nor appears to be, intoxicated. This is because impairment increases gradually; it does not necessarily start at some threshold level of exposure. Also, alcohol's
residual effects (hangovers) are such that even at zero BAC and without causing obvious physical symptoms, work performance can be
impaired the day after a night of heavy drinking.

All the companies we studied had policies prohibiting employees
from working under the influence of alcohol. None, however, had
explicit standards defining "under the influence," except for federally
regulated occupations. Discussions with senior managers indicated an
underlying assumption that worker performance became impaired
only at relatively high levels of blood alcohol and never when BACs
were at or near zero. This is like assuming alcohol-impaired driving

only occurs at or above the legal limit for BAC. Experimental evidence summarized by the National Highway Traffic Safety Administration, however, shows that "there is no threshold for alcohol impairment, i.e., there is no lower level at which impairment starts, or below which no impairment is found."[10]

In contrast to corporate drinking policies, public and private regulations on alcohol use among certain safety-sensitive occupations do acknowledge the performance effects of low-level drinking and hangovers. The Department of Transportation (DOT), for example, prohibits commercial truckers, railroad workers, merchant seamen, and aircraft pilots from operating their vehicles at BACs less than half the level that marks drivers as legally intoxicated under state laws. Moreover, most are prohibited from operating their vehicles within four hours of consuming *any* alcohol, a period extended by the DOT for aircraft pilots to eight hours, by the military for their pilots to twelve hours, and by commercial airlines for their pilots to twenty-four hours.

The survey of employees at sixteen worksites sheds light on the ways in which alcohol affects occupational performance. The data suggest that work-performance problems are associated with both low-level alcohol exposure and hangovers. We examined the independent contribution of three measures of alcohol use to the frequency of self-reported work-performance problems. The measures were any drinking during the work day, alcohol dependency as measured by the CAGE, and frequency of episodes of heavy drinking.[11] Each of the three were significantly associated with frequency of work-performance problems, even when demographics, job characteristics, job satisfaction, and other drug use were accounted for in the analysis.[12]

The relationship between episodes of heavy drinking and work-performance problems indicates the residual effects of drinking the previous night on next-day work performance (the hangover effect). Figure 4.3 shows that the more frequently a nondependent drinker reports episodes of heavy drinking, the more performance problems were reported.

Our interpretation of this calls for some caveats. The relationship between the effects of heavy drinking and work-performance problems could be influenced by some third factor (such as depression) that might cause both heavy drinking and work problems. The study controlled for some, but not all, of these factors. Moreover, the data cannot establish whether heavy drinking causes performance problems at work by way of hangovers, as we believe, or whether such

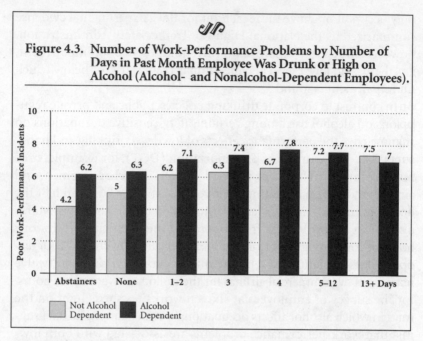

Figure 4.3. Number of Work-Performance Problems by Number of
Days in Past Month Employee Was Drunk or High on
Alcohol (Alcohol- and Nonalcohol-Dependent Employees).

problems lead to heavy drinking. Therefore we relied on the work of
other investigators to support our interpretation.[13] If our findings are
combined with those of other investigators, they support the position
that episodes of heavy drinking leading to hangovers can cause day-
after work-performance problems. Although the mechanism by which
these residual effects impair performance is uncertain, there is evidence that heavy drinking disturbs rapid-eye-movement sleep and
that even without the classic physiological symptoms of hangover
(such as headache, nausea, and irritability) hangovers may leave workers exhausted on the job.[14]

Although it is conventional wisdom that hangovers affect work performance the next day, the findings from this study and those of other
investigators document this relationship. They demonstrate the limitations of corporate drinking policies that only prohibit on-the-job
drinking and working under the influence.

Corporate drinking policies will be more effective in reducing
alcohol-related performance problems if they address both low-level
exposure, such as drinking at lunch, and the residual effects of heavy
drinking on next-day performance. As already discussed, many performance problems due to low-level exposure and hangovers occur
among workers who may not have alcohol-dependency problems.

MYTH THREE

Hourly Workers Are More Likely to Drink During Work Hours than Managers or Supervisors

Our survey of 6,540 employees at sixteen worksites showed that, with one exception, this perception is incorrect. As Figure 4.4 indicates, upper-level managers were three times as likely to report drinking during working hours within the last thirty days than either first-line supervisors or hourly workers (23 percent, 11 percent, and 8 percent, respectively).

Also, about 80 percent of the workday drinking incidents reported occurred during lunchtime or at company-sponsored functions. Only a small fraction of the incidents involved drinking just before coming to work, on a break, or while working. Managers clearly have more opportunities to drink during lunch, because they have more license to leave the worksite and can take more time for lunch. They also are more likely to attend company-sponsored functions where alcohol might be served. This accounts for the higher rates of workday drinking among managers.

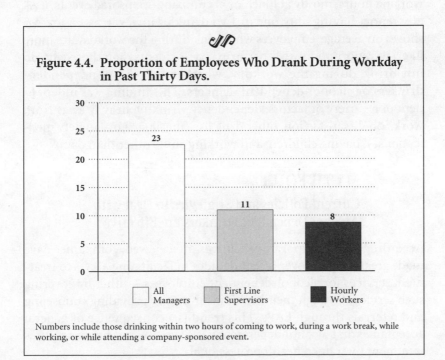

Figure 4.4. Proportion of Employees Who Drank During Workday in Past Thirty Days.

Numbers include those drinking within two hours of coming to work, during a work break, while working, or while attending a company-sponsored event.

However, even though the rates of drinking during the workday are lower among hourly workers than among managers and supervisors, the majority of workday drinking incidents are experienced by hourly workers because there are proportionately more of them. Taken from this perspective, senior executives were correct in their assumption that most workday drinking incidents come from hourly workers.

In our discussions with corporate executives, we found that most drinking policies prohibit alcohol use on the worksite unless a function is specifically granted a waiver. However, these policies leave a loophole concerning drinking at lunch. Essentially, corporate policy makers have taken the position that lunch is personal (or unpaid) time and therefore exempt from policy restrictions, as long as the drinking takes place off the worksite. They feel that the potential consequences of drinking too much at lunch are covered by their policies prohibiting working "under the influence." In other words, employees may drink at lunch but are admonished not to get drunk.

Our findings show that even small amounts of drinking during working hours can affect work performance, regardless of where it occurs or by whom. Employees who acknowledge drinking during working hours, mostly at lunch or at company-sponsored events, usually report having only one or two drinks. However, as Figure 4.5 shows, on average, employees who drink during the workday are more likely to report poor work-performance incidents than those who do not drink during the workday, whether they be nondependent drinkers or alcohol-dependent drinkers. This finding was independent of a variety of factors: dependency, drinking heavily away from work, job dissatisfaction, other drug use (marijuana or "anxiety medications"), having children, and working shifts other than days.[15]

MYTH FOUR
Current Policies and Strategies to Deal with Alcohol-Dependent Drinkers are Effective

According to the corporate executives interviewed, companies have made great progress over recent decades in facilitating access to treatment services for alcohol-dependent employees—either by covering such services through their health insurance or providing counseling and referrals through EAPs. This trend is a consequence of general acceptance that alcohol dependency is a disease and hence requires treatment by trained health professionals.

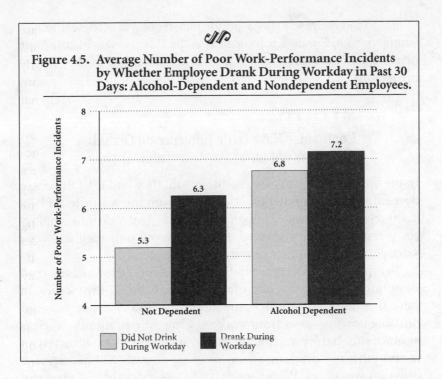

Figure 4.5. Average Number of Poor Work-Performance Incidents by Whether Employee Drank During Workday in Past 30 Days: Alcohol-Dependent and Nondependent Employees.

In general, corporate executives felt their companies had accomplished a lot by developing policies on alcohol use and providing treatment services to employees. They felt, for the most part, that these services were working effectively.

Our survey of 7,255 managers and supervisors from 114 worksites, however, showed that those responsible for implementing drinking policies and making referrals to EAPs were less sanguine about the effectiveness of the policies and services. For instance, only 16 percent of supervisors thought their efforts were "very effective" in identifying and referring employees with serious alcohol problems. A comparably small percentage believed their efforts were "very effective" in preventing heavy drinking by employees who were not yet dependent on alcohol.

The managers identified a range of barriers to successful intervention with alcohol-dependent employees.[16] They mentioned organizational barriers such as senior managers who thought that tough stands on alcohol were not important; interpersonal barriers such as confrontations with union officials protecting problem drinkers; and personal barriers such as managers feeling that they needed more training in how to intervene with poor-performing employees. These findings, summarized in Figure 4.6, indicate that the effectiveness of corporate drinking policies and programs is often compromised in their implementations.

MYTH FIVE
Companies Have Little Influence on Drinking Behaviors of Employees Away from Work

In the interviews, corporate executives said they had little influence over employees' drinking practices away from the worksite. In fact, many felt it was not the company's business to intrude into employees' private lives. They believed intervention was only required when work performance suffers or policies are violated.

The study showed large variations in levels of overall alcohol consumption by supervisor and managers across the 114 worksites. In some sites nearly two-thirds of the supervisors and managers reported drinking heavily—away from work—during the past month, whereas at other sites hardly anybody reported such behaviors. A variety of factors influence drinking behaviors of supervisors and managers at different worksites. Worksites vary in the proportion of men and women, in types of religious backgrounds, in the ages and marital status of supervisors and managers, in education levels, and in the region of the country in which they are located.[17] All of these factors can affect

---

ℐℐℰ

Figure 4.6. Managerial and Supervisory Perceptions of Barriers to Implementation of Alcohol Policies.

Organizational Barriers	Interpersonal Barriers	Individual Barriers
■ 58% say the company is tough on illicit drugs but soft on alcohol	■ 49% say a manager pays a price for confronting a worker who has a problem with alcohol	■ 80% say managers don't have enough training in how to confront employee performance problems
	■ 43% say unions protect problem drinkers	■ 73% say employees who are abusing alcohol are often doing an adequate job

the rates of heavy drinking. But, after statistically "removing" these effects, substantial variation in heavy drinking still remained across worksites. The implication is that worksites develop their own micro-cultures—that is, norms about drinking—that influence individual drinking practices at work as well as away from work.

The exact mechanism by which worksite cultures produce their effects on drinking behaviors is not clear. The fact that employees interact and communicate their values may play a role. Also, employees may observe each others' drinking behaviors directly. In the study, nearly a third of the supervisors and managers reported drinking with their coworkers during the last month alone.

The study also showed that coworkers' attitudes about drinking strongly influenced an employee's own attitudes about drinking. In turn, these attitudes (both an employee's own attitudes and that of his or her coworkers) were very strongly correlated with an employee's own drinking behavior. These worksite influences are predictable when the behavior in question concerns drinking during working hours or at lunch. It was more surprising, however, to see the influence coworker attitudes had on an employee's own attitudes about drinking away from the worksite.

The fact that such variations in drinking behaviors across work-sites is seen (even after adjusting for other influences) belies the belief that companies don't influence employee off-site drinking. It suggests that companies could utilize the power of workplace norms to moderate employee drinking behavior during the workday and heavy drinking away from work. Harnessing the power of small group norms to affect behavior is an underutilized strategy for influencing employee drinking practices.

MYTH SIX

Workers Perceive Additional Company Interventions About Alcohol Behaviors as Intrusive

In the interviews with corporate executives, some were found who would be eager to try additional ways to reduce the negative consequences of employee alcohol use. However, most executives were of the opinion that employees would resist more vigorous company attempts to change their drinking behavior. As an example, they cited disputes with unions when they attempted to intervene with alcohol-dependent or alcohol-abusing employees.

The sixteen-site survey, however, indicates that employees are more open to alcohol interventions than corporate executives imagine, particularly where employees feel endangered by the actions of their coworkers. Employees were asked whether they would be in favor of testing for alcohol use under three different circumstances—preemployment testing, after an accident, and random testing. Surprisingly, there was little difference in the level of support for these measures among managers, supervisors, and hourly workers. A second surprise was the high percentage of employees who supported alcohol-testing strategies. Over 80 percent supported testing after an accident, two-thirds supported preemployment testing, and half supported random testing for alcohol during the workday. Support for random testing climbed to nearly two-thirds of the employees when only those working in dangerous jobs were considered. Nearly three-quarters of the employees who worked in manufacturing or transportation jobs supported random testing.[18]

There was strong support among all employees for company assistance to employees who have drinking problems, particularly when work performance was affected; almost universal support for company insurance covering treatment services; and large majorities of employees who supported the idea that both supervisors and their coworkers should try to help employees with drinking problems. These findings indicate that employees are not as resistant to expanded alcohol interventions as senior executives perceive.

SUMMARY OF KEY FINDINGS

The key findings from the study can be summarized as follows:

- The majority of alcohol-related work-performance problems are associated with nondependent drinkers who may occasionally drink too much—not exclusively by alcohol-dependent employees.
- Two specific kinds of drinking behavior significantly contribute to the level of work-performance problems: drinking right before or during working hours (including drinking at lunch and at company functions), and heavy drinking the night before that causes hangovers during work the next day.
- Upper-level managers are more likely to drink during the workday than either first-line supervisors or hourly workers.

- Managers and supervisors report a variety of organizational, interpersonal, and individual barriers to implementing corporate alcohol policies and procedures.

- Workplace culture and norms have the potential to influence drinking behaviors at work and beyond the workplace.

- There is broad support among managers, supervisors, and hourly workers for assisting employees whose drinking behavior causes problems for themselves, their coworkers, or the company.

IMPLICATIONS

The study suggests a shift is needed in perspectives on corporate alcohol policies and practices. First, the findings suggest that policy makers could expand their focus beyond alcohol-dependent employees to look at employees who drink heavily from time to time. Employees who are *not* alcohol dependent account for 60 percent of the alcohol-related work-performance problems reported in the study. This paradox occurs because the size of the lower-risk group (nondependent drinkers) is substantially larger than that of the high-risk group (alcohol-dependent employees). Therefore, any corporate strategy aimed only at reducing the consequences of alcohol-dependent employees, even if it is totally effective, will miss the opportunity of reducing problems caused by the alcohol consumption of nondependent drinkers.

Second, the findings suggest policy makers could expand the corporation's definition of the types of drinking behaviors that cause problems in the workplace and set policies regarding these behaviors. They show that *any* drinking during or immediately before working hours has consequences for work performance. Corporate decision makers could consider adopting policies that more explicitly address the consequences of drinking before work, at lunch, at company functions, and before driving company vehicles.

The findings also indicate that heavy drinking the night before work has consequences for work performance the next day. This poses the greatest challenge to current corporate perspectives about alcohol, because it implies that employers have reason to be concerned about the personal lifestyle of their employees. It raises issues of personal privacy and the potential difficulty employers might have in encouraging workers to curtail occasional heavy drinking practices when they must work the next day. However, by illustrating the connection between hangovers and subsequent workplace performance, we have provided corporations with a rationale for expanding their focus to this area and for undertaking efforts to increase employee awareness of the negative consequences of hangovers on work performance. Companies currently use such education strategies for other health-related lifestyle issues such as fitness, cholesterol, and smoking.

Third, the study indicates that the methods for estimating alcohol's impact on the workplace could be expanded. Research that calculates the economic costs of alcohol to corporations uses estimates based on the proportion of alcohol-dependent workers in the workplace. It attributes to alcohol only those accidents or production errors associated with acute alcohol exposure. Our data suggest that a significant share of work-performance problems are attributable to employees who drink heavily *the night before.* Employees who are impaired by hangovers will not necessarily test positive for alcohol in their bloodstream following an accident. Furthermore, cost estimates miss secondhand effects. For instance, 14 percent of our survey employees said they had to redo work within the last year because of a coworker's drinking.

Fourth, the study suggests that the corporate culture itself can contribute to employee drinking behaviors. Corporate policy makers can play a role in shaping worksite norms about alcohol use. By acknowledging responsibility for worksite drinking cultures, companies may effectively develop norm-based intervention strategies for reducing the impact of alcohol on work-performance problems.

We feel optimistic about the potential success of such new strategies because they target employees who are not necessarily dependent on alcohol, but who may abuse alcohol on a fairly regular basis or drink from time to time in ways that impair work performance. These employees may be more responsive to educational and normative messages about changing the pattern of their drinking behaviors than alcohol-dependent employees.

Notes

1. This study, the Worksite Prevention of Alcohol Problems, was jointly funded by The Robert Wood Johnson Foundation and the National Institute of Alcoholism and Alcohol Abuse. In addition, The Robert Wood Johnson Foundation provided funding to support continuing analyses and dissemination of findings. Research activities were conducted at the

Harvard and Boston University Schools of Public Health and the
John Snow Research and Training Institute in Boston, Massachusetts.

2. Eighth Annual Report to Congress, NIAAA, 1995, p. 257.

3. Although the CAGE instrument is short and easily administered, it has
been shown to have robust reliability and validity in screening individuals
with alcohol dependencies. Various studies in different populations have
shown it to have very high sensitivity and specificity scores; that is, an
accurate designation of who has and does not have a dependency (for
example, 86 percent sensitivity and 93 percent specificity in B. Liskow
and others, "Validity of the Cage Questionnaire in Screening for Alcohol
Dependence in a Walk-In (Triage) Clinic," *Journal of Studies of Alcohol*
56(3), 1995, 277-281; 85 percent sensitivity and 89 percent specificity in
B. Bush and others, "Screening for Alcohol Abuse Using the Cage Questionnaire," *American Journal of Medicine* 82(2), 1987, 231-235; and 84 percent
sensitivity and 90 percent specificity in C. A. Soderstrom and others, "The
Accuracy of the Cage, the Brief Michigan Alcoholism Screening Test, and
the Alcohol Use Disorders Identification Test in Screening Trauma Center
Patients for Alcoholism," *Trauma* 43(6), 1997, 962-969).

The fact that we included anyone who scored two or more on the CAGE
as "dependent" whether or not they reported they were currently drinking
is consistent with the treatment perspective that people don't lose their
dependency even if they have been sober for a while. Therefore, since some
of our "dependent" workers were currently abstaining, the demonstrated
relationship (shown in Figure 4.1) between different types of drinkers and
work-performance problems may understate the impact of current alcohol
consumption per se.

4. For comparative results, see R. R. Crowe and others, "The Utility of the
'Brief Mast' and the 'Cage' in Identifying Alcohol Problems," *Archives of
Family Medicine,* 1997, 6, 477–483.

5. The exact wording of the work-performance question and items was as
follows: "In the past 12 months, how often did the following happen to
you?" (Response categories: never, 1-2 times, 3-5 times, 6 or more times.)
a. You missed work; b. You did poor quality work; c. You arrived late or left
early; d. You did less amounts of work; and e. You had arguments with a
coworker.

6. T. Blum, P. Roman, and J. Martin, "Alcohol Consumption and Work
Performance," *Journal of Studies on Alcohol* 54, 1993, 61-70.

7. G. M. Ames, J. W. Grube and R. S. Moore, "The Relationship of Drinking
and Hangovers to Workplace Problems: an Empirical Study," *Journal of
Studies on Alcohol* 58, 1997, 37-47.

8. In creating a total poor work-performance problems score, we recoded the ranged response categories to the midpoint amount and then added answers equally weighted from each item to get a total number of incidents per employee.

9. An exception to this standard are the employees engaged in the safety-sensitive occupations that are federally regulated and prohibit blood alcohol counts lower than those required to be intoxicated.

10. National Highway Traffic Safety Administration, *Alcohol and Highway Safety, 1984: A Review of the State of Knowledge.* Technical Report DOT-HS-806-569 (Washington, D.C.: United States Department of Transportation, 1985).

11. We used two different measures of heavy drinking and the results were the same for both. One measure was based on the quantity consumed and asked whether in the past month there was at least one day when five or more drinks were consumed (four or more for females). The other measure asked how many times in the past month the worker got high or drunk from consuming alcohol.

12. T. W. Mangione, J. Howland, B. Amick, J. Cote, M. Lee, N. Bell, and S. Levine, "Employee Drinking Practices and Work Performance," *Journal of Studies on Alcohol,* forthcoming.

13. Genevieve Ames and colleagues at the Prevention Research Center in Berkeley, Calif., for example, recently published a study of drinking practices and work performance at a large manufacturing site. These investigators asked workers specifically about their experience of hangovers and found a significant association between frequency of hangovers and the frequency of work-performance problems, controlling for drinking on the job (see G. M. Ames and others in note six). Perhaps more compelling is experimental evidence of decrements in occupational performance the day after intoxication. These effects have been demonstrated in randomized trials involving simulated aircraft piloting performance and simulated industrial tasks (R. C. Wolkenberg, C. Gold, and E. Tichauer, "Delayed Effects of Acute Alcohol Intoxication on Performance with Reference to Work Safety," *Journal of Safety Research* 7(3), 1975, 104-118). See also J. Yesavage and V. Leirer, "Hangover Effects on Aircraft Pilots 14 Hours after Alcohol Ingestion: a Preliminary Report," *American Journal of Psychiatry* 143(12), 1986, 1546-1550.

14. T. Roehrs, J. Yoon, and T. Roth, "Nocturnal and Next-Day Effects of Ethanol and Basal Level of Sleepiness," *Human Psychopharmacology* 6, 1991, 307-311.

15. See note 12.

16. N. Bell, T. W. Mangione, J. Howland, S. Levine, and B. Amick, "Worksite Barriers to the Effective Management of Alcohol Problems," *Journal of Occupational and Environmental Medicine* 38(12), Dec. 1996, 1212-1219.
17. J. Howland, T. W. Mangione, M. Lee, N. Bell, and S. Levine, "Worksite Variation in Managerial Drinking," *Addiction* 91(7), 1996, 1007-1017.
18. J. Howland, T. W. Mangione, M. Lee, N. Bell, and S. Levine, "Employee Attitudes Toward Worksite Alcohol Testing," *Journal of Occupational and Environmental Medicine* 38(10), Oct. 1996, 1041-1046.

Increasing Access
to Care

CHAPTER FIVE

Influencing Academic Health Centers

The Robert Wood Johnson Foundation Experience

Lewis G. Sandy
Richard Reynolds

Editors' Introduction

This chapter takes on a big topic: the interaction between the Foundation and the nation's academic health centers. These centers, which train most of the clinicians who deliver health care in America, have been the engines of innovation, specialization, and technological change in the health sector. As a dominant force in the health care world—perhaps *the* dominant force during the 1970s and 1980s— it is not surprising that academic health centers would be an important focus of the Foundation's grant making.

This chapter by Lewis Sandy, the Foundation's current executive vice president, and Richard Reynolds, the executive vice president between 1987 and 1996, traces the interaction between the Foundation and the nation's academic health centers over the past three decades. In their assessment, the authors observe that the Foundation's strategies have not always converged with those of academic health centers. In particular, the Foundation has long promoted the importance of educating generalist physicians; academic health centers—often responding to large amounts of money coming from clinical practice and the

National Institutes of Health—have tended to concentrate on training specialists and subspecialists. This chapter explains that early grant making pursued an "augmentation strategy" in an attempt to persuade academic health centers to add generalist training to the medical school curriculum, whereas more recent grants tried to get academic centers to make fundamental changes in their educational approach. Regardless of the prevailing strategy to influence medical education, Sandy and Reynolds note the Foundation's consistent investment in individuals within academic health centers. Such support reflects the value placed on individual leadership to effect institutional change.

This analysis of the Foundation's efforts to influence academic health centers complements the chapter written by Stephen L. Isaacs, Lewis G. Sandy, and Steven A. Schroeder, "Improving the Health Care Workforce: Perspectives from Twenty-Four Years' Experience," that appeared in last year's *Anthology*. It can also be read in conjunction with Terrance Keenan's review of the Foundation's experience in promoting the fields of nurse practitioners and physician assistants—some of which took place in academic health centers—that appears as Chapter Eleven of this year's *Anthology*.

Academic health centers,[1] or AHCs, are an American success story. The envy of the world, AHCs have created an explosion of knowledge in both basic biomedical science and clinical research. AHCs are also the locus of training for the next generation of physicians, nurses, pharmacists, and other health professionals, and they run the specialty and subspecialty training programs that create the practitioners of the most advanced medical care in the world. Not only are AHCs uniquely American in their grand scale and aspirations, they have developed a quintessential American trajectory, reflecting the American faith in technology, a can-do spirit, and even a bit of the Wild West.

Before World War II, AHCs were relatively modest in scope, had a main emphasis on education and research, and by contemporary terms were modest clinical enterprises. In the 1930s and 40s, the scientific era of medicine began to flourish, with the discovery of insulin, the initial success of antibiotics, and new technologies such as blood transfusion. World War II catalyzed further advances in medicine and surgery, and it was logical to believe that more research would produce effective treatments for cancer, heart disease, and other killers. Also, the success of the Manhattan Project, which led to the rapid development of the atomic bomb, suggested that combining world-class talent with modern facilities and generous financial support could lead to similar success in conquering disease.

After the war, the expansion of the National Institutes of Health, or NIH, and further advances in medical science provided fertile soil for accelerated growth. In the 1960s, the creation of the Medicare program and its support for graduate medical education, coupled with the national mood of faith in science and technology that led to continued increases in funding for the NIH, created further support for specialty training and research and continued expansions of the clinical enterprise. AHCs began to develop such technologies as intensive care units, burn centers, heart transplant programs, and comprehensive cancer centers. Academic health physicians became household names and even celebrities—Denton Cooley, Michael De Bakey—and the nation's AHCs enjoyed unparalleled prestige, power, and influence.

In that context, the relationship of AHCs to The Robert Wood Johnson Foundation was initiated. When the Foundation became a national philanthropy in 1972, AHCs were viewed as the center of the health and health care universe. It was only logical that the leadership of the Foundation should be sought from that sector, and David Rogers, a former chairman of medicine at Vanderbilt and dean of the Johns Hopkins University School of Medicine, was recruited as the Foundation's first president.

Although the new president was a rising leader in academic medicine, the Foundation's initial view was that what was needed to improve health and health care was not perfectly congruent with the activities of AHCs. The Foundation's staff and board felt that there was an imperfect fit between the mission of AHCs and the needs of the nation. Although not denying the importance and the value of specialty training and practice, the Foundation felt that the declining interest in primary care and the need for a health care workforce that could care for a population's health needs were critical issues not being addressed by AHC leaders. The application of epidemiological principles to health care itself, or health services research, did not find a natural home either in AHCs or in the NIH. Public health, cleaved from medicine earlier in the century, had minimal input into the training of the nation's health care workforce. At the same time, the policy environment, seven years after the passage of Medicare and Medicaid legislation, looked promising for the extension of health entitlement programs to the rest of the population.

Most of David Rogers's academic colleagues thought he would use the Foundation's funds to support biomedical research. Rogers noted, however, that the NIH was putting billions of dollars into research funding, compared with the Foundation's $50 million grant-making capacity at that time. The Foundation thought more leverage could be gained by fostering the public and community responsibility of AHCs. Rogers was strongly criticized by his colleagues for this move. It did, however, represent his own beliefs about what AHCs should do. From that beginning, then, emerged a series of Foundation grants and programs with the aim of influencing academic medicine. What follows is a decade-to-decade analysis of these efforts, their achievements, limitations, and lessons.

EARLY EFFORTS: THE 1970S

In our view, two additional strategic factors also influenced the relationship of the Foundation to AHCs: first, the recognized position of the AHCs as the leadership institutions in health care, and, second, the desire to work with the nation's leading people and institutions to ensure quality grant making. The more pragmatic requirement of initiating grant making expeditiously was also an important, but secondary, consideration.

The earliest grants made by The Robert Wood Johnson Foundation (see Figure 5.1), then, supported people. It made a series of awards to provide scholarships for medical and dental students, and adopted the Clinical Scholars Program, which had been started by the Carnegie Corporation and the Commonwealth Fund to provide training opportunities in the social, behavioral, and management sciences and other nonbiomedical disciplines for postresidency physicians. This strategy not only met the pragmatic requirements of the time but also was consistent with an academically oriented worldview of change. In brief, this view held that leaders of AHCs were masters of their fate, and had the power and the influence to mold their institutional agendas as they saw fit. Therefore, an appropriate philanthropic strategy was to shape and influence the next generation of leaders in the areas of primary care, public health, and health services research.

A second dimension of the strategy is what we term the augmentation strategy—that is, building new programs on an existing base. In an expansive time of funding for health care, this was reasonable and logical. It also minimized resistance within AHCs: Why not continue to train specialists and also add new primary care residency programs? Why not train baccalaureate nurses and also develop the new nurse practitioner model? With this approach, the Foundation supported the Primary Care Residency Program and the Nurse Faculty Development Program to develop primary care capacity in medicine and pediatrics, and to build capacity for training nurse practitioners. The Foundation also authorized the Teaching Hospital Group Practice Program to help reorganize academic general internal medicine into a model that reflected the primary care principles of continuity, coordination, and access.

The Foundation's investment in primary care residency programs in the 1970s fit the augmentation model to a T. The clear expectation at the time was that the demonstration and training programs funded by the Foundation would be sustained by federal or institutional support, or both. In fact, most of the residency programs funded by the Foundation continued with new federal grant support, and the teaching hospital group practice model became the norm as well. However,

Figure 5.1. RWJF - Authorized AHC Programs in the 1970s (Millions of Dollars).

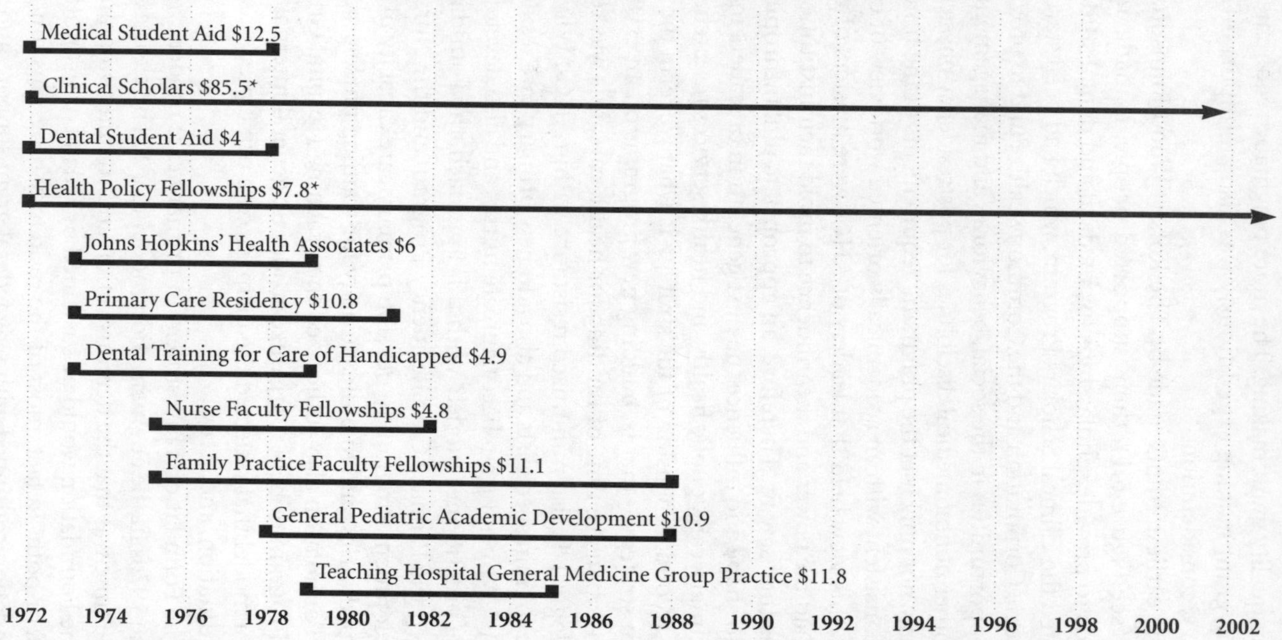

Medical Student Aid $12.5

Clinical Scholars $85.5*

Dental Student Aid $4

Health Policy Fellowships $7.8*

Johns Hopkins' Health Associates $6

Primary Care Residency $10.8

Dental Training for Care of Handicapped $4.9

Nurse Faculty Fellowships $4.8

Family Practice Faculty Fellowships $11.1

General Pediatric Academic Development $10.9

Teaching Hospital General Medicine Group Practice $11.8

1972 1974 1976 1978 1980 1982 1984 1986 1988 1990 1992 1994 1996 1998 2000 2002

Note: Dollars are for sites only and do not include administrative and evaluation costs. An arrow indicates that not all sites have been awarded grants. An asterisk indicates that decisions about possible additional funding will be made at a later date. Dollars indicate the total authorization.

the Foundation-supported attempt by the Johns Hopkins University to create a new kind of provider, a health associate, did not succeed. Beginning in 1973, the Foundation provided five years of support to Johns Hopkins to establish an institution that would train these health associates. This program did not survive the combination of a budget crisis at the university, a lack of clarity over the differences between health associates and physician assistants and nurse practitioners, and the lack of continued funding either from the Foundation or from the federal government.

A third dimension of the initial strategy was investment in faculty development. The Robert Wood Johnson Foundation not only invested in the Clinical Scholars Program but also launched programs to support faculty development in the emerging discipline of family medicine and, subsequently, in general pediatrics. The Foundation also initiated the Health Policy Fellows program, which it continues to support. The original purpose of this program was to train future leaders of AHCs in the politics of health care and health policy making at the federal level by offering mid-career academics the opportunity to work for a year in a Washington legislative or executive office.

Assessment

Did the Foundation's strategy work? Yes, in the sense that it supported programs that attracted talented young people at elite institutions and promulgated the importance of health services research, primary care, and public health. Yes, in the sense that these efforts got the Foundation off to a solid start in grant making and demonstrated that it was an institution of quality and rigor.

Did these efforts significantly influence AHCs? The hope at that time was that, over a decade or two, people supported by the Foundation would rise to prominence within AHCs and steer them toward goals that advanced the health of the public. AHCs did begin grudgingly to accept health services research and clinical epidemiology as legitimate areas of inquiry. However, the Health Policy Fellows had limited impact in influencing the course of their home AHCs. It was becoming clear that the Fellows were not senior enough within their AHCs to initiate change, and that, in any case, single agents for change faced difficulties in altering well-entrenched organizational behavior of AHCs.

And, of course, the policy environment itself did not behave as forecast. The nation did not expand national health insurance nor did primary care become the national norm. Federal support for primary care training programs, although institutionalizing the Foundation's investments, may have masked underlying economic trends and other forces that continued to favor specialty training, research, and care.

For example, it became increasingly clear that the health care financing environment strongly encouraged specialty care and training as opposed to primary care. Medicare, Medicaid, and generous third-party payments for clinical care provided the monetary fuel for huge increases in the clinical enterprises of AHCs. Faculty members could both raise AHC revenue and increase their own productivity by developing clinical and research fellowships, with explicit support by Medicare graduate medical education funding and NIH funding. In turn, this federally funded group of trainees created a local workforce to develop new and ever-expanding clinical programs that would raise further revenue for subsequent expansion. This "positive-feedback" loop led to a tenfold expansion of medical school clinical faculty, from 7,200 in 1961 to 73,400 in 1995, with an accompanying fourfold expansion, from 4,000 to 16,600, in basic science faculty and only a doubling of medical school enrollment.[2] Medical school clinical revenues grew from 5 percent of total medical school support in 1961 to 49 percent of total support in 1995, while federal support has progressively declined to around 20 percent of total support. This increasing reliance on growing clinical revenues and on the specialty training and delivery infrastructure necessary to sustain growth, combined with the protechnology bias in fee-for-service reimbursement, has accounted for AHCs' consistent emphasis on specialist training and on high-technology care delivery as opposed to primary care. It also helps explain why issues important to the population's health—public health, substance abuse, universal access to care, behavioral change—have not been priorities for AHCs.

THE 1980S

As the 1980s began, AHCs were strong, growing, and relatively autonomous. Yet a few ominous clouds began to appear on the horizon. Medicare's Diagnostic Related Group Reimbursement was the first significant change to the reimbursement of usual, customary, and reasonable costs that had fed the growth of fee-for-service medicine practiced at academic medical centers. Although teaching hospitals managed the transition without incident (and even profited), this change was a harbinger of a more fundamental restructuring of health care financing. Health-care costs were continuing to escalate, and academic centers increasingly began to experience adverse effects of their expanded specialty training programs. Many of these trainees, upon finishing their fellowships, promptly set up competitive programs in their local markets.

Nevertheless, the Foundation's strategy of investing in people and in augmenting academic programs seemed quite solid. Graduates of the Clinical Scholars Program were obtaining notable positions in medical schools and were ascending the academic ladder. By the early nineties, the majority of the leaders of divisions of general internal medicine were former clinical scholars. The faculty development programs were also bearing fruit, yielding new leadership in family medicine and general pediatrics.

Given this solid track record, the Foundation's strategy was to stay the course (see Figure 5.2 for a summary of Foundation programs supported in the 1980s). In 1982, it supported the Dental Services Research Program and the Clinical Nurse Scholars Program, which essentially applied the idea of the physician-oriented Clinical Scholars Program to dentistry and nursing.

The Foundation also began to focus attention on curricular change within medical schools. The rapid development of molecular and cellular biology was transforming basic science and raising questions about the educational focus of academic departments' teaching of medical students. More than ever there was need to integrate the teaching of basic science and clinical training throughout the four years of medical school. New pedagogy such as computer-assisted learning and the use of surrogate patients was rapidly evolving. Behavioral, social, probabilistic, and information sciences were deemed as important as the traditional basic science in the general education of medical students. With the current emphasis on general medicine, the establishment of ambulatory practice sites for training in prevention and primary care made sense.

The Foundation was repeatedly asked to fund another Flexner Report. Since its publication in 1910, the Flexner Report has shaped medical education for most of the twentieth century. Though the report had had a major impact on medical education, its postulates were thought now to be archaic and even an impediment to needed change. The Foundation's response was to support an extensive survey of medical educators. A majority of respondents indicated a need

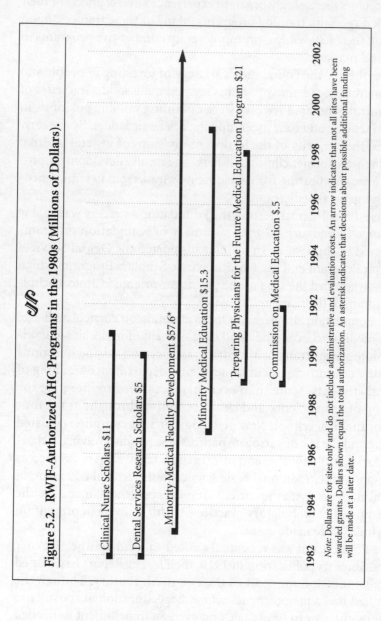

Figure 5.2. RWJF-Authorized AHC Programs in the 1980s (Millions of Dollars).

Note: Dollars are for sites only and do not include administrative and evaluation costs. An arrow indicates that not all sites have been awarded grants. Dollars shown equal the total authorization. An asterisk indicates that decisions about possible additional funding will be made at a later date.

Clinical Nurse Scholars $11

Dental Services Research Scholars $5

Minority Medical Faculty Development $57.6*

Minority Medical Education $15.3

Preparing Physicians for the Future Medical Education Program $21

Commission on Medical Education $.5

1982   1984   1986   1988   1990   1992   1994   1996   1998   2000   2002

for "fundamental changes" and "thorough reform" in medical education. Against this background the Foundation initiated two programs—the Commission on Medical Education: The Science of Medical Practice, and Preparing Physicians for the Future: A Program in Medical Education.

The recommendations of the commission included the integration of basic and clinical sciences, the need for students to have a better comprehension of the role of behavioral and social aspects of disease, the expansion of clinical training into ambulatory care sites, and a medical school governance to make curriculum change feasible. These were thought to be modest in scope, and all had been already noted by previous commissions or task forces. The thrust of the commission's report, however, was to challenge the departmental segmentation and control of the curriculum and to suggest that medical education could be improved from its present status.

What was different from earlier efforts at curricular reform, however, was that the Foundation followed through with the Program in Medical Education that was designed to support the implementation of the commission's recommendations for curricular change, something no other task force or commission had done.

Rather than just tinkering with the existing scheme of medical education, the Foundation supported eight schools through the Program in Medical Education over a five-year period to make fundamental changes in their curriculum in keeping with the commission's recommendations. An extensive evaluation indicated that they were successful in doing this. The continuation of these changes remains to be seen, but the initial indications are promising.

Assessment

Through its various programs, the Foundation succeeded in supporting new kinds of medical school faculty. Reforms in medical education also proved to be successful,[3] but the Foundation's catalytic role is less clear. One might reasonably view the Foundation's role as one of facilitating trends that already existed rather than creating any fundamental shifts.[4] Perhaps even more significant is the Foundation's sustained investment in scholarship in the areas of health services research, clinical epidemiology, biomedical ethics, and other disciplines. This extensive and continuing investment, which occurred through both explicit training programs and Foundation research initiatives and demonstration programs on specific topics, has had the effect of legitimizing these disciplines within AHCs. This effect, which may transcend individual programs and eras, may be the Foundation's most lasting contribution to academic health centers.

The Foundation's success in creating new kinds of academic physicians did not extend to dentistry and nursing. As one of us has argued elsewhere,[5] the Clinical Nurse Scholars program may have been terminated prematurely. Additionally, the disparate paths available in nursing education may have made efforts at change significantly more difficult. Dental education was buffeted by forces—including falling student demand for dental education and a reduction of dental diseases such as caries—more powerful than those areas of the Foundation's modest investment. Perhaps the clearest example of philanthropic impact was the Program for Training Dentists in the Care of Handicapped Patients, which led to widespread curricular reform in this area.

The Foundation's mixed record in the areas of nursing and other health professions may reflect a profound ambivalence about power within AHCs. Although the notion was never explicitly articulated, it was generally believed at the Foundation that the major source of power and influence within AHCs was the medical school and its leadership. Egalitarian impulses contributed to the desire to work across a variety of disciplines, but the tension between egalitarian desire and the search for leverage may have contributed to the Foundation's limited impact beyond medicine.

THE 1990S

By the early nineties, the prevailing winds of change had increased to near-hurricane force. Health care costs had continued to rise, and, in certain areas of the country, managed care growth had begun to affect the clinical operations of academic health centers significantly. For example, contracts for managed care patients were not as lucrative and limited AHCs' ability to cross-subsidize teaching, research, and indigent care. Interest in primary care among medical students and faculty fell dramatically,[6] and academic health centers continued to expand their clinical programs to support the service requirements of expanding specialty training programs and to increase clinical revenue. The number of medical school clinical faculty, for example, increased 11.9 percent from 1992–93 to 1994–95 alone.[7]

Ultimately more disturbing for AHCs, however, was the gradual erosion of their place at the center of power and influence in health care. By training too many specialists (who in turn set up competing tertiary-care programs), AHCs lost their natural monopoly on specialty care. The growth of managed care created powerful new corporations in the health care arena—organizations with no special reverence for the products and the values intrinsic to AHCs. Many AHCs neglected community concerns, and were viewed as arrogant and insular institutions. Finally, the dramatic growth of overall health care spending led to a continued monetarization of the health care sector,[8] with the ascension of economics, business, and politics over medicine. With such developments in mind, the Foundation created a new generation of programs that were, perhaps paradoxically, both more ambitious and more circumscribed than previous efforts (see Figure 5.3).

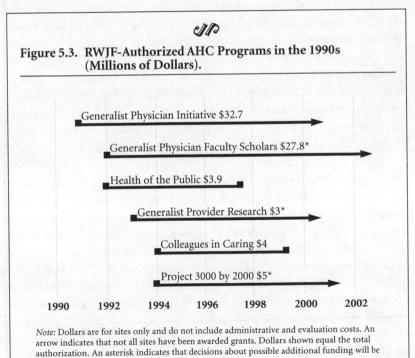

Figure 5.3. RWJF-Authorized AHC Programs in the 1990s (Millions of Dollars).

Generalist Physician Initiative $32.7

Generalist Physician Faculty Scholars $27.8*

Health of the Public $3.9

Generalist Provider Research $3*

Colleagues in Caring $4

Project 3000 by 2000 $5*

1990   1992   1994   1996   1998   2000   2002

Note: Dollars are for sites only and do not include administrative and evaluation costs. An arrow indicates that not all sites have been awarded grants. Dollars shown equal the total authorization. An asterisk indicates that decisions about possible additional funding will be made at a later date.

First, the Foundation developed programs to encourage medical schools to shift their educational focus toward generalism and away from a predominance of specialists. This move away from a strategy of augmentation was quite explicit, for example, in the Generalist Physician Initiative, whose program guidelines insisted on fundamental changes in the school's overall admission process, curriculum, and career path of graduates to encourage generalism. This ambitious program was launched in parallel with a more traditional faculty development program, the Generalist Physician Faculty Scholars Program, and a generalist-oriented research program, the Generalist Provider Research Initiative.

Second, the Foundation's programs to encourage generalism had another thrust—that is, the beginning of an outside-in strategy. Previous efforts to influence AHCs through direct grants to individual agents of change within institutions evolved into grants to support the effort both of AHCs and of potentially influential partners outside the AHCs. For example, the Generalist Physician Initiative insisted that AHCs have external partners such as HMOs, group practices, or insurers. Early experience in the program suggests that these partners have a considerable influence in the production of generalists, in pointing out deficiencies in the preclinical and clinical curricula, and in highlighting the "hidden curriculum"[9] of academia that encourages excessive specialization and expensive care. The Generalist Provider Research Initiative supports policy and analytic studies in generalism, but also serves as a way to provide information to shape the policy levers that affect specialty choice.

Third, the Foundation provided support to the Health of the Public Program. This program was designed to encourage AHCs to come up with new ideas for their mission and functions, so that teaching, research, and care would be aligned to better meet the needs of the health of defined populations, such as the community surrounding the AHC. The initial two phases of the Health of the Public Program had been supported by the Rockefeller Foundation and the Pew Charitable Trusts. The Robert Wood Johnson Foundation, in collaboration with Pew, funded a third phase to extend and institutionalize the community partnerships and curricular reforms.

Another target of Foundation grant making to influence AHCs in the 1990s included better matching of supply and demand for nurses. The Colleagues in Caring program was designed to bring together employers of nurses—such as hospitals, clinics, home health providers—with educational institutions to plan more rational responses to the way the market operates.

Finally, the Foundation has continued and expanded its support for educating minorities in the health professions. The Minority Medical Education Program, the Minority Medical Faculty Development Program, and other efforts reflect the Foundation's long-standing and continuing commitment to diversity in these professions. An analysis of demographic data suggests that the nation's health workforce is getting less diverse and less representative of the nation overall. The Association of American Medical Colleges' program called 3000 by 2000, partially funded by the Foundation, recognizes that the solution to this problem lies in expanding the pipeline by investing in educational programs in secondary schools, and even earlier, to enlarge the pool of minorities that enter the health professions.

Assessment

Although current Foundation efforts are ambitious in their goals, they are more modest in their ability to change the overall course and nature of AHCs. As the twentieth century draws to a close, AHCs are enormous engines of clinical care, training, and research, fueled by public and private reimbursement, the NIH and other research funders, and federal and state subsidies for graduate medical education. In spite of the concerns about the effect of marketplace changes and managed care growth on AHCs, most are fiscally and programmatically robust, continue to expand, and have yet to undergo a critical reexamination of their mission and function. The Health of the Public Program, for example, was successful in articulating the argument for a new vision of academic health centers and in supporting a number of important local efforts at curricular reform and community service. But it lacked sufficient leverage to affect the way AHCs responded to enormous economic and market forces. The Health of the Public grants were modest, often funding only one faculty member at an institution, with limited funds to support innovative programs beyond their initiation. Even larger-scale Foundation investments, such as the Generalist Physician Initiative, are seeing positive trends emanating more from market forces than from direct program effects. In addition, the institutional tendency remains to add on programs rather than fundamentally change core activities.

The Foundation itself has evolved as well. From an initial emphasis on health care institutions and health care delivery, it is currently supporting a widened array of programs and projects that are tackling the challenging issues of substance abuse at the community level, enhancing consumer-directed approaches to care for the disabled, and integration of housing and social services, to name just a few. Many of these efforts are quite remote from AHCs, and efforts to influence AHCs are now probably best viewed as one of a number of areas of Foundation action rather than as a central thrust.

THE FUTURE

Given this experience, what is The Robert Wood Johnson Foundation's current approach to AHCs? First, in addition to continuing the generalist programs developed in the 1990s, the Foundation is investing in an effort to encourage a long-range strategic assessment of the mission and the function of the AHCs. The Forum on the Future of Academic Medicine, sponsored by the Association of American Medical Colleges, is bringing together leaders of AHCs with leaders from outside health and health care to debate the mission, the function, and the role of AHCs in the twenty-first century. The Forum has already identified important areas for further work, such as a better understanding of AHC financial affairs and the need for leadership development. Work in these areas may hold great promise. In parallel, the Commonwealth Fund's Commission on Academic Medicine is contributing important policy analysis to the field, and helping to focus attention on the question of how best to support the mission of AHCs in the current turbulent environment.

Second, the Foundation, with Pew, is supporting a transformation of the Health of the Public Program into a sustainable network. Third, the Foundation is supporting a new nurse executive leadership program, which, although not exclusively focused on academic nursing, will identify and help develop the next generation of nursing leadership. Finally, the Foundation continues to support scholarly endeavors in the areas of health care organization and finance, home care, substance abuse policy, and others that help influence the direction of research within AHCs.

LESSONS LEARNED

After twenty-five years of grant-making experience, a number of lessons have emerged.

- First, investments in people pay off. Clinical Scholars, for example, now hold a variety of leadership positions in AHCs, in government, and in the private sector. In part, this may be because of the Foundation's sustained commitment to the program over twenty-five years, and the fact that approximately 750 Clinical Scholars have been trained, more than 60 percent of whom remain in academe. Although fellowship programs are expensive, supporting bright young people early in their career may be a more effective institutional change strategy than direct institutional grants.

- Second, AHCs, like most academic institutions, do not follow a logical, planned process of change. As is true of most complex systems, AHCs react to a variety of external changes—political, economic, social, and scientific. For example, the postwar environment encouraged a dramatic growth in specialty training and research, and today managed care is encouraging joint ventures, mergers, and other changes in the clinical systems of care in AHCs. Efforts to influence AHCs may perhaps best be accomplished by shaping those broader social and economic forces, as well as by supporting talented individuals through training and research programs.

- Third, both a strategy of augmentation and one of fundamental change can work, with appropriate targeting and resources. An augmentation strategy can succeed if funding can be sustained over time, and a strategy of fundamental change can work if it is targeted to a fairly specific area and sufficient resources are committed.

- Fourth, it is important to work with both elite and nonelite AHCs, although it may be appropriate to pursue different strategies for each. For example, an augmentation strategy is most appropriate for elite institutions, where adding a new program to a premiere institution enhances the program's visibility. But a fundamental change strategy has a greater chance of succeeding in a nonelite setting, where barriers to reform may be fewer and where there may be greater interest in moving the institution in new directions.

• Finally, the role of philanthropy in influencing large and powerful institutions should be kept in proper perspective. Unlike earlier in the century, when philanthropic resources were a much larger fraction of resources devoted to academia, modern AHCs are multibillion-dollar enterprises. Multimillion-dollar foundation grants, although welcome, cannot by themselves transform AHCs or their directions.

For the Foundation, whose mission is to improve health and health care for all Americans, AHCs have a special role and place. Their role in creating new knowledge, in providing advanced care and specialty training, and in educating the next generation of health professionals is unquestioned. Their role in improving community health, in caring for the underserved, and in being held accountable for societal goals is undergoing vigorous debate. In addition, the commitment of the AHCs to diversity is undergoing both internal and societal challenges at a time when such a commitment is needed more than ever. Nevertheless, AHCs remain in large part a public trust[10] and should be held accountable for their contributions to the society's health. By investing in people, by identifying and shaping those forces that have an impact on AHCs, and by carefully targeting philanthropic investment in the right areas at the right time, The Robert Wood Johnson Foundation continues to seek to influence AHCs to improve health and health care for the American people.

As the twenty-first century draws near, perhaps what is needed is a new concept of the AHC and its function and purpose. A soul-searching look at mission, at function, and at structure may help catalyze creative responses to the future that are not merely reactive but make a compelling case for continued public trust, support, and acclaim.

Notes

1. According to the Association of Academic Health Centers, AHCs vary in their organization and structure, but all centers include a medical school, at least one other health professional school or program, and one or more owned or affiliated teaching hospitals.

2. D. Korn, "Reengineering Academic Medical Centers: Reengineering Academic Values?" *Academic Medicine* 71(10), Oct. 1996, 1033-1043.
3. An evaluation of the Program in Medical Education by Gordon Moore indicated the funded schools did indeed change, but so did comparison schools. The funded schools felt strongly that the Foundation had made a major impact in updating their curriculum.
4. N. A. Christakis, "The Similarity and Frequency of Proposals to Reform US Medical Education: Constant Concerns," *JAMA* 274(9), Sept. 1995, 706-711.
5. S. L. Isaacs, L. G. Sandy, and S. A. Schroeder, "Grants to Shape the Health Care Workforce: The Robert Wood Johnson Foundation Experience," *Health Affairs* 15(2), Summer 1996, 279-295.
6. J. M. Colwill, "Where Have All the Primary Care Applicants Gone?" *NEJM* 326(5), Feb. 1992, 387-393.
7. J. Y. Krakower, J. Ganem, and P. Jolly, "Review of US Medical School Finances, 1994-1995," *JAMA* 276(9), Sept. 1996, 720-724.
8. E. Ginzberg, "The Monetarization of Medical Care," *NEJM* 310(18), May 1984, 1162-1165.
9. F. W. Hafferty and R. Franks, "The Hidden Curriculum, Ethics Teaching, and the Structure of Medical Education," *Academic Medicine* 69(11), Nov. 1994, 861-871.
10. S. A. Schroeder, J. S. Zones, and J. A. Showstack, "Academic Medicine as a Public Trust," *JAMA* 262(6), Aug. 1989, 803-812.

CHAPTER SIX

~~ The Strengthening Hospital Nursing Program

Changing Organizations to Improve Patient Care

Thomas G. Rundall
David B. Starkweather
Barbara Norrish

Editors' Introduction

The Strengthening Hospital Nursing program described in this chapter was planned in the mid-1980s and has unfolded in some unexpected ways over the past ten years. The impetus for the program during its planning phase was clear and simple: to help hospitals address the problems caused by shortages of nurses in the 1980s. However, the cofunders of the program—The Robert Wood Johnson Foundation and the Pew Charitable Trusts—quickly widened the scope of this expensive and highly visible program. It became, over time, a focal point for increasing the role of nursing and transforming the basic approach to patient care within hospitals.

In the 1990s, as the program was unfolding, it faced two substantial environmental obstacles: first, the nursing shortage that had motivated the program evaporated, leading to serious questions about the purpose of the program; and second, the spread of managed care and ever-increasing financial pressures facing hospitals became more dominant forces in shaping approaches to patient care than the approaches offered by this program.

It is difficult to assess the success or failure of this program definitively because it addressed ambitious, difficult-to-measure goals and because so much change was taking place in the nation's hospitals. There have been constant concerns within the Foundation, however, that the goals of the projects selected were too broad and that the theory that nursing could lead fundamental changes in overall hospital structure is not viable.

Partly because of these concerns, The Robert Wood Johnson Foundation and the Pew Charitable Trusts asked Thomas Rundall, David Starkweather, and Barbara Norrish from the University of California, Berkeley's School of Public Health, to take an outside look at the program. In this chapter, they summarize the results of their evaluation and present an in-depth report on three of the twenty Strengthening Hospital Nursing sites. The authors conclude that even though the program was overtaken by changes in the health care field and may not have accomplished what it was supposed to, it still led to many positive results in the sites where it was undertaken.

In the 1980s, there were widespread reports of a nursing shortage in the United States. Hospitals had difficulty recruiting and retaining nurses. The increasing use of complex biomedical technology, the demand for hospitalization by a growing elderly population, and changing patterns of medical care resulting in shorter but more acute hospital stays contributed to the need for more hospital nurses—and for more intense and skilled nursing care. Despite a nationwide supply of more than two million registered nurses, or RNs, and a hospital RN-to-patient ratio that had doubled over the previous twenty years, hospitals across the country reported critical vacancies for budgeted nursing positions. Many hospitals were forced to delay admissions, or even close beds, because of an inadequate number of nurses on staff. Many factors contributed to the nursing shortage of the eighties, but two of the most frequently cited were the high level of job dissatisfaction caused by nurses' seeming lack of control over their work and poor working relationships with physicians and non-clinical staff members. To respond to these concerns, the Secretary of Health and Human Services appointed a special Commission on Nursing to study the problem and make recommendations. In 1988, the Commission published sixteen specific recommendations and eighty-one strategies to relieve the nursing shortage in the United States.

That same year, The Robert Wood Johnson Foundation and the Pew Charitable Trusts announced a jointly funded national initiative to provide better patient care through innovative, hospital-wide restructuring. From the outset, the foundations recognized the inherent connection between quality hospital patient care and strong hospital nursing services, and entitled their national program Strengthening Hospital Nursing: A Program to Improve Patient Care, or SHN. The SHN Program rested on two fundamental principles. First, SHN projects were to restructure hospital working environments to use nursing resources optimally, improve care in a cost-effective manner, and provide satisfying service designs for patients as well as nurses and other staff. Second, participating hospitals would be given great flexibility in the means they chose to identify organizational and operational problems having an impact on their current nursing services and in the measures they would take to remedy these problems and improve patient care.

Early in the development of the SHN Program, the SHN national program director, Barbara A. Donaho, and its associate director, Mary Kay Kohles, wrote, "The Strengthening Hospital Nursing Program seeks to bring about a fundamental change in the U.S. hospital—from a discipline-driven, departmentalized institution to a patient-driven, unified one. It seeks an awakening by the hospital to the understanding that the patient is why it exists. It seeks a metamorphosis—a shedding of the old, tired image of the nursing profession and constructing a better-fitting image in keeping with what the profession actually contributes to patient care."

Clearly, this was an ambitious program, and it was designed and overseen with recommendations from an advisory board of nationally recognized leaders in nursing and medical care. The supporting foundations provided not only monetary resources but also institutional legitimacy to the effort. The challenges facing the grantee hospitals were to a significant extent understood by the program planners and the national governing staff, and these challenges were anticipated in many features of the program. At each site, a considerable investment was made in the education, training, and empowerment of a team of people who could facilitate change. In short, there were good reasons to believe that the SHN Program would be successful.

The flexible nature of the program meant, however, that success could be assessed only in the local context of each hospital's circumstances. Each hospital was planning a unique project tailored to its particular problems. Moreover, given the five-year term of the program, it was likely that planned projects would have to be modified over time, and that unplanned strategies and projects would emerge.

The total financial commitment of The Robert Wood Johnson Foundation and the Pew Charitable Trusts to the program was $26.8 million: $4 million for one-year planning grants, $20 million for the five-year implementation grants, and $2.8 million for technical assistance, program administration, and monitoring. Many of the hospitals ultimately selected as grantees augmented their foundation grant with their own funds.

In October 1990, the two foundations announced that twenty projects—twelve hospitals and eight consortiums of hospitals—had been selected to receive five-year SHN implementation grants of up to $1 million each. The hospitals and the hospital consortiums selected to receive implementation grants are identified in Exhibit 6.1 at the end of this chapter. The group of grantee hospitals was diverse, including rural and urban, large and small, academic and community hospitals.

The proposals of the grantee hospitals shared some common themes, including the following:

- The development of institution-wide initiatives for change, and communications networks that would last beyond the grant's planning and implementation phases
- The use of planning and implementation processes that relied on collaboration and consensus building horizontally as well as vertically within the hospital
- The use of organizational and management consultants to facilitate the hospital planning team's ability to envision new models of nursing and patient care
- A focus on providers' relationships with patients rather than with one another
- Cross-training of professional staff
- Unbundling hotel services from patient care services
- Self-governance for individual nursing units
- New models of nursing care

PREPARING SHN GRANTEES TO CREATE CHANGE

To help the grantees acquire the tools to change their hospitals effectively, the national office of the SHN Program sponsored a number of educational workshops. Teams from the grantee hospitals, consisting of the chief executive officer, the nurse executive, members of the board of trustees, a medical staff representative, and the SHN project director, were required to attend an initial educational conference held in September 1989 in Orlando, Florida, and a follow-up two-day workshop. These educational sessions were an integral part of the year-long planning process. A consultant to the National Program Office, Russell L. Ackoff, emeritus professor of systems science at the Wharton School of the University of Pennsylvania, led the project teams through the principles and applications of systems thinking. Each planning phase grantee then prepared a detailed five-year plan for restructuring the workplace to strengthen hospital nursing and improve patient care.

EVALUATING SHN

The authors conducted an evaluation of the SHN program between 1994 and 1997.[1] The specific projects for change at each of the nine study sites are presented in Exhibit 6.2 at the end of this chapter. To enable us to see the larger picture, we classified each project by whether it was aimed primarily at a change in a patient care process, in a service, in administration, or in human resources.

Changes in Patient Care Process

All nine SHN study sites implemented process changes such as redesigning patient care pathways and creating new pathways for cardiovascular, cancer, maternity, pediatric, intensive care, and emergency patients, among others. The changes in the patient care process were often accompanied by an increased use of nonprofessional patient care assistants, cross-training of professional staff people, and the use of a case manager to coordinate care across the continuum of services. Another major theme of the changes in patient care process at SHN hospital sites was the emphasis on creating and supporting a team approach to care. In several instances, new centers were created to provide an organizational mechanism for supporting the team approach to patient care and the integration of the care of patients across traditional disciplinary boundaries.

Typically, changes in the patient care process were the most difficult ones for hospitals to adopt, because they were the ones most likely to be resisted by physicians and nurses, who often viewed them as threatening to their current job responsibilities and their autonomy. Moreover, changes in patient care processes often required changes in the activities of many ancillary and support personnel, which significantly complicated the process.

Service Changes

Six of nine SHN study sites supplemented their changes in the patient care process with the introduction of new services. These varied greatly, with each site creating new services uniquely tailored to its patients' needs and the existing services. Some new services added to the array of direct patient care services available at the hospital, such as special attention to the victims of domestic violence and sexual assault, hospice care, outpatient chemical dependency treatment, cardiac rehabilitation, and a program to give patients more control over their hospital care. Other new services were designed to expand the continuum of care to include prehospital and posthospital services, such as an informational video for patients about to be admitted to the hospital, referral programs linking the hospital to the patients' home-town nursing services, and a faith ministry. Two sites established new patient education centers to help patients and their families learn more about their health problems and participate more fully in the planning and carrying out of their treatment regimens.

Administrative Changes

The changes in the SHN hospitals' patient care processes and services were often accompanied by changes in the administrative structures and processes of the hospital. Eight of the nine study sites adopted such changes. In several sites, the organizational structure of the hospital was changed through the implementation of shared governance, the creation of new committees, the use of matrix organizational structures, and the introduction of new administrative roles to support the clinical staff. The introduction of shared governance in hospitals was one of the most favored changes, because it decentralized decision making, giving staff members more control over their work. However, even this change was resisted by some nurses and others who preferred simply to "do their job" and not be burdened with the responsibility of participating in making work process, staffing, and personnel policy decisions.

One common administrative change was to strengthen the hospital's information systems. This was accomplished in a number of ways. More information and feedback from patients was acquired through the use of patient questionnaires and focus groups. In one hospital, the site of much patient-related data collection and storage was moved to the patient's bedside. Additionally, two hospitals designed and adopted new computer-based information systems to support the care providers. The task of making information systems more useful for clinical and managerial work was complex and difficult, affecting virtually every department in the hospital. However, staff at several study sites commented that the inadequacy of their information systems was a barrier to making administrative and other changes, indicating that significant value could be added to the patient care process with an improved information system.

Human Resources Changes

Seven of the nine study sites created human resources development programs to provide administrative and clinical staff with the conceptual tools and the practical skills necessary to bring about change. These programs developed staff members' knowledge of the process of organizational change, introduced them to new approaches to patient care, taught effective communications skills, emphasized the importance of teamwork, and reinforced the values and beliefs supportive of a patient-centered focus for the hospital. Frequently, these human resources activities were packaged as leadership development programs. Other human resource changes included the development of new training programs for clinical nurses, staff performance recognition programs, and training in continuous quality improvement techniques.

THREE CASES

Perhaps the best way to gain an understanding of the changes adopted by the SHN hospitals, and of the impact those changes had on nursing and patient care, is to examine three distinctly different cases: Beth Israel Hospital in Boston, D.C. General Hospital in Washington, D.C., and the Rural Connection, a consortium of Idaho Hospitals.

Beth Israel Hospital

Beth Israel Hospital, in the center of Boston's medical metropolis, serves as one of the primary teaching hospitals for the Harvard School of Medicine. It is nationally recognized as one of the nation's premier health care institutions. The 408-bed hospital provides a full range of acute care services. In addition to its reputation as a leader in the field of medicine, Beth Israel Hospital is recognized both nationally and internationally for its professional nursing practice model (primary nursing) and the quality of its nursing care. Under the leadership of Joyce Clifford, the hospital's vice president for nursing and nurse-in-chief, the nursing division at Beth Israel successfully developed and adopted primary nursing in 1974. This model of professional practice has been emulated widely in hospitals throughout the United States. Elements of this model of nursing practice at Beth Israel include an individualized patient relationship, twenty-four hour accountability for nursing care, admission-to-discharge accountability for a patient by one nurse who cares for that patient when present, case-based management of care through the use of nursing care plans as well as direct communication between care givers, and associate nurses who provide care in the absence of the primary nurse consistent with the plan of care developed by the primary nurse.

Underlying the primary nursing model was the value the organization placed on the clinical practice of nursing. Dr. Mitchell Rabkin, the president and chief executive officer, or CEO, of the Beth Israel Health System, said his philosophy "is that the hospital is fundamentally a nursing institution," and added, "Doctors don't like to hear me say that. Basically, we are nurturing the patients for a variety of perturbations that are carried out by doctors." The Strengthening Hospital Nursing Program enabled Beth Israel to change its patient care model from primary nursing to a new model referred to as integrated clinical practice.

WHY CHANGE? The awareness of the need for change at Beth Israel was stimulated by factors both internal and external. Two of the major internal forces were the increasing severity of patients' illnesses and the decreasing length of stay, which resulted in greater demands on the nurses. Jane Ruzansky, the director of nursing for surgery, commented on the importance of these factors: "With managed care, patients' conditions have become very complex—patients were staying for shorter periods of time, and a lot [of the care] was happening outside the hospital. We knew that new graduates were having a harder time managing the complexity of the patients. We heard from clinical instructors that they were overwhelmed with the difficulty of patients and figuring out assignments."

External factors also pressured Beth Israel to change. At the time of the planning grant—1989—it was clear that managed care was on the horizon. Increasing competition for managed care contracts required the hospital to reduce its costs. According to Joyce Clifford, "None of us had any notion of how difficult that environment was going to get." In 1994, the nursing division budget was reduced by

127 positions, mainly from inpatient nursing. During this period, the hospital experienced an increased volume and a decreased length of stay.

The theme of loss was frequently identified as an experience affecting the nursing staff in a variety of ways. The closure of a nursing unit resulted in "losing friends that we have worked with for ten years" as well as the loss of a manager. Some nurses experienced monetary losses with the elimination of ten-hour shifts. Also, as one nurse reported, it was "really painful for nurses to watch patients going home much sooner than they thought they should be going home. It was sad for nurses to be sending patients out when the nurses would like them to stay [so they could] take care of them."

THE SHN PROGRAM AT BETH ISRAEL. The SHN program at Beth Israel was a five-year project designed to redefine the role of the professional nurse in caring for patients across the continuum of care. The program title, Integrated Clinical Practice, stressed the complex interdisciplinary approach believed to be necessary to enhance patient care. Four major goals were articulated to guide SHN grant activities.

- To span the system of care and the spectrum of illness so that continuity in patient and family care is improved and experienced, advanced practitioners of nursing are utilized effectively in achieving a consistent quality and standard of care. The development of care teams was one of the principal mechanisms by which nursing was able to span the continuum of care.

- To restructure the organizational framework of hospital nursing practice based on professional and career development concepts for novice through expert nursing practice. The Clinical Nurse Entry Program was the major initiative adopted to achieve this goal. This program was a two-year first work experience for new nurses. New nursing graduates were provided with a preceptor and a guided orientation to the hospital work environment and the job expectations for a clinical nurse.

- To refine and strengthen interdisciplinary collaboration, especially that of physician and nurse, through integrated systems for the planning and the management of patient care. The creation of care teams, previously described, was the principal initiative to accomplish this goal.

• To develop institutionally focused, patient-centered support systems for the delivery of care. Two new patient-centered positions were created to provide support to professional staff. The support assistant performed tasks previously done by housekeeping, dietary, and transportation staff. The practice coordinator provided support to the nurse manager by coordinating the administrative activities of a nursing unit.

CARE TEAMS. Care teams were designed to improve the continuity of care for different services and at various sites, and to promote an interdisciplinary approach to patient care. Membership on the Care Teams was fluid, flexible, and inclusive; any care provider who wanted to participate was welcome. Care Teams were given latitude to redesign patient care so that they could achieve the goals of the grant: continuity, career development, interdisciplinary collaboration, and spanning the spectrum of illness and the system of care.

The Hematology/Oncology Care Team illustrates the effects of care teams on nursing and patient care. This team involved everyone in the department, including physicians, nurses, and support staff members. The major work of this group was "breaking down the barriers between [inpatient and outpatient] settings and really looking at ourselves as an integrated practice," one of the team members remarked. Group activities were designed to "make a patient's experience seamless, so that from a patient's perspective, receiving care in any setting, or from anybody in the department feels like it's the same focus, the same themes, the same materials. This included improving communications, and, from the patient's focus, making it feel very coordinated."

One strategy to improve communications and the coordination of care was integrating the role of nurses so that they could practice in both the ambulatory and the inpatient oncology settings. The nurses involved had a caseload of patients they cared for in both settings. By the fourth year of the grant (1993–94), four nurses were practicing in the role. As this model evolved, practice groups were formed that linked a small group of inpatient nurses with a physician's ambulatory practice. A team member commented on the impact of this change on patients: "We've put one integrated practice nurse in each practice group. For any patient seen in that ambulatory practice, there is a nurse who also takes care of patients on the inpatient unit who has some knowledge of them. From a patient's point of view, that's been very reassuring—to see a familiar face, to know someone who has known them in an ambulatory setting."

Other strategies were used to improve communications between the inpatient and ambulatory staff about the care of patients. Patients newly diagnosed on the inpatient unit were referred to the ambulatory unit by the primary nurse, and an ambulatory nurse who would care for the patient after discharge was identified before discharge. Information about the patient's hospital stay was shared with the ambulatory nurse, and, if possible, the nurse met the patient before discharge. Another method to improve communications was the implementation of the same patient assessment tool in the radiation oncology unit, the inpatient oncology unit, and the ambulatory hematology-oncology unit. Further, patient education materials were made consistent among the three units.

The major source of resistance to Care Teams came from the nursing staff. According to Ellen Powers, the nurse manager for hematology/oncology, staff members were able to understand the external pressures for creating change. "I think people understood that piece," she said. "These are experienced clinicians who are very good at adaptation and who have very appropriate values around patients and practice. So I think they could logically understand the grant and the changes in health care, and the reasons for this. However, the change was threatening to staff at a personal level. It was just that they didn't like how it felt to them to have to change. They had been in a certain pattern for a long time, and nobody had ever examined it or asked them to examine it, and now they were being asked to look at things very deeply." Resistance was eventually overcome by providing staff time to adjust to the changes. Also, the grant provided an opportunity to showcase the achievements of the Care Team at meetings and in the newsletter, thus providing positive feedback to the members.

SUPPORT ROLES. During the first year of the grant, 1990–91, a work analysis team was formed to determine how best to support the nursing staff in caring for patients. The goal was to relieve the nurses of chores that they didn't need to be doing so they could spend more time taking care of patients. Out of the planning the work analysis team did, two new roles were created: the support assistant and the practice coordinator.

Support Assistant. The people in these new positions were assigned to a patient care unit, becoming part of the patient care staff, and were trained to clean patient rooms, deliver and collect meal trays, and transport patients to and from tests. "I think the patients supported this," the SHN project director, Laura Duprat, noted. "When things were going tough and we could look at those [patient] comment cards and realize that it really impacted patients in a great way, we couldn't *not* move the program forward. It was very important to have that feedback from patients."

By 1996, however, the role of support assistant had been adopted only by three demonstration nursing units. A major obstacle to the hospital-wide adoption of the program was the cost. Although the cost of the program was lower than the centrally based support services on weekends and holidays, it was slightly more expensive during the week. Full implementation was contingent on moving the program forward in a way that didn't cause budget increases.

Practice Coordinator. The practice coordinator was responsible for "making sure the unit has what it needs to run smoothly and if it doesn't, to work on those systems to make things happen," Laura Duprat commented. "We found that nurse managers were spending so much time worrying about [operational matters], they couldn't do their jobs, and we decided they really needed to be focusing on nursing." In addition to overseeing all nonclinical functions, the practice coordinator planned and organized the work of unit-based support staff, developed systems to enhance unit operations, devised policies and procedures to ensure efficient processing of work, and prepared and monitored supply and expense budgets.

CLINICAL NURSE ENTRY PROGRAM. The hospital traditionally hired new graduates immediately upon graduation and, after a brief orientation, expected them to function as full members of the nursing staff with no additional formal career development. The typical orientation acquainted graduate nurses with hospital policies and procedures and prepared them to fulfill the job description for registered nurses on a particular patient care unit. What was lacking was systematic, ongoing, formalized attention to the professional development of the nurse beyond the orientation period.

The Clinical Nurse Entry Program was designed to provide new graduates with clinical skills and to ensure that they adopted professional values. New graduates were hired for a two-year residency. During this period, they received a standardized residency experience that emphasized not only clinical competence but also systematic career planning and orientation for the role of the nurse. As part of this orientation, the new graduate had a clinical nurse mentor—an experienced nurse who understood the importance of value-based practice. Nurse residents functioned as members of the nursing staff and maintained a caseload of primary patients. However, the planned process of acquainting the new graduate with the nursing profession was the distinguishing characteristic of the entry program.

District of Columbia General Hospital

The District of Columbia General Hospital is a 482–bed acute care hospital in Washington, D.C. Established in 1806, the hospital provides health services for the residents of the community regardless of their ability to pay and serves as a safety net for vulnerable populations within the District of Columbia. Frequently it is the provider of last-resort care. The hospital also provides medical education through affiliation with the medical schools of Georgetown University and Howard University.

The patient population served by D.C. General consists predominantly of patients who, for reasons relating to poverty, social circumstances, health (including mental health) status, employment, race, and culture, make up the community's most vulnerable populations. These patients tend to be high-risk, complex patients who experience multisystem disease. In addition to providing specialty inpatient care, the hospital is a major provider of primary and other ambulatory care.

D.C. General also provides emergency and trauma services, and at the time of the planning grant—1988–89—the Emergency Department was the busiest in the Washington, D.C., metropolitan area with an average of 200,000 visits a year. Some 88 percent of the inpatient population was admitted through the Emergency Department.

As the only acute care public hospital located in the nation's capital, D.C. General was responsible both to the District of Columbia government and to the United States Congress, and this dual responsibility resulted in a highly politicized governing structure subject to the changing nature of political control. The hospital staff was highly unionized. Staff physicians were unionized, and so were nurses and other professional, technical, and support staff people.

WHY CHANGE? The recent history of D.C. General reveals an organization fighting for survival and buffeted by the winds of political change, including a changing governing structure. In the late 1960s, the hospital became the responsibility of the District government, losing its federal status. In 1977, a semi-independent commission, named by the mayor, was created to manage the hospital. This commission had the authority to make physical, personnel, and policy changes. Fiscal crises have been the focus of more recent concerns, and further changes in the governing structure have been proposed to address the financial situation. Plagued by chronic budget deficits, the District of Columbia government had repeatedly called for budget cuts and staff reductions to cope with an almost yearly operating loss at the hospital. At the time of the planning grant in 1989, the organization was experiencing an increasing emphasis on cost containment, quality of care outcomes, and productivity.

In addition to extreme turbulence from the outside, a great deal of disturbance occurred on the inside. Four different chief executive officers served during the grant funding period, and this turnover contributed to a lack of consistent organizational mission and vision. The hospital historically suffered from staff shortages, inadequate non-clinical support systems, and underutilization of automated labor-saving mechanisms. At the time of the planning grant, the hospital had had to reduce the number of beds it could make available. Staff morale was low, and there was a high turnover of registered nurses.

In short, D.C. General displayed few of the characteristics one would expect to see in a hospital undertaking successful organizational change. In the midst of this turbulence, however, the appointment of Nellie Robinson as the associate administrator for nursing in 1987 served as a catalyst for change. Nellie Robinson was identified as a charismatic leader who was able to articulate her vision of a patient-centered hospital, and to mobilize people to bring about change. The combination of visionary leadership and highly unsettled conditions created a sense of a fighting spirit in the organization, and provided the motivation to rise above the challenges.

THE SHN GRANT AT DISTRICT OF COLUMBIA GENERAL HOSPITAL. The Strengthening Hospital Nursing grant activities at D.C. General focused on the goal of creating a system emphasizing the patient as the key stakeholder in the health care system. Achieving this goal meant restructuring of services at the unit level. The four major SHN projects undertaken by the hospital were collaborative care project teams, patient focus groups, guest relations, and the hospital staff recognition program. The project most fundamentally affecting patient care was that of the collaborative care project teams.

These teams provided a structured, administratively supported forum for interdisciplinary discussion, collaboration, and problem solving. Representatives from many departments were invited to provide their expertise in designing a more efficient, patient-friendly environment. Group members attended an educational session conducted by consultants from the Center for Applied Research, and were thus provided with a common language and tools to accomplish the work of the group. Teams were authorized to take responsibility for certain problems and to arrive at solutions.

Five project teams were established during the third year of the grant, in 1992, but only four of them survived to the fourth year of the grant. Each project team functioned in a unique way, and most were able to accomplish some significant changes in care delivery. For example, the pediatric team addressed and solved more than twenty problems affecting patient care, such as decreasing the waiting times in the pharmacy from more than sixty minutes on average to fifteen minutes, decreasing triage time by initiating triage coding, and decreasing waiting time to see a physician in the outpatient clinic from sixty minutes to twenty. The surgery unit project team decreased the length of stay and the cost of caring for two groups of patients.

Unfortunately, the project teams were not sustained, for several reasons. Some physicians resisted the creation of the teams from the outset. The associate administrator for nursing noted, "Physicians were not used to spending time in meetings; they were used to giving orders, not working things out as a team." The hospital's medical director also noted that involving physicians was difficult because they regarded the grant as being specifically for nursing.

Other factors causing the demise of the project teams were related to the general turmoil affecting the hospital. In 1993, during the third year of the grant, the project staff was administratively transferred from the Nursing Division to the Office of the Executive Director. The associate administrator for nursing believed that by having those responsible for the grant report to the hospital's chief executive officer the program "would get proper attention and we would be able to achieve 100 percent cooperation." She wanted to get away from the "stigma of this being a 'nursing grant.'" When the grant was administratively transferred to the CEO, however, he did not have time to provide the necessary direction for it because of the demands external issues imposed on his time. According to one of the consultants, the CEO did not view the grant as strategically important. Nellie Robinson was able to provide leadership and support to the project team's activities, but in 1993 she left D.C. General, and the leadership of the project was assumed by Rachel Smith, who had been actively involved in the unit-level activities of the project teams. Smith continued to provide enthusiastic leadership for those teams, but she left in 1994, and there was no one to continue to champion the project teams. The SHN project director also left the organization in 1994 and was not replaced.

During this same period, the hospital CEO and other members of senior management had to focus not on the grant but on tremendous external changes that threatened the survival of D.C. General. The movement to Medicaid managed care resulted in a decline in patient volume at D.C. General, and, with more hospitals in Washington willing to care for Medicaid patients, many in the community intensified the debate about the need for a public hospital. In the fall of 1995, an interagency task force was appointed by Washington's mayor to create a public benefit corporation to govern the hospital. At the same time, members of Congress were calling for the closing of the hospital. In response to the resulting instability, the hospital began experiencing tremendous personnel turnover. In May of 1995, the city government called for a reduction in force of 200 employees and 60 physicians. Fear of the unknown caused many staff people to resign. Because of a hiring freeze, new nurses were not recruited to fill vacancies created by the turnover. Many of the unit aide positions were lost in the reduction, and nonnursing tasks once again fell to the staff of registered nurses. In 1995, registered nurses took a 12 percent salary reduction, and the management staff experienced a 4 percent across-the-board salary reduction—this after a four-to-five-year period without any salary increase. Essentially all of the major participants in the grant activities left D.C. General before the grant ended. According to the hospital's executive director, the hospital employed one-third fewer employees in 1996 than it had when the grant began.

Activities related to the Strengthening Hospital Nursing grant effectively ceased in the latter part of 1994, during the fifth year of the grant. The organization was not able to complete its SHN implementation plan, and never fully adopted the SHN grant projects. The only bright note is that despite the cessation of grant-related projects, many staff members are convinced that life is different at D.C. General as a result of the grant. According to the director of social work, "[Something] very powerful has happened to those involved in the program and their relations with other disciplines. . . . They are able to reach out and speak to each other. . . . This has permeated to line staff, who are buying in as a philosophy and a way of life."

The Rural Connection

The Rural Connection was a consortium project that included an urban medical center, a rehabilitation hospital, four rural hospitals, and a university. The initiating organization was St. Luke's Regional Medical Center, a 252-bed hospital in Boise, Idaho. Other hospitals that made up the consortium included Idaho Elks Rehabilitation Hospital (Boise), Holy Rosary Medical Center (Ontario, Oregon), McCall Memorial Hospital (McCall, Idaho), Walter Knox Memorial Hospital (Emmett, Idaho), and Wood River Medical Center (Sun Valley, Idaho). The four rural hospitals are separated by many miles of mountain ranges and desert. Travel among them is complicated by harsh and unpredictable winter weather conditions.

WHY CHANGE? The initial interest in using the Strengthening Hospital Nursing grant to support change came from the relatively new leadership of St. Luke's Hospital—its president, Edwin Dahlberg, and its vice president for patient care services, Sharon Lee. St. Luke's Regional Medical Center was founded in 1902 by an Episcopal bishop who wished to provide a facility to care for the sick in his parish. Since its founding, St. Luke's has been a regional leader in health care. In 1968, the first open-heart surgery performed in Idaho was done at St. Luke's. In 1993, 1994, and 1995, St. Luke's was named one of the country's top hundred hospitals by HCIA, Inc., and William M. Mercer. Clearly, the staff of St. Luke's took great pride in being recognized as an industry leader, and the new executives at the hospital wanted to maintain the status of St. Luke's.

This desire was acknowledged by Edwin Dahlberg, who attributed interest in the grant to "the fact that I was relatively new at that time, and Sharon was new." He added, "The folks who were new were willing to take it on. The new people were expecting some change." Sharon Lee believed that the grant had great potential, and her enthusiasm was infectious. Joe Caroselli, the administrator of Idaho Elks Rehabilitation Hospital, said of Lee, "You would get around her and she would start talking about the grant like it was a religion. She knew it was a lot of work, and she was going to do some and you were going to do some, too. She was able to engage others and get them involved."

THE SHN PROJECT AT THE RURAL CONNECTION. The SHN projects involving the Rural Connection included those set up within each participating organization and a consortium-wide project. The goal of the consortium-wide project was to develop an interagency system of rural health care delivery—specifically, to develop regional standards of care for patients experiencing a heart attack and requiring thrombolytic therapy.

During the first two years of the grant, the Rural Connection focus was on projects at each of the consortium hospitals. At the end of 1991, however, the Rural Connection received a wake-up call from the SHN National Office. At that time, the Rural Connection project director was frustrated by what she believed to be a lack of progress on grant initiatives and a lack of organizational focus on the grant. Rather than focusing on the progress that had been made, she submitted a report to the national SHN project office that emphasized what had not been accomplished. The result was a surprise visit from Mary Kay Kohles, the deputy director of the SHN National Program, during which the threat of losing the grant was identified as a possibility unless further progress was achieved.

After that visit, the work of the Rural Connection took on a much broader focus. The members of the consortium began to look at improving the health care of the larger community, rather than concentrating on issues specific to an individual hospital. As Connie Perry, the project's coordinator, explained, "We knew that there were patients who go back and forth between our hospitals and we knew we were not doing a very good job of managing them. And we knew we were caring for them in the most expensive way—repeating every test, collecting the same information. The right hand did not know what the left hand was doing. The patient would come back, no one knew they were back, no one knows what had happened. So we said, 'How can we build a continuum of care?'"

THE CONSORTIUM THERAPY PROJECT. The first regionwide project of the rural consortium was the development of regional standards of care for patients experiencing a heart attack and requiring therapy. The end result was a protocol of care for these patients that described standards of treatment in the rural hospitals. These included standards for identifying patients with chest pain who were candidates for thrombolytic therapy, standards for the timing of the administration of thrombolytic therapy, and standards for appropriate transfers and community-based follow-up care.

The success of this project was in large measure due to the ability of the project leader to bring together a group of skilled and knowledgeable people who would not normally have worked together. For example, Joe Caroselli at Idaho Elks Hospital described his involvement: "I think there was a lot of effort to try and get different people into different roles. The idea of getting disinterested people involved was visionary. I quickly became aware that these people representing these various hospitals really were concerned about this cardiac patient population. They began to see they could make a difference in the lives of these people and the basic purpose of the group was that we were going to add muscle to the community." Additionally, this group brought together people involved in different aspects of the care of cardiac patients who had not previously collaborated in planning for patient care, including physicians, emergency medical services personnel, hospital nurses, and patient care staff at the rehabilitation hospital.

The Rural Connection myocardial infarction/thrombolytic therapy regional design group was so focused on improving the care of these patients that its work easily crossed over organizational boundaries, even to the point where consortium hospitals worked collaboratively with competing hospitals. "About three-fourths of the way through the project, it was clear that St. Luke's and its network was definitely in control of the cardiac patient," Caroselli said. "But there was a competing hospital across town. Through this vision of this particular group, who had all the protocols established, they said, 'If anyone in this community has an infarct and did end up at [the competing hospital],' this group wanted to make sure the patient was attended to. So that barrier broke down." The competing hospital was approached, and it agreed to participate in the protocols. Involving the competing hospital "put the focus on what we're really here to do," Caroselli said.

In 1996, a year after the grant funding terminated, the work of the Rural Connection was continuing. Moreover, the model was in the process of being applied to three other patient groups: obstetrics, stroke, and breast cancer.

CONCLUSION

The nursing shortage of the 1980s appears to have given way to a more complicated picture in the mid-1990s. During the early nineties, new market forces, including the increasing use by payers of per diem and capitated hospital reimbursement and competition among hospitals for contracts with managed care plans, changed the demand for hospital nursing. As managed care techniques were adopted by health plans and providers, hospitals were required to cope with declining patient days, fewer admissions, and lower payments. Many diagnostic tests and treatments were routinely provided on an outpatient basis and in outpatient settings separate from the hospital. The use of the hospital for the observation of patients as part of the diagnostic regimen was greatly reduced. Similarly, hospitals were little used for bed rest of patients, as more out-of-hospital exercise-oriented regimens for treatment and rehabilitation of both acute and chronic diseases were adopted. Although the patients who were admitted to hospitals were typically sicker and more complex cases than was true through most of the 1980s, pressure from payers of all sorts to reduce hospital costs caused hospitals to attempt to redesign hospital work to reduce lengths of stay while maintaining quality of care. Increasingly, hospitals sought to cut costs by reducing the number of full-time equivalent employees, cutting nursing hours per patient, and lowering overall wages by employing fewer high-cost registered nurses.

There continues to be significant pressure on nursing staffs to use more nonprofessional assistants for mundane tasks, while maintaining a highly trained professional workforce to care for an increasingly acutely ill inpatient population. If anything, in the mid-1990s the forces acting on hospitals to transform the patient care process have strengthened.

The changes implemented by the Strengthening Hospital Nursing sites ran deep and wide. Using patient-centered care as a conceptual touchstone, the clinical and administrative staff in these hospitals adopted many innovations, and in some cases true organizational transformation was realized. Core patient care processes were redesigned, affecting the practice patterns and the working relationships among many different clinical care providers. In many cases, patient care practice was for the first time standardized. Serious efforts to create an integrated continuum of care were observed, with further restructuring of long-established turf boundaries and work roles. Cross-training of staff and the use of assistants to provide nonprofessional aspects of patient care further challenged the personal beliefs and institutional norms regarding best practices and improving patient care. It is important to note, however, that the changes in patient care processes were adopted at the same time that new services and products were being introduced and new administrative and human resources structures and processes were being put in place to support the changes in patient care.

Among the SHN study hospitals, the importance of the resources made available by the SHN planning and implementation grants was frequently cited as the key to building the capacity to change. "People say, 'It wasn't so much the grant money,' but it *was* the money," one project director said. "This is what allowed us to learn the process, stretch the rules, learn how to develop others, undertake training around the patient care process. Without the grant, we would not have been as rich, nor as sustainable, nor as spirited."

The importance of larger environmental forces on hospital decision making cannot be ignored, however. The penetration of managed care and competition among hospitals for contracts to provide care to patients covered by managed care plans were important stimuli for hospitals to reduce costs, improve care, and increase patient satisfaction. On the negative side, as demonstrated in the case of District of Columbia General Hospital, dramatic budget cuts, large numbers of personnel layoffs, and rapid turnover in senior management positions can be devastating to a hospital's efforts to improve patient care. The Strengthening Hospital Nursing Program was not designed to solve such problems, and it did not.

Our eight other SHN study sites did make lasting improvements in patient care, however, and in most cases created new models of nursing practice and new relationships among nurses and other providers of care. Perhaps the most fundamental changes observed in SHN hospitals was a reaffirmation of the importance of the patient and a reorganization of hospital activities around the patients' needs. These changes will surely strengthen the role of those care providers having the most contact with patients—hospital nurses.

Note

1. Case study methodology was used to study the SHN Program. The five-year SHN implementation grants were funded in 1990. The research team conducting the case studies of the SHN Projects was assembled and began work in 1994, and continued to conduct site visits to selected grantee institutions and collect data via other means through July 1997. Because of limited resources, only nine of the original twenty SHN grantees could be studied. Hence, in 1994 we selected nine of the sites for maximum variability in key program, organizational, and environmental characteristics. The nine selected sites were

- Abbott Northwestern Hospital, Minneapolis, Minn.
- Beth Israel Hospital, Boston, Mass.
- D.C. General Hospital, Washington, D.C.
- Health Bond (a consortium of hospitals), South Central, Minn.
- Providence Medical Center, Portland, Ore.
- Rural Connection (a consortium of hospitals), Boise, Idaho
- University Hospitals of Cleveland, Cleveland, Ohio
- University Hospital, Salt Lake City, Utah
- Vanderbilt University Medical Center, Nashville, Tenn.

ગ્JP

Exhibit 6.1. Strengthening Hospital Nursing Program Implementation Grants.

- Harbor-UCLA Medical Center, Torrance CA

- Hartford Hospital, Hartford CT

- District of Columbia General Hospital, Washington DC

- Tallahassee Memorial Medical Center, Tallahassee FL

- St. Luke's Regional Medical Center, Boise ID
  Idaho Elks Rehabilitation Hospital, Boise ID

- Mercy Hospital and Medical Center, Chicago IL

- Beth Israel Hospital, Boston MA

- Boston Department of Health and Hospitals, Boston MA
  Mattapan Hospital, Boston MA

- Penobscot Bay Medical Center, Rockland ME
  Camden Health Care Center, Camden ME
  Kno-Wal-Lin Home Health Care Center, Camden ME
  Knox Center for Long Term Care, Rockland ME

- Mercy Health Services, Farmington Hills MI
  Battle Creek Health System, Battle Creek MI
  Catherine McAuley Health Center, Ann Arbor MI
  Marian Health Center, Sioux City IA
  Mercy Health Center, Dubuque IA
  Mercy Health Services North
      Mercy Hospital, Cadillac MI
      Mercy Hospital, Grayling MI
  Mercy Hospital, Muskegon MI
  Mercy Hospital, Port Huron MI
  Mercy Hospitals and Health Services of Detroit, Detroit MI
  Our Lady of Mercy Hospital, Dyer MI
  Samaritan Health System, Clinton IA
  St. Joseph Mercy Hospital, Mason City IA
  St. Joseph Mercy Hospital, Pontiac MI
  St. Lawrence Hospital and Healthcare Services, Lansing MI
  St. Mary's Health Services, Grand Rapids MI
  Traverse City Osteopathic Hospital, Traverse City MI

Ⓙ𝄢

Exhibit 6.1. Strengthening Hospital Nursing Program Implementation Grants, *continued*.

- Abbott-Northwestern Hospital, Inc., Minneapolis MN
- Health Bond, Mankato MN
    Grantree: Immanuel-St. Joseph's Hospital, Mankato MN
    Arlington Municipal Hospital, Arlington MN
    Waseca Area Memorial Hospital, Waseca MN
- The Montana Consortium
    Columbus Hospital, Great Falls MT
    St. Patrick Hospital, Missoula MT
    St. Vincent Hospital & Health Center, Billings MT
- St. Luke's Hospital-MeritCare, Fargo ND
- University Hospitals of Cleveland, Cleveland OH
    Geaga Hospital, Chardon OH
    Lakewood Hospital, Lakewood OH
    Lorain Community Hospital, Lorain OH
    University MEDNET, Cleveland OH
- Providence Medical Center, Portland OR
- The Pennsylvania State University/The Milton S. Hershey Medical Center, Hershey PA
- Vanderbilt University Hospital, Nashville TN
- University Hospital/University of Utah Health Science Center, Salt Lake City UT
- The Vermont Nursing Initiative
    Copley Hospital, Inc., Morrisville VT
    Brattleboro Memorial Hospital, Brattleboro VT
    Central Vermont Medical Center, Barre VT
    Fanny Allen Hospital, Colchester VT
    Gifford Memorial Hospital, Randolph VT
    Grace Cottage Hospital, Townshend VT
    Medical Center Hospital of Vermont, Burlington VT
    Mt. Ascutney Hospital and Health Center, Windsor VT
    North Country Hospital, Newport VT
    Northeastern Vermont Regional Hospital, St. Johnsbury VT
    Northwestern Medical Center, St. Albans VT
    Porter Medical Center, Middlebury VT
    Rutland Regional Medical Center, Rutland VT
    Southwestern Vermont Medical Center, Bennington VT
    Springfield Hospital, Springfield VT

ઝૐ

Exhibit 6.2. Types of Changes Made in Strengthening Hospital Nursing Study Sites.

Abbott Northwestern Hospital

Patient Care	Service	Administrative	Human Resource
• ICU Epicenter • Cardiovascular Epicenter • Sister Kenney Institute Epicenter	• Hometown Nurse Program • CV Referral Program	• President's Quality Council • Bedside point of care information system • Patient Care Community	• Personal Mastery Institutes • Clinical models in nursing

Beth Israel Hospital

Patient Care	Service	Administrative	Human Resource
• Integrated Clinical Practice	• Patient and Family Learning Center	• Support roles for clinical staff	• Clinical Nurse Entry Program

District of Columbia General Hospital

Patient Care	Service	Administrative	Human Resource
• Patient Centered Hospital Environment— Collaborative Care Project Teams		• Patient Focus Groups	• Guest Relations • Hospital Staff Recognition Program

Health Bond Consortium

Patient Care	Service	Administrative	Human Resource
• Behavioral Services Integration of Care (ISJ) • Primary Nursing Implementation (ISJ) • Managed Care for Arthroplasty Patients (ISJ)	• Victims of Domestic Violence and Sexual Assault • Displasia Program: Implementation (ISJ) • Hospice: Meeting the Needs of Families and Patients (AMN) • Surgical Patient Care, Inpatient and Outpatient Services (WAMH)	• Oncology Resources Data Base Development (ISJ) • Education Resource Network Remote Access to ISJ Library (ISJ)	• Maternal Child Services: Training (ISJ) • Culture Change/ Empowerment (ISJ) • Culture Change/ Empowerment • Assess Educational Needs of Regional Health Care Providers (SCTC, ISJ) • Teaming Up for Better Eldercare (ISJ)

♫

Exhibit 6.2. Types of Changes Made in Strengthening Hospital Nursing Study Sites, *continued.*

Health Bond Consortium, *continued*

Patient Care	Service	Administrative	Human Resource
	• Family Focus Outpatient Chemical Dependency • Cardiac Rehabilitation Implementation (AMH) • Heart Health Care Notebook (ISJ) • Faith Health Ministry (ISJ)		• Culture change in Nursing (AMH) • Rural Health Strategic Planning Day • Tri Hospital Board and Medical Staff Visioning (Region 9 Dev. Comm., ISJ) • Education for Crisis Intervention and Grief Counseling (ISJ)

Providence Portland Medical Center

Patient Care	Service	Administrative	Human Resource
• Patient Care Delivery Redesign			

Rural Connection Consortium

Patient Care	Service	Administrative	Human Resource
• Pre-hospital cardiac pathways • Patient Care Redesign		• Organizational restructuring • Shared governance councils	• Nurse exchanges

University Hospitals of Cleveland

Patient Care	Service	Administrative	Human Resource
• Collaborative care—critical pathways • Care Manager • Emergency Department Redesign • Women's Health Center Design	• Patient Education Center		• Leadership Institute

ঔ৹

Exhibit 6.2. Types of Changes Made in Strengthening Hospital Nursing Study Sites, *continued.*

University Hospitals of Cleveland, *continued*

Patient Care	Service	Administrative	Human Resource
• Labor and Delivery Redesign • Pediatric Intensive Care Unit Redesign • Breast Center			

University of Utah Health Science Center

Patient Care	Service	Administrative	Human Resource
• STARS	• U Choose • First Impressions	• Multi-disciplinary Apprentice Program	

Vanderbilt University Hospital

Patient Care	Service	Administrative	Human Resource
• Orthopedics Unit Redesign • Myelosuppression Unit Redesign • Perinatal Project: MOM • Cardiology Service Project • Patient Care Centers • The Vanderbilt Clinic	• Pediatric Round Wing Redesign • Case Management/ Collaborative Care	• Radiology Project • Collaborative Organization Design • Project Evaluation • Integrated Advanced Medical Informatics System/IAMS Grant • Shared Governance System	• Support for Mission • Center for Patient Care Innovation • Facilitative Leadership and CQI Courses

Note: The acronym in parenthesis represents the name of a particular organizational member within a consortium in which the organizational change was implemented. ISJ = Immanuel–St. Joseph's Hospital; AMH = Arlington Municipal Hospital; WAMH = Waseca Area Memorial Hospital; SCTC = South Central Technical College.

Improving Chronic Care

CHAPTER SEVEN

⟨⟨⟨ Faith in Action

Paul Jellinek
Terri Gibbs Appel
Terrance Keenan

Editors' Introduction

Faith in Action is a program that encourages voluntarism as a strategy for meeting the needs of chronically ill people. The Foundation sees voluntarism as one leg of the three-legged stool needed to build an effective system of chronic care. The first leg is public programs that provide home care and other supportive services, because many people with chronic conditions lack the resources to pay for services themselves. The second leg is private financing tools that let people plan for the services they will need if and when they become frail. Perhaps the most important leg is volunteers. Informal mechanisms—particularly families and friends—have been the main source of care for the chronically ill. The number of people engaged in this kind of work needs to be expanded as the aging of the population increases the number of people with chronic illness.

Over the past few years, the Faith in Action initiative has attempted to build a large service program—not just a demonstration—quickly. It has now given grants to more than 1,100 religious coalitions around the country. In this chapter, Paul Jellinek, a Foundation vice president;

Terri Gibbs Appel, a former Foundation program officer; and Terrance Keenan, a senior consultant to the Foundation, discuss the logic of this approach and the issues that arose in implementing it.

Faith in Action is the Foundation's largest initiative encouraging voluntarism, but it is not the only one. For many years, the Foundation supported a concept called Service Credit Banking, in which healthy elders would volunteer to provide services to frail elders and receive "service credits," which the caregivers could cash in later in life when they themselves might need volunteer services. Another major initiative—the Reach Out Program—supports volunteer efforts by physicians to care for uninsured and indigent patients. More recently, the Foundation has begun to explore how volunteers might help improve the after-school lives of young people. The importance of mentors is becoming clear from recent research, and voluntarism—especially in urban areas—is often seen as one way of increasing contact between young people and caring adults.

Certainly, voluntarism has received national attention through the efforts of General Colin Powell and others to promote community volunteering. Nationwide, his America's Promise campaign has received widespread publicity and praise. The groundswell movement may gather even more momentum over time.

In the same way, the Faith in Action program may be entering a new phase of development. Even as this book is being published, the Foundation is considering the next steps in its support of this initiative, and of voluntarism in general.

Bob Barclay, a sixty-nine-year-old retired research chemist, is a quiet, unassuming bachelor who lives alone in a house he bought twenty-six years ago in a working class suburb of Trenton, New Jersey. He serves as a lector at Our Lady of Sorrows Church on East State Street, and over the years has done some volunteer work for Catholic Charities, but other than that he has kept pretty much to himself. "I'm a very private person," he said not long ago.

Yet in the winter of 1995, in his own quiet way, Bob Barclay became something of a hero to a small group of people in need in his community when he signed on to become an interfaith volunteer caregiver. "I saw a notice in the church bulletin, and I knew I could do this," he said. What Barclay knew he could do was become a volunteer driver for people who had chronic health problems or disabilities that made it hard for them to get out of the house.

"I had done this for my mother for many years, and she had only recently passed away," he remarked. Barclay's mother, who had lived with him for more than twenty years until she died at age ninety-one, had suffered from increasingly debilitating arthritis and had needed a great deal of help getting around, "including a lot of chauffeuring," Barclay said.

There were plenty of other services Barclay could have signed up to provide as an interfaith caregiver—shopping, respite, home repairs, personal care, meal preparation, or even just visiting—but others in the congregation had already volunteered to do those things. What was missing was somebody who could provide transportation, especially in the daytime, because that's when people need to get to the doctor or the bank or the hairdresser. "That's what attracted me—the notion of transportation," Barclay said. "It would be quite impersonal and, as I said, I've always been a private person."

But Bob soon discovered that it wasn't always so easy to keep things impersonal. One of his regular passengers was Mary, an eighty-five-year-old widow who lived alone and needed transportation for her medical appointments. "There was the dentist, the cardiologist, several eye doctors, and the psychiatrist," Barclay said. "Actually, she seemed to me to be in reasonably good health for someone her age, but she suffered from panic attacks. She would often think she was having a heart attack or a stroke."

Barclay said that after a while, despite his natural reserve, "we did get to know each other quite well, and it was a pleasant surprise. When I brought her back from her appointments, she would want me to stay and talk to her for a while. Sometimes as long as two hours."

Mary had no real social contacts anymore, Barclay said, because she could no longer drive and many of the people she had known had died. "But I was always surprised at what she would know about what was going on in the parish and in the township," he said. "Mostly, I think she was just lonely."

Another of Barclay's regular passengers was a woman named Karen—"a quiet, private person like me, on the other end of the scale from Mary," Barclay recalled. Eighty-four years old and unmarried, "she lived alone in a house on Vincent Avenue, a couple of blocks from the church. She had a real bad heart, and she died suddenly just before Christmas last year," he said.

With Karen, Barclay said, the conversation was always "strictly business—just the time and the place she had to be." But as her condition worsened and she became increasingly frail, "She would hold onto my arm," he said.

Bob Barclay is not the only quiet hero out there. There were others at Our Lady of Sorrows Church who saw the item in the church bulletin, went to an organizational meeting, and received the necessary training. Including Bob, there are now twenty-five active interfaith volunteer caregivers at Our Lady of Sorrows, up from eighteen last year. And just as Bob Barclay is part of a larger group within his church, Our Lady of Sorrows is itself part of a larger interfaith volunteer caregivers coalition that has come together in the Trenton area with a $25,000 start-up grant from The Robert Wood Johnson Foundation. The coalition, which is made up of thirteen urban and suburban congregations, expects to continue to grow in the coming years, and already has several hundred volunteers—including the twenty-five from Our Lady of Sorrows—and in 1997 provided some 7,470 hours of care throughout the region.

The Trenton-area coalition is not the only one of its kind—it is one of hundreds of interfaith volunteer caregiving coalitions operating in towns and cities all across the country, many of them also initiated with funding from The Robert Wood Johnson Foundation. The National Federation of Interfaith Volunteer Caregivers, a membership organization that provides technical assistance and support to new and established coalitions, currently has 1,378 member coalitions, up from a hundred in 1992, and there are several hundred others—no one is sure exactly how many—that do not formally belong to the Federation. In other words, there are tens of thousands of people out there who, like Barclay, are volunteering their time and their energy to provide care and support to the many Americans, young and old, who have been cut off from their communities and from everyday life by chronic health problems.

THE GROWING NEED

The problem of chronic care in America is staggering. Almost one hundred million people in this country have one or more chronic conditions. More than forty million of them—one in six Americans—have some kind of functional limitation as a result of their condition. And although the elderly are more likely to have a chronic health problem than other age groups, Americans of all ages are affected, including twelve million children.[1]

These large numbers come as a surprise to many of us. Maybe this is because we tend to think of chronic conditions categorically rather than as a group. We are accustomed to thinking of arthritis, paralysis, asthma, heart disease, cancer, diabetes, AIDS, blindness, deafness, mental retardation, Alzheimer's, and the many other chronic illnesses and disabilities as separate and distinct conditions. What we lose sight of is that although these conditions are distinct biologically and clinically, their impact on people's ability to carry on with their everyday lives is often depressingly consistent. No matter what their particular condition may be, people with serious chronic health problems frequently require some level of assistance with ordinary activities of daily living such as feeding, bathing, dressing, housekeeping, transportation, and, for those who live alone, companionship.

A major challenge facing the nation is how to meet that need as we move into the twenty-first century. So far, we have relied largely on family and friends to do the job. In fact, for seven out of ten persons with chronic conditions, family and friends are the only source of support. And although family and friends will undoubtedly continue to be the mainstay of chronic care in this country, the current arrangement is beginning to wear thin. Already, one out of four Americans is providing some form of assistance to a person with a chronic condition, and as the baby boomers age and life expectancy rates for the elderly continue to rise, the demand will grow even greater. At the same time, the capacity of family and friends to shoulder the burden on their own is declining. Over the next several decades, demographic shifts will reduce the proportion of Americans in the average age range for caregiving—fifty to sixty-four. Moreover, women, who until now have done most of the informal caregiving, have been entering the workforce in record numbers, sharply reducing the amount of time that they can make available.

As the contours of this problem come into focus, it seems unlikely that as a nation we will be able to finance our way out of it. Policy makers these days are desperately seeking ways to reduce future spending for health and social programs, not expand it. Moreover, the same demographic forces that are undermining existing informal care arrangements will also make it increasingly difficult to subsidize expanded chronic care services in the future. New ideas are needed, and interfaith volunteer caregiving is one new idea that The Robert Wood Johnson Foundation has been exploring.

THE CONCEPT

The basic notion of helping a neighbor in need is deeply rooted in the world's major faiths. Giving of oneself is widely recognized as a path to spiritual fulfillment, and has been espoused and practiced throughout the ages. Indeed, most religious congregations in America today offer at least some opportunities for members to volunteer their time in the service of others. Given that some two-thirds of all adult Americans belong to a religious congregation, this represents a vast potential resource to support and supplement the caregiving that families and friends currently provide to people who need chronic care. Some level of caregiving does go on in many congregations; however, it is usually on a very small scale, no more than a handful of people who do what they can on an informal basis. This is partly because there is often a range of volunteer opportunities to choose from in any given congregation, and those who are inclined to volunteer disperse themselves accordingly.

But the more fundamental problem is that most congregations by themselves simply don't have the resources necessary to staff and oversee their volunteer programs adequately. As a result, these programs are often poorly organized and not well promoted. Without a paid individual responsible for organizing and managing the program, volunteer efforts of the kind needed to help those with chronic illness will almost invariably fall far short of their true potential.

This is where interfaith volunteer caregiving comes into the picture. As a concept, it is remarkably simple. Rather than each congregation trying to develop and sustain its own volunteer effort to help the chronically ill and the disabled, a group of congregations representing the community's various faiths comes together, hires a paid director, and establishes a single caregiving program that draws its volunteers largely from the participating congregations to serve the entire community. By banding together in this way, in other words, the congregations are able to create a program large enough to justify hiring a paid director and, together with other organizations and individuals in the community, they should eventually be able to share the cost of that position and sustain it over time. Having a paid director who is responsible for the program in turn makes it possible to have a better-organized, more structured program that is more attractive to volunteers, who otherwise might not have come forward or, if they had, might not have been adequately utilized. Furthermore, because of the program's ecumenical character, religious proselytizing by the volunteers is not permitted—and this tends to make their services more acceptable to those in need of care.

The Robert Wood Johnson Foundation began its funding of interfaith volunteer caregiving in 1983 under the directorship of Dr. Kenneth Johnson, an internist who had worked closely with earlier Foundation programs for the elderly as well as for mothers and infants. A national demonstration program was announced under which the Foundation would award three-year grants of $150,000— that is, $50,000 a year—to fifteen communities around the country on a competitive basis. The program received a thousand letters of intent, signaling a strong interest in the concept and prompting the Foundation to increase the number of sites it was willing to fund from fifteen to twenty-five. The twenty-five sites were spread across the map, and included communities ranging from urban New York City, Memphis, and San Antonio to rural La Grande, Oregon, and Belhaven, North Carolina. Over the three-year life of the program, the sites recruited eleven thousand volunteers and served twenty-six thousand people, an average of more than a thousand per site.

Several useful lessons emerged from the initial program. First, it appeared that the concept could be applied successfully in a wide range of communities. Churches, synagogues, and other houses of worship were able to come together, form local governing boards, recruit competent directors, mobilize volunteers, and provide informal care to substantial numbers of individuals in need, including respite to their families. It is also worth noting that a number of the coalitions that were not funded by the Foundation's program were able to obtain funding elsewhere. Some of these did go forward, but those that were not able to obtain sufficient funding to pay a director had real problems implementing the model, and these problems underscored one of the program's underlying premises about the value of having someone responsible on a full-time basis for organizing and managing each coalition.

A second lesson was that it took several years for most of the projects to develop into fully formed interfaith coalitions. Mature projects typically involved twenty or more congregations and served approximately five hundred individuals at any point in time—a substantial return for the cost of one project director. Often, however, projects started with just a handful of active congregations and had to work hard during the first few years to persuade more skeptical clergy that interfaith caregiving was something that their congregations should become involved with. Many already felt overburdened with their existing obligations, and were hesitant to take on new responsibilities; others seemed to be uncomfortable with the interfaith dimension of the program.

Third, the interfaith model did appear to be sustainable financially beyond the three years of Foundation grant support. Of the original twenty-five coalitions, twenty are in operation today, more than ten years after their original Robert Wood Johnson Foundation grants expired, and some have expanded their operations substantially. Principal sources of continuing support typically have included local funding agencies such as the United Way, local civic groups and businesses, and individual contributions, as well as the congregations themselves. Probably part of the reason for the projects' durability is that the operating costs—essentially, the director's salary plus minimal office and support costs—are modest, especially when they are spread across multiple funding sources. The transition period immediately after the conclusion of Robert Wood Johnson Foundation funding was not always easy, however. Often, the project directors were so preoccupied with the day-to-day task of organizing and managing their newly formed coalitions that they did not give their full attention to the issue of postgrant funding until their grants had almost run out. Also, during this initial demonstration program, The Robert Wood Johnson Foundation grants were large enough that very little local matching support was necessary. Consequently, when the grants ended, the shift to local funding sources was abrupt. This, too, made the transition more difficult than it might have been if local funders had been brought in earlier.

Finally, the thousand letters received in response to the program announcement suggested that there did seem to be a market for the idea of interfaith volunteer caregiving. The late Arthur Flemming, former Secretary of Health, Education, and Welfare under President Eisenhower and chairman of the Foundation's national advisory committee for the program, saw the potential for a national movement and urged the Foundation to support the establishment of a new organization, the National Federation of Interfaith Volunteer Caregivers, to guide and nurture that movement. At that time, the Foundation rarely made any follow-up grants to try to broaden the impact of its demonstration programs. In this case, however, largely in response to Flemming's encouragement, the Foundation did provide a modest amount of start-up funding for the Federation, although with the understanding that funding to initiate new coalitions, at least for the moment, would have to be obtained elsewhere.

FUELING A MOVEMENT

Despite The Robert Wood Johnson Foundation's apparent reticence, the new Caregivers Federation was able to obtain additional funding elsewhere—notably from the Pew Charitable Trusts, the Public Welfare Foundation, the Commonwealth Fund, the Colorado Trust, and an anonymous donor. And slowly but surely, between 1988 and 1992, with Flemming as chairman, Johnson, the director of the Foundation's demonstration, as vice chairman, and a staff of two, the Federation helped to launch 150 new interfaith volunteer caregiver coalitions.

In so doing, the Federation not only increased the number of coalitions that had been in the original Robert Wood Johnson Foundation demonstration program by a factor of six; it also demonstrated that new coalitions could be launched with considerably less outside grant funding than the $150,000 that had been awarded to those twenty-five original prototype projects.

The Public Welfare Foundation, for example, provided seed grants of $20,000 each to start fifty new coalitions, and approximately four out of five were still in operation six years after starting up.

THE FAITH IN ACTION PROGRAM

The potential to produce large numbers of sustainable interfaith volunteer caregiver coalitions with relatively modest seed grants caught the attention of staff members at The Robert Wood Johnson Foundation in the early 1990s as they began to consider what the Foundation could do to help improve the organization and delivery of care for Americans with chronic health problems. In truth, the interfaith projects had been largely overlooked by Foundation staff people since the original demonstration had come to a close in 1987. Instead, the focus tended to be on the big picture: doctors and hospitals and the financing programs that supported them. Yet although doctors and hospitals would clearly continue to play a necessary role in the provision of chronic care, it was becoming increasingly clear that medical care alone was not sufficient to meet the needs of the chronically ill and the disabled; there were vitally important supportive services that doctors and hospitals simply couldn't provide.

In describing the role of interfaith volunteer caregivers, Johnson noted, "Their relationship to the people they help is *friend,* not a patient or client relationship. . . . Interfaith volunteer caregiver programs fill gaps in the long-term care system. About 60 percent of their referrals come from agencies that are unable to respond. Who else is there to look after an old person living alone after being discharged from the hospital on a Friday afternoon? Who else will deliver meals on weekends and holidays? Who else can be called after office hours? Who else will transport without charge someone three times a week for chemotherapy at a hospital sixty miles away?"

By tapping into the latent capacity of the nation's faith communities, these caregiver coalitions had shown themselves able to respond to the growing need for informal care. Moreover, the Federation's experience in successfully launching large numbers of new coalitions for a fraction of the cost of the original twenty-five demonstration projects suggested the possibility of funding the start-up of new coalitions on an even greater scale.

In the past, the Foundation had typically limited its role to that of developing and testing new health service delivery models, with the expectation that if a particular model proved to be successful, its broader replication would be supported by others, including the federal government. For example, its demonstration programs to improve health care for the homeless and for people with AIDS had paved the way for the federal McKinney Act and the Ryan White Emergency Care Act, both of which made federal dollars available to help communities across the country replicate the service delivery models tested by those programs.

Interfaith volunteer caregiving, though, did not seem to be a likely candidate for major federal funding. For one thing, the heyday of federal expansionism was clearly coming to an end. Also, the fact that the model was faith-based could raise concerns about separation of church and state. Above all, interfaith volunteer caregiving was truly a community-based enterprise. A sense of local ownership was fundamental to the model. And so, in the summer of 1993, the Foundation announced a new $23 million grant program entitled Faith in Action. Under the direction of Johnson, Faith in Action was designed to make available eighteen-month seed grants of $25,000 to help start up more than 900 new interfaith volunteer caregiver coalitions throughout the nation over a four-year period. The Foundation also provided funding for the National Federation of Interfaith Volunteer Caregivers to offer technical assistance to communities interested in applying to the program. A national advisory committee representing the major faiths and headed by Barbara Jordan, the late U.S. Representative from Texas, provided oversight for the program. Although the Foundation had funded demonstration programs at this dollar level in the past, those programs typically involved much larger but far fewer grants. Never before had the Foundation sought to make such a large number of grants under a single program.

In a way, this was a different kind of demonstration program. Because interfaith caregiving would ultimately have to emanate from and be supported at the local level, Faith in Action was designed to make enough grants throughout the country that over time there would be an interfaith coalition within reach of most communities around the country. The hope was that once people heard by word of mouth what a coalition in a neighboring community was doing, they would be motivated to start one in their own community. Some of this natural diffusion had already been observed among the first generation of coalitions in places such as Austin, Milwaukee, and New Haven.

The logistic challenge of managing a grant program on this scale was formidable, and the Foundation, despite twenty years as a national philanthropy, had little experience to fall back on. Even more daunting was the uncertainty about what the response to the program would be. True, the original demonstration had prompted a thousand letters of intent, but the grants under that program were for $150,000. Would there be as many inquiries for grants one-sixth that size?

The initial response was in fact disappointing. Although there were many inquiries (more than ten thousand by 1997), relatively few completed proposals were received during the first year, and only a handful were funded. Despite a relatively straightforward application process, applicants were expected to do a good deal of work before submitting a proposal, including actually forming a coalition that could receive the funding, establishing a local governing board, and securing local matching support of approximately $10,000. All this appeared to take more time than anticipated, especially for applicants not experienced in applying for grants.

In the fall of 1994, in response to these low enrollment figures, eligibility for the program was extended to include health and social service agencies that wished to apply on behalf of interfaith caregiver coalitions. In addition, efforts to inform potential applicants about the program were stepped up, and periodic application deadlines were established in place of the rolling admissions approach taken initially. Subsequent to these modifications, there was a marked increase in the number of grants. Between June 1994 and May 1995, only sixty grants were awarded. But over the next twelve months, 279 grants were issued, and as of July 31, 1998, a total of 1100 Faith in Action grants had been made.

The coalitions funded under Faith in Action are diverse. Half of them provide care to people of all ages with chronic conditions of all kinds. A third focus primarily on the elderly, one in eight is focused on people with AIDS, and others concentrate on the mentally ill, people with dementia, children with disabilities, and people with chronic substance abuse problems.

Reports received from the first 409 funded coalitions after twelve months of operation indicate that the service most frequently provided is "friendly visit/telephone reassurance" (22 percent), followed by transportation (14 percent). Other commonly provided services include meal preparation and delivery, linkage with community services, shopping, and respite. Almost half the volunteers are employed full-time or part-time, approximately a third are retired, and about one in ten is a student. Among the recipients, 37 percent are over age seventy-four, but one in four is between thirty-one and sixty-four years old, and about one in eight is under age eighteen. Fully two-thirds of the recipients are either poor or "barely managing."

IMPACT

Although hundreds of grants have been awarded under the Faith in Action program and there are more to be made, their cumulative impact on the nation's chronic care problem so far is probably marginal at best. After twelve months of funding, the first 409 Faith in Action grantees had served 25,052 persons, an average of only about 60 per coalition. Although some are serving more and past experience suggests that these numbers will grow as much as tenfold over time, even at that enhanced level the coalitions will meet only a fraction of the total need in this country.

The hope is that over time there will be local and regional ripple effects that will give rise to more new coalitions. Yet, as Rabbi Murray Saltzman, Arthur Flemming's successor as chairman of the Federation of Interfaith Volunteer Caregivers, has pointed out, the full impact of interfaith caregiving could extend beyond simply the number of people served. By providing a structured opportunity for personal fulfillment through service to others, interfaith volunteer caregiving may be seen as part of a broader movement aimed at revitalizing Americans' sense of civic responsibility. This movement reflects a growing sense that although government and the market have important roles to play, they cannot by themselves solve the nation's most pressing health and social problems. At the presidential summit on voluntarism held in Philadelphia in 1997, speaker after speaker underscored how important it was for individual citizens to recommit themselves personally, through active volunteer work, to the well-being of their neighbors and their communities. Voluntarism of this kind was promoted not only as a way to help meet those needs that fall beyond the reach of government and the market but also as a way to restore a sense of purpose and vitality to the lives of those who make the commitment.

Bob Barclay, reflecting on his experience as a caregiver over the past few years, seemed to agree. "It *is* something I enjoy," he said. "In a way, it's a kind of tribute to my mother. She isn't around for me to help anymore, but this gives me a way to help others with the same kinds of needs."

Note

1. C. Hoffman and D. Rice, *Chronic Care in America: A 21st Century Challenge* (Princeton, N.J.: The Robert Wood Johnson Foundation, 1996).

CHAPTER EIGHT

⁓ Providing Care— Not Cure—for Patients with Chronic Conditions

Lisa Lopez

Editors' Introduction

The Foundation's goal of improving the way services are organized and delivered for people with chronic conditions has proven particularly elusive.

The realities are daunting: a disorganized array of actors deliver services that are driven more by financing rules than by the needs of chronically ill individuals. Moreover, because acute care is often covered by insurance whereas more caring services—such as homemakers' visits—are not, the services offered to chronically ill people are skewed toward treating acute episodes of illness rather than coordinated approaches addressing a whole array of their needs. A logical approach to organizing services would be to start with the needs of people who have chronic conditions and then figure out how to meet those needs most effectively.

This chapter by Lisa Lopez, a freelance writer specializing in health care, analyzes the strategies and accomplishments of two significant investments by the Foundation to improve the way services for chronically ill people are organized and delivered. One of the programs—Chronic Care Initiatives in HMOs—attempts to improve the medical care of individuals with chronic illness enrolled in managed care. The second program—Building Health Systems for People with Chronic Illness—focuses on better approaches to coordinating both medical and supportive care services, such as assistance with activities of daily living.

Both national programs underscore the need to expand the services covered by insurance or health plans so that nonmedical as well as medical interventions are covered. They emphasize, as well, the importance of coordinating the different providers needed by a person with complex chronic conditions.

Findings from these two programs have helped define a new generation of Foundation investments aimed at improving services for chronically ill people. Currently, the Foundation is beginning new national programs to improve the clinical management of the long-term medical needs of the chronically ill. Other national programs are being designed to increase the capacity of the long-term care system to meet the supportive needs of the chronically ill.

athy's life in a large group home in Keene, New Hampshire, where she was placed after leaving a state school for the mentally disabled, was more nightmare than reality. She was anxious and couldn't sleep at night. She didn't speak to anyone. Administrators sedated her as often as they could, and she could not see a doctor or a dentist unless she was first sedated. During the day, she spent fitful hours biting and kicking. At one point, neighbors phoned the police when a disruption in the house got out of hand. Even medication could not release her from the attacks on herself. When her family visited, they felt guilty and hopeless. "I used to wonder if this was what Cathy's life was like all the time," her twin sister, Carleen, later recalled.

Like many others before her, Cathy was responding to her environment—a controlled, homelike setting, but one with prescribed conditions and activities and with little, if any, choice for individuals. Carleen and her husband, Chuck, had often thought of bringing Cathy home to live with them and their two young children, but Cathy's unpredictable outbursts made the idea seem unworkable. After much thought, however, they decided on a six-month trial, and Cathy moved in with them in March 1995 with the hope that a new local program, the Monadnock Self-Determination for People with Developmental Disabilities Project, would help them manage her needs. A project team helped them devise a budget using Cathy's Medicaid dollars, with which they would seek the services Cathy needed. In this project, individuals and families—not the state—choose the services a person needs.

In a matter of days, Cathy's responses to her life reversed themselves. She began sleeping through the night and participating in her family's activities—going shopping, playing with the children, and celebrating birthdays and holidays. She no longer required sedation for her medical and dental visits. She communicated her wants through hand and head gestures, and was aware of activities around her. Although the family went through periodic challenges with Cathy, being at home with her loved ones has brightened her life. This resulted from allowing Cathy to have better control over her circumstances. "She is able to cope better, and can handle almost anything,"

Carleen remarked later. "She feels better about herself, and that she is being listened to."[1]

HIGHER AIMS FOR CHRONICALLY ILL PERSONS

The Monadnock project is funded by The Robert Wood Johnson Foundation as part of the Building Health Systems for People With Chronic Illnesses Program. It is just one of many projects the Foundation supports that provide social and medical services for the chronically ill and the disabled. Since 1991, The Robert Wood Johnson Foundation has made more than $200 million in grants in the area of chronic care. Of this, more than $50 million has been granted to three national programs with more than 1100 projects that seek new ways to provide health and supportive care services for chronically ill and disabled people like Cathy. These programs are Chronic Care Initiatives in HMOs; Building Health Systems for People with Chronic Illnesses; and Faith in Action, the interfaith volunteer caregiver project discussed in Chapter Seven.

In some cases, the programs have improved the quality of life for people with chronic illness or with disabilities simply by providing them with more options for care—and for less than the cost of care in traditional programs. In Cathy's case, her life improved significantly, and at a cost that was 75 percent of what the Medicaid system paid for the young woman to live in the group home.

Chronic care became a specific Foundation priority in 1991. Although the Foundation had funded a number of programs in past years that focused on specific diseases such as AIDS, Alzheimer's, and chronic mental illness, Foundation staff members realized that there was a need to look at the challenges all these illnesses shared. These challenges had to be overcome in order to improve care, says Dr. Lewis G. Sandy, the Foundation's executive vice president. "There had to be better integration and coordination of care, focusing on both medical and nonmedical needs," Sandy notes. "The overall orientation of the medical care system is disease specific, powerfully oriented toward acute care, and so pervasive that it is difficult to move people toward different models of care." Moreover, he said, there remains a stigma associated with mental illness and disability.

In the United States, perhaps one hundred million people live with some type of chronic condition such as hypertension, the effects of stroke, HIV, or a mental or physical disability.[2] These conditions cost $470 billion a year for medical services alone.[3]

Even with this investment in what is often considered the best health care in the world, however, the United States has not adequately addressed the needs of chronically ill or disabled people. They are often caught in a fragmented system in which public and private benefits are tailored to those with acute care needs, or limits are placed on the choices that would allow them either to reduce their pain or to improve their quality of life, or both.

Although chronic conditions cannot be cured, private health insurance emphasizes medical services that have a curative focus. Insurance coverage is much spottier for the nonmedical services that people with chronic conditions often need, such as supportive housing, the installation of bathtub railings, getting access to devices that can help them return to work, and help with daily activities that would allow them to make the transition from a nursing home to their own home.[4] The aging of Americans will surely increase the need for care among this population and further burden the current fragmented system of care. By 2030, almost 150 million people are expected to have a chronic condition. Of these, an estimated 42 million will be limited in their ability to work, to go to school, or to live independently.[5]

Changing the structure of our current system of care to meet the care—not curative—needs of people with chronic conditions will mean changing the attitudes and the behavior of health care organizations, federal and state policy makers, physicians, and other health professionals. It will require that these institutions explore new ways of financing and delivering care and services.

Chronic Care Initiatives in HMOs and Building Health Systems for People with Chronic Illnesses examine such alternatives. These programs represent only two of the Foundation's initiatives in chronic care, and each has a distinctive focus. Chronic Care Initiatives in HMOs explores innovations in managed care systems. Building Health Systems for People with Chronic Illnesses funds projects that cut across medical and supportive care sites as well as chronically ill populations. Each of these programs includes a variety of projects that target a number of areas, from primary care and risk assessment for the frail elderly, to independent living for the mentally and physically disabled, to education that encourages doctors to work as teams in managed care plans.

The two national programs demonstrate how care can be delivered using a commonsense approach to building clinician and patient interaction and decision making. In many cases, for instance, the projects funded under the national programs make use of or restructure existing resources within an organization and a community rather than develop new efforts. The project directors hope their experiences will prompt consumers, policy makers, health plans, community-based organizations, and others to begin to discuss new ways to care for the chronically ill, and to learn lessons for the future.

MANAGED CARE AND CHRONIC CONDITIONS

At first glance, chronic illness and HMOs do not seem to be a natural fit. The capitated financing of managed care provides incentives to enroll healthy people who have below-average needs for medical services. In addition, like the fee-for-service system, managed care plans such as HMOs have traditionally operated as systems that are structured more for delivering care to people with acute, short-term needs than for delivering care to people with lifelong chronic conditions such as diabetes and arthritis. Moreover, delivering—and improving—care to people with chronic illness requires providers and health plans to change provider and patient behavior in several ways:[6]

- Moving from a focus on cure to a focus on the relief of symptoms
- Making the patient a critical part of the care process
- Creating active roles for the patient's significant others, such as immediate family
- Expanding the boundaries of care among providers and between traditional medical and social services
- Tying patient satisfaction to clinical outcomes

Despite these challenges, HMOs do have the potential to adopt such approaches. For one thing, HMOs can intervene on a system level rather than an individual level, and this allows a person's care to be coordinated within a health plan's available resources rather than in a fragmented way. Second, the primary care orientation of HMOs emphasizes generalist physicians, nurse practitioners, and other providers, whose care may be more appropriate for patients with chronic illness than specialty practices. Third, the HMO system of paying for care on a prepaid, capitated basis gives these organizations the flexibility to allocate resources where needed, including those that focus on home- and community-based services, outreach, and case management. Fourth, capitated payments can create an incentive for HMOs to provide cost-effective care in the most appropriate settings.[7]

THE CHRONIC CARE INITIATIVES IN HMOS PROGRAM

Chronic Care Initiatives in HMOs, a $5.6 million, four-year program, was begun in January 1993 with the aim of testing innovative projects that focused on six areas:

- Offering innovative ways to provide posthospital care to those with chronic conditions in order to reduce rehospitalizations

- Developing and coordinating services for high-risk populations, such as children with mental or physical disabilities and adults with depression or dementia

- Evaluating ways to provide primary care to HMO enrollees who are in nursing homes

- Coordinating services for people with multiple, complex problems that require multidisciplinary teams of providers, as well as family caregivers and community resources

- Assessing new ways to deliver primary care for persons with chronic conditions

- Conducting cross-cutting assessments of care

The program has funded twenty-one different projects to date.

Peter D. Fox, the national director of the program, notes the importance of three research priorities: evaluating case management in HMOs, reorganizing primary care to enhance the delivery of services, and improving the delivery of primary care to nursing home residents.

Reorganizing primary care is perhaps the best example of how HMOs can use existing resources to manage care for the chronically ill, Fox says. Armed with the ability to provide a more population-based approach to care, he notes, HMOs can identify problems at both the secondary prevention stage (identifying and treating the disease at an early point) and the tertiary prevention stage (reducing impairment, disability, and suffering).

Case management was at the heart of the program, says Teresa Fama, its former deputy director. "We saw case management as being the glue in service delivery for people with chronic conditions," she says. Simply put, that meant influencing physicians to change their traditional approaches to delivering care and helping patients become more active participants in their care. Fama and Fox note that two projects in particular provide good illustrations of how reorganizing primary care and influencing provider behavior can improve health care delivery for chronically ill HMO members. The first—undertaken by the Group Health Cooperative of Puget Sound—works directly by restructuring care around specific chronic conditions. The second— undertaken by the Henry Ford Health System—works indirectly by training physicians in the care of patients with chronic conditions.

The intent was to take the chaos out of the delivery of primary care, and at the same time improve results among its enrollees with chronic conditions. The goal was to integrate the management of chronic care into its existing system of primary care. By 1998, many managed care providers began to experiment with chronic disease management approaches. However, back in 1995, this approach was innovative both in its timing and in its focus on the primary care system.

Group Health Cooperative Reorganizes Primary Care

The Group Health Cooperative of Puget Sound, or GHC, a five-hundred-thousand–member Seattle-based HMO, was one health plan that felt it could reorganize its internal processes to improve care for the chronically ill. In 1995, it introduced a Chronic Care Clinic in an effort to restructure the way physicians and their staff practiced.

"The primary care practices were continuing to function in a lot of ways like miniature emergency rooms," says Brian Austin, the manager of the Sandy MacColl Institute for Healthcare Innovation at GHC. "All the attention was being given to the next patient coming through the door, and at any given time clinicians would have to rotate their attention from condition to condition. It was hard for them to have a concentrated time with either a patient or a single condition. We were trying to find an oasis in the clinicians' day where they could concentrate on a single condition and work as a team, and to allow patients who had similar conditions to meet with one another and share some coping and management skills."

Enter the Chronic Care Clinic. Group Health Cooperative officials had studied and somewhat patterned the Chronic Care Clinic after England's miniclinic days—a system in which the National Health Service organizes practices around a single condition. English providers bring in nonphysician health care practitioners and designate one morning to treat just diabetics or asthmatics or the frail elderly. The efficiency of that model and the positive outcomes among patients led GHC to try it in Seattle, Austin says. The Chronic Care Clinic focuses on four main areas:

- Conducting thorough patient assessments to detect potential complications
- Introducing techniques that help patients manage their own condition
- Providing physicians and their staff with clinical guidelines
- Improving patient satisfaction through education and psychosocial support services

Two chronically ill populations—the frail elderly and diabetics—were chosen to participate in a study to assess this approach. In all, nineteen GHC physician group practices participated in the study; twenty-five physician groups continued their usual practice and were designated the control group. Each of the practices had about twenty chronically ill patients in all, between the two categories. Patients in the study met every three or four months in groups of four to eight. Their sessions with practitioners covered a range of topics, from exercise and general management of their condition to more specific issues the patients wanted to address. They also met individually with their own doctor and nurse. Patients also often met with a pharmacist either before or after the group session, especially during their first Chronic Care Clinic visit. Nurses made follow-up telephone calls to help patients adhere to their care plans and to schedule new appointments.

At the beginning of the study, providers were trained to work together and were encouraged to establish team meetings. They were also given clinical guidelines on basic care for the condition they selected. These guidelines, called Diabetes 101 and Geriatrics 101, were in turn tied to the objectives of The Robert Wood Johnson Foundation grant and to GHC's own clinical guidelines. With diabetes, for example, clinicians measured individuals' physical function, glucose control, reduction of microvascular complications, and changes in patients' behaviors, such as exercise, foot care, and diet.

For the frail elderly, GHC clinicians worked with geriatricians to create a new clinical guide. To measure its effectiveness, physicians were asked to concentrate on reducing falls and on drug side effects, managing depression, managing incontinence in older women, and managing impaired function. "We tried to keep it fairly simple," Austin says.

The first-year results are based on reports by physicians and patients. They show increased satisfaction among clinicians and among the diabetic and elderly patients. Overall, physicians and other staff delivered active versus reactive care, and patients became more involved in managing their conditions and were less passive than they had been before the Chronic Care Clinic was introduced. One benefit was that pharmacists could more easily identify and communicate potential drug interactions to both providers and patients, and could more readily discuss prescription needs with the physicians, who were better able to follow up with their patients.

During the study, Austin points out, providers demonstrated a surprising willingness to try new ways of organizing their practices in order to communicate better with and more actively treat their patients, even in a time of enormous change. (GHC's central region was undergoing a major reorganization.) "All seemed to feel that they weren't doing as good a job with their chronic care patients as they thought they had"—before the Chronic Care Clinic—"and that there was a lot more they could do," he says. By the end of 1998 the GHC project expects to have results indicating how often patients use the clinic's services. The findings should provide a picture of the extent to which the primary care doctors and other providers improved their services.

When the findings become available, the HMO plans to distribute them both internally and externally. A "how-to" packet on the chronic care clinics has been prepared and is being shared with other practices. The plan is also considering the Chronic Care Clinic approach for patients with other chronic conditions such as asthma.

Managed Care College Targets Physician Behavior

The Henry Ford Health System, which serves residents of southeast Michigan, includes a 500,000-member HMO, the Health Alliance Plan, or HAP. In 1993, the Metro Medical Group, which at the time was a division of HAP, launched the Managed Care College, an on-site medical education program for primary care physicians within the medical group. The idea was to combine medical education and actual clinical practice on site in order to improve patient care and results for patients with chronic conditions who were being treated by the health plan's primary care clinicians. Moreover, the medical group's leadership believed that this approach would encourage physicians to practice more cohesively, bring about changes that would improve care, and reduce inappropriate practice variations among the clinicians. At that time, the Metro Medical Group had 80,000 members and 120 physicians, 65 percent of whom were in primary care, and eight ambulatory sites. In the Managed Care College's second year, the Metro Medical Group merged with the larger multispecialty Henry Ford Medical Group, which was also affiliated with the Henry Ford Health System. The merger signaled the need to adapt the college to the needs of the larger physician group.

In the initial year of the program, enrollment was mandatory for all primary care physicians in the Metro Medical Group. Physicians—and some nurses—attended one four-to-five-hour session each month covering topics such as the role of primary care physicians in managed care, epidemiology, clinical practice improvement, and courses targeting the care and management of specific chronic conditions—type II adult diabetes mellitus, for instance.

After the two medical groups merged, the college faced the challenge of maintaining the core elements of the program while expanding to meet the needs of the larger health system. Although the sheer size of the Henry Ford Medical Group precluded mandatory enrollment, the college was expanded to include a two-track curriculum: an administrative track and a clinical one. Classes involved more hands-on learning, and the program was shortened to better accommodate physicians' schedules. In subsequent years, the college has added specialists to its enrollment and merged the two-track curriculum. Although specific courses vary each year, the core concepts have remained the same: clinical practice based on proven methods, teamwork, the clinician's role in managed care, and quality improvement. Supplementing this core list are electives in ethics, finance, customer service, and other topics. Core classes generally run from October through June on weekday afternoons and occasionally Saturday mornings. Since the college's inception, some 240 physicians, nurses, administrators, and others have participated in the college's core curriculum, and some 500 have taken the elective courses. The college has seventy-six clinicians enrolled in the 1997–98 session.

What distinguishes this approach from current continuing medical education, according to project staff members, is the effort both to improve the physicians' understanding of managed care and to enhance the clinical skills of medical staff members in order to improve patient care. "What we know is that it has caused our staff to realize that managed care is more than capitation and cost containment," says Jennifer Elston-Lafata, a research scientist for the Ford System's Center for Clinical Effectiveness. "What they're gaining is a much broader perspective on what's involved with managed care."

The results have been fruitful in both administrative and clinical areas. After the first year, physicians were more likely than they had been to accept clinical guidelines in treating patients with chronic conditions (72 percent precollege versus 86 percent postcollege); 21 percent indicated that their clinical practice had changed for the better in the last year as a result of using the guidelines. Moreover, 41 percent of the physicians said they had changed their approach to treating their diabetic patients.

After the second and third year, significant changes occurred in the knowledge that physicians had about existing resources and in their ability to use them. For example, they indicated that they had become better informed about where to turn when they needed assistance with clinical resources (19 percent precollege, 85 percent postcollege).

The college is still analyzing data, but preliminary results show that third-year enrollees have already applied the lessons learned. For example, a number of physician teams devised a primary care guideline for managing depression and a standardized coding for depression, and are seeking ways to improve prescribing patterns. Other clinics established education programs for diabetic patients. Some medical teams worked on improving retinal examinations. One clinic offered counseling programs for teenagers as part of its childbirth program.

"There is a general impression here that the Managed Care College has made a cultural change in all quarters and has been instrumental in helping reorient the Henry Ford Health System's agenda and the approaches we take to working with staff on improvement projects," says Dr. John J. Wisniewski, the system's assistant medical director. "We did not anticipate that, and did not design any explicit way to measure that."

The Managed Care College is sharing its model of education and its preliminary findings with organizations outside its own health system. These include the Jefferson Medical College in Philadelphia, the Cleveland Clinic, the Armed Services University, and Michigan State University. The college signed an agreement with the Medical College of Ohio in January 1998 to help it develop similar programs, Wisniewski says, and continues to expand a special curriculum for managed care nursing.

THE BUILDING HEALTH SYSTEMS FOR PEOPLE WITH CHRONIC ILLNESSES PROGRAM

The other national program directed at improving chronic care focuses on the difficult challenge of better coordinating the delivery of medical services and supportive services for the chronically ill. Building Health Systems for People with Chronic Illnesses is a $13 million five-year initiative that began in 1993 and has supported twenty-four different projects around the country. The aim of the program is to identify new approaches for better coordinating the work that medical providers and supportive care providers—such as home care agencies, nursing homes, and social service organizations—do for the chronically ill.

The program tackles a key anomaly with our caring system referred to earlier: insurance systems tend to fund acute medical care rather than supportive care for chronically ill individuals. The challenge is to find ways to reshape financing and service delivery systems so that the two types of services are coordinated and accessible to people in need.

Under this national program, the Foundation sought projects that have these goals:

- Integrating services so that care is provided across diverse settings, and systems of care link clinical and nonclinical support services

- Reallocating resources by redirecting existing and acute-care-focused delivery and financing to better serve the chronically ill

- Promoting early medical and non-medical interventions

- Helping individuals maintain their independence for as long as possible in their own homes and communities

• Giving the chronically ill and their caregivers a role in designing and improving their health care and support services

• Reflecting models of care that can be used by people with different chronic health conditions

Initially designed to look at a range of people with chronic illness and accommodate them within a single system, the program now focuses on three specific populations, project officials say: children with special health care needs, the physically and mentally disabled, and the frail elderly.

"The dream was to address the disorganization of health care systems for people with chronic illness," says Dr. F. Marc LaForce, the national program director of Building Health Systems for People With Chronic Illnesses. "The program was based on the understanding that, given the tools and the support to live independently, disabled and other chronically ill persons could have a better quality of life." As the program matured, housing and employment issues were recognized as important barriers to living independently.

One of the early projects run by Monadnock Developmental Services in Keene, New Hampshire, had such an immediate and significant impact on care for the developmentally disabled that The Robert Wood Johnson Foundation decided to establish a new national program, also called Self-Determination for Persons with Developmental Disabilities, that now funds twenty-three projects in twelve states.

The Monadnock project was funded as a pilot project of Building Health Systems from November 1993 to October 1996, and it tested whether giving people with disabilities the freedom and the resources to make decisions about their own needs, with the help of friends and family, would improve their care and their quality of life. The project targeted people who had been institutionalized in state facilities. As a result of the program, some participants are now living independently and are employed. "The lesson we learned here was to throw away the old prejudices, and that even people with severe disabilities are capable of managing much of their lives," LaForce says. In this project, a case manager works with individuals and their friends and families to develop a plan for all needed services, as happened with Cathy, who was able to move in with her twin sister's family. The disabled person and his or her so-called circle of support—family and friends—develop a budget from Medicaid and state dollars, not to exceed 75 to 90 percent of previous service costs. The individual or the support network, or both, choose from an array of local resources—transportation, job skills training, physical therapy—to help the person live as independently as possible.

Besides Cathy, other individuals have had their lives changed for the better. An independent evaluation of the project by James W. Conroy, of the Center for Outcome Analysis in Ardmore, Pennsylvania, found that the quality of life improved significantly among thirty-eight individuals who were studied after one year of the program. All those enrolled in the program said that their quality of life had improved in each of these nine areas: health, making personal choices, family relationships, seeing friends and socializing, getting out and around, day activities, food, happiness, and comfort.

Researchers also found positive results among those enrolled, such as working with others and a reduction in challenging behaviors—self-injury, damaging property, social withdrawal. "This was an initiative that put control of resources in the hands of individuals who in the past had been taken care of paternalistically by systems that didn't empower them to do much of anything," LaForce says.

Another effort that is attempting to integrate individuals into the community is called Enabling People with Disabilities to Reestablish Life in the Community, in South Portland, Maine. This project focuses on helping people with physical disabilities who are living in nursing homes move back into the community. As part of the program, the Alpha One Center for Independent Living, a local independent living center, is working with local housing agencies to improve access to assistive devices and housing for these people.

Often, disabled persons can receive Medicaid services only if they prove that they cannot live in the community without them, Jay M. Wussow, the deputy director of the program, points out. "But they can't do that until they move into the community," he says, and moving from the nursing home into the community involves a transitional cost. People in nursing homes who could live in the community can't make the transition without that assistance—and that takes money, Wussow says. To address the financing issue, Alpha One is using profits from a for-profit durable medical equipment subsidiary it runs to cover the actual care costs of transitional services, such as skills training. Because the project has the potential to be replicated elsewhere, the University of Southern Maine will evaluate it for the Foundation.

Addressing barriers to the employment of the physically disabled is the goal of Health Systems for Work Force Enhancement, a project funded with an eighteen-month grant to Employment Resources, Inc., or ERI, in Madison, Wisconsin. The project is a public-private partnership that explores ways·to break the health insurance barriers disabled people face when they return to work. Specifically, ERI is studying how disabled people can continue to receive Medicaid, health insurance, and long-term care insurance after they get jobs. It also works to enhance opportunities to employ disabled persons. The project attempts to reduce the fears people have when they face losing benefits after they return to work. ERI found that this fear was the greatest barrier to returning to work. "The way the system works now encourages individuals to stay unemployed because of the risk of losing home and attendant services as they earn salary dollars," LaForce says.

The thirty people enrolled in the program received Supplemental Security Income and Social Security Disability Insurance benefits that continued while they were undergoing rehabilitation, but faced the loss of their Medicaid benefits, which cover health care and the personal care services of daily living, if they were employed. These people will be guaranteed publicly funded health insurance and long-term care insurance, whereas a control group will not. As with the Alpha One project, the ERI project's potential to be replicated led to a separate Robert Wood Johnson Foundation grant to evaluate the project. In this case, the Oregon Health Sciences University will measure rates of employment and insurance coverage among people in the intervention and control groups.

Only anecdotal evidence now exists on the exact cost savings to the system, but ERI has found that there are some cost savings as people move off the disability rolls. Once the results are available, project officials will work with the Social Security Administration and the Health Care Financing Administration to provide ways to overcome the health insurance barriers that inhibit people with chronic disabling conditions from seeking employment. The long-term goal of a project like this one is to affect government regulations so that people can keep their benefits for a longer period of time, Wussow says.

Another project that attempts to empower chronically ill individuals is called Development of an Integrated Housing, Health, and Support Services Network for Disabled Adults. Launched by the Corporation for Supportive Housing in Oakland, California, in July 1995, this three-year project aims at developing mental health and substance abuse treatment services for 750 previously homeless individuals with HIV/AIDS, mental illness, and/or substance abuse problems. The Corporation for Supportive Housing has worked with community agencies to establish housing for people with these conditions in order to help stabilize their environment. Often, people recovering from drug addiction don't have stable housing—a critical component in helping them recover. The project is now in its third year. The aspect of combining health care and housing has already had preliminary success, program officials say. "Many of these people have gone from being homeless to more stable arrangements in a matter of a couple of years," Wussow says.

Given the project's focus on housing and support services to help people live as independently as possible in the community, officials are currently considering the next step, Wussow says: how to ensure the same employment opportunities for these individuals that anyone else in the community would have.

LESSONS LEARNED

Although it is too early to offer a definitive assessment, program directors and Robert Wood Johnson Foundation program officers for both Chronic Care Initiatives in HMOs and Building Health Systems for People With Chronic Illnesses cite a variety of lessons learned from the programs:

• *Existing systems and resources can be reorganized to enhance care.*

As the examples cited in this chapter demonstrate, existing resources—whether HMO physicians and nurses, social services organizations, or community-based agencies—can be coordinated in order to link individuals with the medical and social services they need. HMOs can effectively provide chronic care management if they organize their systems so that they have a case management function in place, give physicians more clinical guidance and education, and provide patients with more tools for self-care. Beyond managed care systems, linking medical and nonmedical services can be important. Housing is a good example. "When I was thinking about issues of chronic care four or five years ago," says Marc LaForce, "I wasn't thinking about housing but how we could better integrate systems of medical care. One of the lessons we learned was that medical care is just one piece of a complex system that must be in place."

- *The behavior and attitudes of physicians can be modified to improve the care that they offer.*

Few physicians are taught in medical school how to manage chronically ill patients. The Managed Care College and the GHC Chronic Care Clinic showed that physicians could work in teams and use their collective resources to better serve their patients. Although the doctors at the Chronic Care Clinic were initially concerned about the time a new process would add to their already busy schedules, the core concepts of the clinic—giving physicians' groups the time to work as a team and to focus on a specific condition and giving patients an opportunity to come together—succeeded in increasing physicians' acceptance of the group-care model.

- *Encouraging independent living and supporting consumers' choice in their own care services hold promise as ways of improving care of individuals with chronic conditions.*

The models tried under the Building Health Systems for People with Chronic Illnesses Program have given individuals greater control over their care. They range from self-care techniques that can help patients cope with their illness to innovative financing mechanisms where individuals, not professionals, are given the resources to manage their own care.

- *Flexibility is needed to cope with marketplace changes, such as mergers, that can disrupt program and research efforts.*

In the projects undertaken under the Chronic Care Initiatives in HMOs Program, research designs had to be changed frequently to accommodate changes in the health care system. For example, University of Colorado researchers had difficulty obtaining data for its patient care management project after the HMO where they were conducting research changed hands. And when the Metro Medical Group in Detroit merged with the Henry Ford Medical Group, it added a sizable and geographically diverse population to the Managed Care College, forcing changes in the project design.

• *Clinicians from different HMOs can work together to advance the field.*

One example is the development of a new screening tool developed under the Chronic Care Initiatives in HMOs Program. In the fall of 1994, a group of twelve HMO representatives, along with two university-based geriatricians, began to meet to share ideas for providing care to their frail elderly members. Within two years, the group had developed a standardized tool and basic comprehensive geriatric assessment plan for identifying high-risk elderly patients. Today, more than three hundred health care organizations have asked to use the screening tool for the elderly patients in their plans.

• *Sharing experiences publicly can help expand awareness of innovations.*

The Chronic Care Initiatives in HMOs Program was aimed at evaluating innovative HMO programs, but it went beyond that mandate and disseminated information widely. To this end, the program sponsored two chronic care conferences that gave clinicians and managers the chance to discuss their models of care, problems, and potential solutions; those involved in the program published articles in professional journals, wrote books, and issued reports.

Perhaps the most significant element to emerge from these programs, according to Rosemary Gibson, senior program officer for The Robert Wood Johnson Foundation, is the development of improved indicators to measure the quality of chronic care in HMOs. Researchers at six HMOs are testing the use of measures for four chronic conditions: childhood asthma, coronary artery disease, diabetes, and major depression. Once tested and evaluated, some of these may be included in future versions of the Health Plan Employer Data and Information Set (HEDIS), a set of quality indicators published by the National Committee for Quality Assurance and widely used by health plans and employers. "If these measures become generally accepted," says Gibson, "they will affect the entire field."

Notes

1. E. Cummings, "Whatever It Takes: Stories of Self Determination from the Monadnock Region," Monadnock Self Determination Project.
2. C. Hoffman and D. P. Rice; estimates based on the 1987 National Medical Expenditure Survey, University of California, San Francisco, Institute for Health & Aging, 1995.
3. See note two.
4. *Chronic Care in America: A 21st Century Challenge,* The Robert Wood Johnson Foundation, Aug. 1996.
5. See note two.
6. P. D. Fox and T. Fama (eds.), *Managed Care and Chronic Illness: Challenges and Opportunities* (Gaithersburg, Md.: Aspen Publishers, 1996).
7. See note six.

—ʌʌ— The Mental Health Services Program for Youth

Leonard Saxe
Theodore P. Cross

Editors' Introduction

Between 1985 and 1995, the Foundation funded a number of national demonstration programs that relied on communities rather than on institutions to care for people with a range of persistent health-related problems. Providing care in the community was a theme of Foundation-funded programs to serve people with chronic mental illness and with HIV or AIDS, the frail elderly, and children with chronic mental health problems.

Leonard Saxe and Theodore Cross, as faculty members at the Heller School of Brandeis University, led a team that evaluated the Mental Health Services Program for Youth, or MHSPY. They place MHSPY within the broader context of efforts to reform services for children with mental health problems and then examine what happened under the program. The chapter takes the reader through the program's attempts to address the challenges related to creating, financing, and coordinating community services.

As in the case of many Foundation-supported initiatives to support innovation in service delivery, it is difficult to reach bottom-line assessments:

Were the new systems of care better or worse than their predecessors? Did youth fare better under the new systems of care? For better or worse, the initiatives vary with local conditions that make scientific assessment difficult if not impossible to make. And the initiatives often do not address all of the issues needed to assess outcomes. Questions remain, but Saxe and Cross do conclude that MHSPY was able to provide services in the community and to keep children with mental health problems from being institutionalized.

Children are cherished as our most precious resource, but if we are judged by how the health system treats them, there is a contradiction between our words and our deeds. The neglect of children is particularly evident in the mental health care system, where children's services have often languished as a stepchild of adult mental health, which is itself a resource-starved sibling to physical health care. Although reform efforts have improved children's services over the past twenty-five years—from a time when large numbers of children were institutionalized without *any* effective treatment—they remain woefully inadequate. An attempt to develop services was made in the 1970s, but by the early eighties it was clear that children with emotional disorders were often not able to get access to these services.

The recognition that children were underserved catalyzed a coalition of parents, professionals, and researchers to press for reform. There was consensus that existing services inappropriately removed children from their homes and their community and served only a fraction of the children in need.[1] The reformers proposed the development of comprehensive systems of community-based care, oriented to providing appropriate care to each child with a mental disorder and including parents as key caregivers.

The disturbing findings of a 1982 Children's Defense Fund report by Jane Knitzer, entitled *Unclaimed Children*,[2] provided an early prompt for reform. Knitzer's survey of state agencies documented the deplorable state of children's mental health services available nationwide. She found that only a minority of the more than two million American children with severe emotional disturbances received adequate mental health services. The report concluded that children's services were not coordinated and were not provided to children within their homes and communities.

These conclusions were substantiated in a study that we and our colleagues developed for Congress's Office of Technology Assessment.[3] Epidemiological estimates indicated that more than 12 percent of the nation's children had a diagnosable mental disorder, with half of these children conservatively estimated to have a serious mental disorder. Yet the mental health care system concentrated almost all of its resources on a small number of children placed in institutional settings (such as psychiatric hospitals and residential treatment centers), while the needs of the majority were inappropriately ignored.

Child and Adolescent Service System Program

In 1986, the federal government established the Child and Adolescent Service System Program, or CASSP, to help states reorganize their agencies responsible for providing mental health services to children and their families. A goal was to ensure collaboration among child-serving agencies. Typically, although children with serious emotional disorders were served by education and child welfare agencies as well as traditional mental health providers, the collaboration among these agencies had been minimal. The CASSP philosophy envisioned the child as the focus of mental health services and the professional caregivers as partners with the families serving these children. It promoted individualized care provided in the least restrictive setting and in the community. Ideally, the services available in the community would make it unnecessary to place children in institutional settings. And, in theory, limited reliance on psychiatric hospitals or residential treatment centers could reduce the cost of care.

The system of care would contain a continuum of services of varying intensity and intrusion in children's lives. The services would range from outpatient psychotherapy and parental guidance, day treatment, therapeutic foster care, and intensive case management to intensive services such as residential treatment and psychiatric hospitalization. Unnecessary duplication and gaps in service were to be avoided. Case managers, interagency planning, and case review teams would be used to ensure coordination and a close fit of services to child and family needs. In addition, parental experience and involvement was valued and needed to ensure the responsiveness of those services to a child's needs.

Although CASSP had a profound effect on how states organized care through an unprecedented degree of interagency coordination, it was a small program constrained in scope and power. Its funds were both limited and restricted, and could not be used to support services directly or to fill gaps in existing services. All told, the initiative had a fiscal life span of ten years.

THE MENTAL HEALTH SERVICES PROGRAM FOR YOUTH

The Robert Wood Johnson Foundation saw a need to help communities develop more effective mental health services for children with emotional disorders and to help fill the funding gaps. In 1988, two years after CASSP was established, the Mental Health Services Program for Youth, or MHSPY, was conceived. It was intended to put into effect the reforms that had broad support among professionals and parents but that had not been widely adopted. Structured by the Foundation as a national demonstration, MHSPY was designed to test coordinated, community-based mental health care for children. Parallel to CASSP, the implicit theory was that children, even those with the most serious mental disorders, could be treated within their community, provided that a broad range of services was available and that the family, the school, and the other settings in which these children lived were made partners in developing supportive services. Creating a system of care was designed to reduce reliance on out-of-home placements for children with serious mental disorders, and to make more efficient use of limited mental health resources.

Because the idea of coordinated community-based mental health services was consistent with broader efforts during the 1980s to reduce the federal government's responsibility for health care, communities were given considerable latitude. Each participating community was expected to develop a structure and program that fit its needs and could eventually be supported by the community, independent of The Robert Wood Johnson Foundation's support. Developing cost-effective solutions was central to the program's design. Institutional care for children with serious emotional disorders was too expensive, and resources were not available to expand it. Community-based care was thought to be less resource-intensive. Thus, the program idea appealed both to those who were concerned with reducing the costs of health and social programs and to those who wanted more effective and accessible services for children. It was, perhaps, an unusual alliance between budget-conscious officials and advocates for children.

The MHSPY demonstration aimed explicitly at changing the organization, the financing, and the agency responsibility for providing mental health services. Eight communities participated, representing diverse geographic and demographic areas. The sites ranged from portions of large cities, such as Cleveland and San Francisco, to the entire state of Vermont and several rural and semi-urban counties of North Carolina, as well as communities in Kentucky, Wisconsin, Pennsylvania, and Oregon (see Table 9.1 for a listing of MHSPY sites). Each project was a joint endeavor between state agencies and local communities. The Foundation initially invested $20 million in the program, with funds designed to help participating communities reorganize services and develop new services.

Each of the communities that participated was funded to serve the children with the most serious emotional and behavioral problems. These included specific psychiatric disorders such as conduct disorder, major depressive disorder, borderline personality disorder, and pervasive developmental disorder. Many children had dual or multiple diagnoses. The children's histories were compelling and, perhaps, more telling than their diagnoses. Many had experienced severe abuse or neglect, multiple residential or foster care placements, or a long history of problems and unsuccessful interventions in schools, outpatient clinics, child welfare agencies, and juvenile courts.

Sites aimed at avoiding the hospitalization of children with serious mental illness through a number of methods: expanding the community's continuum of care, providing case management with an individualized care philosophy, and financing strategies that allowed

ℐℛ

Table 9.1. MHSPY Sites.

State	Area	Project
California	San Francisco	Family Mosaic Project
Kentucky	Bluegrass region	Bluegrass IMPACT
Ohio	Cleveland	Connections
Oregon	Multnomah County (Portland)	The Partners Project
North Carolina	Blue Ridge and Smoky Mountain regions	The Children's Initiative
Pennsylvania	Philadelphia region	Parent and Child Cooperative
Vermont	Entire state	New Directions
Wisconsin	Madison	Children Come First

the flexible use of treatment money. Collaborations among mental health, child welfare, education, and, with one exception, juvenile justice agencies, were common in all the sites. Projects had to create mechanisms for interagency coordination, involve parents and other caregivers, and expand community-based services. Expanded services often required the development of new or pilot services, such as therapeutic foster care, crisis intervention, independent living programs, and intensive home visiting. The emphasis was on flexible, intensive interventions provided in the community.

The development of a system of care was not a discrete intervention, but a complex organization of people, resources, and procedures. The particular system developed depended on the specific demographics, geography, economics, history, law, policy, and individual relationships present in a site. The Foundation, realizing that different models were necessary, encouraged diversity. MHSPY sites resembled one another in their development of specific services and mechanisms for providing and coordinating care—for example, case management, interagency treatment planning and programming, flexible funding, individualized care, and community-based interventions. But the organization of the projects varied greatly, making it difficult to develop an organizational chart for a system of care.

Thus, for example, Vermont developed a system structured around state and local interagency planning teams as well as interagency treatment teams, all based within the Department of Mental Health and using more or less traditional funding sources. Similarly, Kentucky based its system on a statewide interagency system, mobile case managers, and interagency treatment teams at the local level. The Madison, Wisconsin, site developed its system around a private agency contracting with multiple private providers, using a capitated managed care approach. The San Francisco, California, project developed a new organization with workers from various agencies coming together to develop ethnically diverse, neighborhood-based programs; that project also used a new managed-care model. The Cleveland, Ohio, site based its system on an effective partnership between a private human services program with strong community ties and a forward-thinking county mental health board. North Carolina relied on strong county public mental health organizations backed by a strong state mental health department. It joined a state-run managed care experiment toward the end of the project. The Oregon project centered on a social welfare agency with skilled clinical social workers. In

Pennsylvania, the site relied on a long-standing local interagency planning team. The specific organizational strategies each site used to move toward a system of care varied, even though the system principles were uniform across sites.

EVALUATION

The evaluation of MHSPY was designed to assess the feasibility of the program and its impact on service delivery. The focus was on how changes in the organization of a community's mental health system for children could allow children to be treated in their normal environment and could reduce the need for placements in hospitals and residential treatment centers. The evaluation, which was conducted over a five-year period beginning in 1990, monitored program implementation in each community and tracked program effects. The evaluation emphasized the description of the diversity of forms of an effective system of care and how implementation of systems of care varied by population, geography, financing, administrative and legal structures, and local history. The evaluation also sought to determine whether there were common lessons across communities.[4]

The evaluation data support the hypothesis that systems of care are indeed feasible with the appropriate organizational and financial support.[5] All sites expanded the range and the flexibility of services available to children. Therapeutic foster care providing homes with specially trained and supported foster parents was increasingly available. Weary parents of children with mental disorders had greater access to respite care, and emotionally troubled teenagers with inadequate homes had greater access to independent living programs that helped them learn to live on their own. Specific services that became available to more youths and families included crisis intervention and child mental health screening. Over the course of the project, case management became universal. All sites seemed to have at least one frequently used, intensive, intermediate service between outpatient services and residential or hospital treatment. The specific intermediate services varied from site to site and included intensive home-based intervention, therapeutic foster care, group homes, and independent living programs. For example, a majority of Kentucky clients received intensive home-based treatment during their first three months, and nearly half in Vermont received therapeutic foster care.

Community-Based Care

A key issue was whether care could be provided in the community. Each MHSPY site tried to maintain children at risk of psychiatric hospitalization in the community by providing for their multiple service needs. There is substantial evidence that the demonstration accomplished this goal. Service data from the client information system indicate that hospitalization and residential treatment were rarely used. For most sites, the percentage of MHSPY children in residential or hospital treatment was 5 percent or less (with one exception, where 10 percent were hospitalized at the beginning of treatment and 8 percent at twelve months of treatment). Low hospitalization rates were achieved despite the fact that many of the children and adolescents had histories of residential or hospital treatment, and were selected because they were at high risk for institutional placement. Indeed, some sites explicitly selected children who were in residential or hospital settings at the beginning of the demonstration and brought them back to the community.

Changes in financing services were instrumental to offering a wider range of services, avoiding hospitalization, and providing a better fit between needs and services. In six sites, different agencies in the system of care pooled funding for services, so that money originating from mental health, child protection, and education agencies could be used together for a wide array of services. Accounts for funds were created, providing money to cover the needs of individual children. Thus, sensible interventions could be provided, such as a yard fence for an impulsive child who had no place to play safely at his home or cooking lessons for an adolescent with emotional problems who had found this a productive outlet. Most sites made innovative use of federal entitlements, in particular the Medicaid 1915(a) option. This option allows states to pay for "services not included in the state plan." The money can be used flexibly for whatever services are needed. Altogether, these funding mechanisms were used to address the totality of the physical health, mental health, educational, and social needs of children and families. Therapeutic, family support, and other services are essential if children are to be maintained in their home environments. That children are not hospitalized does *not* diminish their need for services; in some cases, it may increase the demands.

Systems of Care

Whether sites could function as systems of care was also a central question. The expectation was that child-serving agencies would change to work in partnership with families, coordinate with other organizations, and provide child-centered treatment. During the five-year implementation of MHSPY, many of these changes were evident. Some sites consolidated existing interagency structures and extended their influence on local practices. They developed new services, set up training programs in system of care models, and adapted innovative financing methods. Interagency working groups emerged from the central interagency structures to deal with specific issues such as training, outcomes, programming, case review, management of specialized services, and technical assistance to local communities. By the end of the project, most of the sites had broadened the range of children served. In many cases, administrative changes were accompanied by changes in governance, with increased local management of services and use of funds.

In addition to the development of interagency structures, most sites reported a qualitative increase in the degree of collaboration. Staff in several sites reported a process in which the different organizations in the system of care became more engaged over time and more productive working together. Local community agencies in each site gradually absorbed system-of-care principles that were previously little known. In Cleveland, Ohio, for example, the child welfare agency and private agencies that traditionally had contracts for residential beds gradually developed an investment in community-based alternatives. Kentucky increased collaboration by training education officials in how to access mental health and social service funding.

Interagency relationships flourished in part because MHSPY projects had funds and services to offer and case managers with skills in individualized care for children that other agencies found difficult to manage. In Cleveland, for example, child welfare workers came to rely on MHSPY case managers because they were able to provide support to clients, design individualized services, and use flexible Medicaid funds. In San Francisco, empowered by control over flexible Medicaid funds, the MHSPY project developed a culturally sensitive model of care that worked with neighborhood agencies to create packages of services for clients.

Nevertheless, despite the substantial development of services and systems, the sites fell short of fully developed systems of care. One issue was the difficulty of establishing services to cover more than a few well-chosen points on the continuum of care. Typically, each site had at least some gaps in the continuum of care as it was originally envisioned. Often, this was because some child-serving agencies remained outside the interagency agreement and systems of care, or financing innovations produced limited funding pools, or both. In one case, there was a struggle to maintain even a small number of residential treatment beds for those children who temporarily needed such services. There were also chronic problems linking the social welfare system to other agencies responsible for children with emotional disorders. By the time support from The Robert Wood Johnson Foundation had ended, each site was still working to adopt system of care principles.

Continuation

One striking accomplishment was the staying power of the partial systems of care that were developed by the projects. At every site but Pennsylvania, most of the services and structures created by MHSPY survived beyond the end of Foundation support. The sites replaced MHSPY funds from a variety of sources, including county and state money and federal grants. Several innovations developed in part or wholly through MHSPY were incorporated into managed mental health care plans developed by the states.

Collaboration between Health Professionals and Parents

The partnership between professionals and parents that was one goal of MHSPY was partly realized. The close relationship between case managers and parents at many sites was evident from parent interviews, so parents often felt comfortable reaching out to their case managers for a variety of needs. Parent participation in the development and the management of the system of care was, however, underdeveloped in most sites, although in Vermont a strong family advocacy group took the initiative to begin and maintain a respite program for parents, and had a strong presence on the state interagency planning team.

Case Example

The case of a child referred to as Iola illustrates how the system of care functions in the community. Iola was an adolescent whose childhood was marred by trauma and instability: her father's death when she was a toddler, placement in foster care at age three, incest at the hands of her adoptive father, placement in four foster homes over six months as a twelve-year-old, neuroleptic medication at age thirteen, residential treatment from age thirteen to sixteen, and finally placement in the community at age seventeen. Her school records showed a history of destructive and aggressive behavior, inattentiveness, tantrums, and self-abuse. She abused drugs and alcohol and developed a cocaine dependence that led her to trade sex for drugs. Outpatient treatment, foster care, psychiatric medication, residential treatment, and juvenile detention were all inadequate. Serving her was a challenge because of her hostile, manipulative, and suicidal behavior and her tendency to run away from placements.

Iola was placed in an independent living program with multiple services. The treatment team doubted that she could avoid incarceration unless she developed the capacity to live on her own. The project provided her with an apartment, allowances for groceries and clothes, and daily advice and monitoring from a case manager. Her treatment team included staff members from mental health, child protection, school, and juvenile justice agencies as well as a motorcycle policeman that she had befriended. Her mother was also included, but could not contribute much because of her own difficulties. The team shared responsibility for the support she needed, and worked with school and probation officials to help them respond to her emotional disturbance. Only after months of support from the team was she able to tolerate individual psychotherapy to address her trauma. With support, she completed high school, obtained a job, began to write about her life, and started taking care of daily living. Interwoven with these positive developments, however, were occasional encounters with the police and the intermittent use of alcohol and drugs. The case of Iola illustrates how the MHSPY system of care developed flexible, multipronged methods for dealing with very difficult adolescents with a poor prognosis. It shows how a continuum of services and interagency coordination can make community care feasible, and how an evaluation must take into account how profoundly these young people have been hurt.[6]

Building Programs Around Children's and Their Families' Needs

The evaluation did not allow for an objective assessment of treatment effectiveness. Efficiency is not equivalent to effectiveness, and it is unclear, given the current knowledge base in children's mental health, whether making available a set of desirable services is going to ameliorate the disturbance of children with serious emotional disorders. Some researchers have argued that there is little data to support the real-world effectiveness of mental health treatments for children, and, therefore, organizing effective systems is not going to have much impact.[7]

Qualitative evaluation data suggest that the sites most successful in programmatic terms seemed to be those that were able to adapt systems to the needs of children and their families. All sites conducted elaborate assessment and decision making about treatment programs and planning for individual children and families. Perhaps such programs and plans are the key to effective treatment. Thus, MHSPY's most important idea may *not* be coordinated systems of care but the idea that services must be designed specifically around the needs of children and families.

LESSONS LEARNED

America's health care and social systems have undergone profound change, fueled not only by the need to control costs and expand services but also by political changes that place increased responsibility on those who seek help for health care problems. MHSPY's lessons need to be understood in terms of these larger changes. What was clear is that, although individuals and families have a potentially important role, the way professional services and community resources are used is critical.

When MHSPY was launched, the gap between the rhetoric and the reality of children's mental health care was substantial. Professionals, parents, and advocates believed that they knew what was wrong with services, and the promise of MHSPY was that it was going to demonstrate how reforming delivery would provide more effective and efficient care. In part because MHSPY was established as a nonexperimental demonstration program—that is, there were no comparisons with control groups—it is difficult to draw definitive conclusions about whether it was successful in terms of ultimate outcomes. In several ways, external events outpaced the demonstration and made its lessons even more difficult to discern.

Treatment Effectiveness: Lessons from the Fort Bragg Experiment and MHSPY

The Fort Bragg Child and Adolescent Mental Health Demonstration began in 1990, after MHSPY, and was explicitly developed as a quasi-experiment to test the effectiveness of system-of-care services to children with emotional disorders. Funded by the Department of Defense and the National Institute of Mental Health, the Fort Bragg demonstration was conducted with children of military personnel. In collaboration with the state of North Carolina, the demonstration developed a full continuum of children's mental health services for military dependents. An independent evaluation was conducted to assess the conduct of the demonstration and its impact on the children served. The evaluation compared outcomes in the Fort Bragg community with outcomes at two comparable military sites.

Like MHSPY, the Fort Bragg continuum of care was designed to offer a wide range of services to be more responsive to the needs of children and families and avoid unnecessarily restrictive treatments, such as psychiatric hospitalization. The demonstration emphasized intermediate services such as in-home crisis stabilization, after-school group treatment, therapeutic foster care, and crisis management to help fill the gap between outpatient psychotherapy and institutional treatment. However, unlike the MHSPY sites, the Fort Bragg demonstration was conducted within a closed system of health care provided by the military for its dependents, an environment that more closely resembled a managed health care organization than the MHSPY sites.

The results of the evaluation indicate that care provided during the demonstration expanded dramatically.[8] Compared with baseline data, it served three times the number of children, far more than were served at the two comparison sites. As was the case with MHSPY, there is strong evidence that the continuum was put in place, and there is further evidence that services were of high caliber. Children in the demonstration were less likely to use hospital and residential treatment but more likely to use intermediate services. They also had significantly more therapy visits and longer time in treatment. Clinical outcomes were generally no different, however; children at both demonstration and comparison sites improved, but the demonstration did not lead to better scores on mental health measures. Moreover, the demonstration was more expensive, spending 1.5 times as much per child as the comparison site.[9]

The Fort Bragg evaluation attracted considerable attention because it challenged the assumption that a continuum of care improves access to care and enhances children's mental health outcomes. To the consternation of those who advocate coordinated systems of care, the results suggest that children are not necessarily better off as a result of being served by the continuum. Is it possible, as Bickman and others suggest, that we have misplaced our focus, and that we need to return to basics and develop more effective treatments?[10] Or is this a narrow view of the findings from the Fort Bragg demonstration, one that overgeneralizes the results?[11]

Although the Fort Bragg study did not find differences in outcomes between the demonstration and comparison groups, the findings are consistent with the MHSPY results showing that a comprehensive continuum of care can be developed and can increase access to services for children in need. Moreover, the children's improvement on outcomes were relatively impressive in both the demonstration and comparison groups, suggesting positive effects of mental health treatment across the study.[12] A problem with the study was that the comparison group—other military communities—actually received intensive and coordinated services far better than those typically available to children outside of military families. The rates of hospitalization and residential care were, however, lower in the treatment site, and confirm that children, even those with the most serious mental illness, can be effectively treated outside of institutional settings.

The lack of superiority in clinical outcomes and high costs suggest that health professionals are only at the early stage of understanding how to provide effective and cost-efficient mental health care. Clearly, we need to better understand how the delivery of services affects outcome. If, in fact, the present assumption is correct—that the effectiveness of treatment is linked to how closely one can match treatments with children's and families' needs—it is essential that we develop a continuum of research. The continuum needs to include basic research studies as well as efforts to test models of caregiving in actual communities. The MHSPY demonstration and the Fort Bragg study make clear that experiments with managing mental health care for children are still very new and that the question is not whether they should be done, but how.

Patient-Focused Care

Although there are many ways to describe the new perspective incorporated in the systems-of-care model to providing services to children with mental disorders, it is clear that a system of care embodies fundamental changes in the way services are provided. For present purposes, it will be characterized as a patient-focused approach for restructuring health services, where clinical needs are placed at the fore and health professionals have to form a partnership with patients and families to make key decisions. The claim cannot yet be made that this will bring about more effective care, but it provides a way to think about developing and testing more effective treatment.

Patient-focused care should not be revolutionary, but the nation has experienced several decades of rapid progress in health technology and a concomitant institutionalization of health services, where the patient's needs were often subordinated. Decision-making power is now shared in an uneasy balance between those responsible for financing care and the institutions that provide health services. The new patient-centered approach to children's mental health services takes back this authority and gives a central role to parents and, in some cases, children and adolescents.

The development of a new model has not happened *de novo*. Many have pointed to the need to reshape health and social systems to respond to the needs of those served.[13] For children, the guiding principles are that care must be community- and family-based *and* comprehensive.[14] This is because families have the responsibility for children, but it is clear that they cannot cope alone with problems such as serious mental illness. They need the help of professionals, but professionals cannot have the sole responsibility.

One of our observations in MHSPY was that the new service most often used by families was respite. Respite care enabled a family with a child who had a mental illness to have help at home. Sometimes, a respite worker was simply an extra hand; in other cases, the respite worker was able to relieve the parents and allow them to work or deal with other responsibilities. Anecdotal evidence suggests that respite was a critical service that allowed children in MHSPY sites, even those whose behavior required constant attention, to be maintained in their community. Respite care exemplifies the interdependence of families and professionals.

There has been a major change in perspective by those responsible for federal and state initiatives. Categorical federal programs have been replaced by block grants to the states, and mandates have been replaced with broad new local authority. Centralized health care reform is not being discussed now, and, instead, smaller reforms have been introduced. In most cases, individuals have more responsibility, financial and other, for obtaining care. One of MHSPY's lessons is that there is an alternative to the two extremes of centralized health care and individually directed health care. MHSPY and Fort Bragg suggest that local communities can develop systems that help individuals. Because families cannot deal with serious health problems alone, some way to provide professional support and resources to those in need must be found. MHSPY-sponsored programs were able to mobilize a variety of resources to provide individually tailored services, and not all of these were from traditional health care providers.

CONCLUSION

Children have been victims of our society's inability to resolve fundamental problems with our health and social systems. They are more likely than adults to live in poverty and to lack health insurance, and they have the most difficult problems getting access to appropriate health care. Improving children's health and their ability to function should be a cornerstone of any reform of the health system, if for no other reason than the long-term benefits for child development.

Whether the issue is education, juvenile justice, or mental or physical health, the MHSPY approach of taking an integrated view of children's needs seems a useful way to reconsider the help we provide. The Robert Wood Johnson Foundation's experience with MHSPY does not provide unequivocal evidence to support the MHSPY approach, but the idea of children as part of a family and a community seems so obvious that one wonders how we could have allowed our programs to stray from it. The village cannot raise the child, perhaps, but neither can the family do so without the support of its community. Children with serious mental illness are an extreme example, but how we treat them is symbolic of how we regard all children. Our failure to provide effective and efficient services for these children make them more visible, but the underlying principles are universal. All children need both their homes and the support of those in the communities in which they live.

Notes

Appreciation is expressed to the colleagues who collaborated with us on the development of this study, most importantly the late Dr. Judith Gardner and Gretchen Lovas. Appreciation is also expressed to Andrea Kabcenell and Marjorie Gutman, who served as program officers at The Robert Wood Johnson Foundation for this study.

1. Institute of Medicine, *Research on Children and Adolescents with Mental, Behavioral, and Developmental Disorders: Mobilizing a National Initiative* (Washington, D.C.: National Academy Press, 1989).
2. J. Knitzer, *Unclaimed Children* (Washington, D.C.: Children's Defense Fund, 1982).
3. L. Saxe, T. P. Cross, N. Silverman, and W. F. Batchelor, with D. Dougherty, *Children's Mental Health: Problems and Services* (Durham, N.C.: Duke University Press, 1987; originally published by the Office of Technology Assessment, U.S. Congress, OTA-BP-H-33; Washington, D.C.).
4. Three types of data were collected:
   Organizational Assessment: Detailed case studies were developed for each of the eight communities to provide an understanding of how care was organized and financed. Site documents were reviewed and interviews, focus groups, and observational studies were conducted.
   Client Information: A common information system was developed and later adapted for each site to provide data on demographics, mental health problems, treatment plans, and services provided.
   Clinical Assessment Conferences: Conducted by expert clinicians on a sample of patients and their families at each site, clinical assessment conferences provided an analysis of the quality of care and an appraisal of the contribution by the interagency system of care to the child's treatment.
5. T. P. Cross and L. Saxe, "Many Hands Make Mental Health Systems of Care a Reality: Lessons from the Mental Health Services Program for Youth," in C. T. Nixon and D. A. Northrup (eds.), *Children's Mental Health Services: Research, Policy, and Evaluation* (Thousand Oaks, Calif.: Sage, 1997), pp. 45–72.

6. A. J. Solnit, J. Adnopoz, L. Saxe, J. Gardner, and T. Fallon, "Evaluating Systems of Care for Children: Utility of the Clinical Case Conference," *American Journal of Orthopsychiatry* 67, 1997, 554.

7. J. R. Weisz, B. Weiss, S. S. Han, D. A. Granger, and T. Morton, "Effects of Psychotherapy With Children and Adolescents Revisited: A Meta-Analysis of Treatment Outcome Studies," *Psychological Bulletin* 117(3), 1995, 450; J. R. Weisz, S. S. Han, and S. M. Valeri, "More of What? Issues Raised by the Fort Bragg Study," *American Psychologist* 52, 1997, 541.

8. See, for example, L. Bickman, "Reinterpreting the Fort Bragg Evaluation Findings: The Message Does Not Change," *Journal of Mental Health Administration* 23(1), 1996, 137–145.

9. L. Bickman, P. R. Guthrie, E. M. Foster, E. W. Lambert, W. T. Summerfelt, C. S. Breda, and C. A. Heflinger, *Evaluating Managed Mental Health Services: The Fort Bragg Experiment* (New York: Plenum, 1995).

10. See note seven.

11. L. B. Behar, "The Fort Bragg Evaluation: A Snapshot in Time," *American Psychologist* 52, 1997, 557–559; see also note six.

12. K. Hoagwood, "Interpreting Nullity: The Fort Bragg Experiment: A Comparative Success or Failure?" *American Psychologist* 52, 1997, 546–550.

13. See, for example, L. B. Schorr, *Within Our Reach: Breaking the Cycle of Disadvantage* (New York: Anchor Books, Doubleday, 1989).

14. Children's Defense Fund, *The State of America's Children: 1992* (Washington, D.C.: Children's Defense Fund, 1992); National Commission on Children, *Beyond Rhetoric: A New American Agenda for Children and Families,* final report of the National Commission on Children (Washington, D.C.: Government Printing Office, 1991).

Communications

CHAPTER TEN

~~~ The Foundation's Radio and Television Grants, 1987–1997

Victoria D. Weisfeld

Editors' Introduction

Traditionally, communications departments of philanthropies try to inform the public about the foundation and its work through press releases, annual reports, and dissemination of findings from grantees' work. In recent years, The Robert Wood Johnson Foundation has also taken a somewhat different and parallel approach—using communications itself as a strategy for attacking some of the nation's health problems. Just as some grants use demonstration or research projects to advance a goal of the Foundation, the grants discussed in this chapter use communications as a strategy.

As the chapter makes clear, the Foundation has experimented with a broad range of media approaches. Some represent core funding to encourage better and more extensive reporting of health news, whereas others support a television or radio production aimed at a specific health issue. There have been successes and failures, and, as is typical, not everyone scores successes and failures in the same way.

The communications office at The Robert Wood Johnson Foundation and its grantees have received numerous awards in honor of its efforts in the emerging field of philanthropic communications.

Victoria Weisfeld, the author of this chapter, has been a key player in the communications unit of the Foundation for over ten years, and has been responsible for a range of grants to radio and television for health-related programming.

Information comes to The Robert Wood Johnson Foundation from many sources—the experiences of the Foundation's grantees, the deliberations at conferences that the Foundation funds, the knowledge base of the fields the Foundation works in. Information of different types can be used to raise awareness about a problem or an issue, to describe promising innovations that others may want to adopt, to encourage collaboration among people working in similar areas, and to report on outcomes, good or bad. Properly used, information is capital—even more valuable, on occasion, than the dollars the Foundation awards.

Just as there are many sources of information, so there are many different places to distribute it: to other grantees, to professionals and policy makers, to the public. The appropriate place to distribute information will depend on what it is, what problem or issue it addresses, who may need to act on it, and how timely it is. Information for its own sake is not very interesting to the Foundation, which is more concerned with information that people can act on.

Putting these two ideas together—the type of information and who needs it—creates an almost limitless array of communications possibilities. Just like every other organization and individual in the country wanting to reach audiences with a message, the Foundation works with the full array of news and information media. How it has worked with radio and television between 1987 and 1997 is the subject of this chapter.[1]

In a nutshell, the Foundation's communications strategy is built around activities that foster its programmatic goals. In its relations with broadcast media, the Foundation tries to capitalize on the different roles of broadcasters, some of which aid and some of which inhibit its work.

- Both the news and information side of broadcasting and the entertainment side hold potential in *health education*—conveying new information about preserving health and treating illnesses or about getting access to health care. The Foundation tries to encourage such messages through grants to the media or to other organizations that work with them, through briefings for journalists, and through continued media relations activities.

- The media also portray people engaged in *risky behavior* (tobacco, drug, and alcohol use, for example), which the Foundation hopes to counter. The Partnership for a Drug-Free America and the Center for Tobacco-Free Kids are good examples of grantees that try to change the media climate.

- The broadcast media are an important source of *public information* regarding key health policy questions—in fact, their coverage of an issue at all is essential to *public agenda setting*. A grant enabling National Public Radio to increase its coverage of health care reform and to award small grants to local stations to do the same are two such activities.

Although the Foundation's informal interactions with the news media are numerous, it has seen a special opportunity to make grants in certain areas:

- To broadcasters themselves
- To independent producers for broadcast programs

WE DON'T FUND MEDIA—DO WE?

In the mid-1980s, the Council on Foundations and the Benton Foundation produced a landmark video, *We Don't Fund Media*. The title reflected the typical response that producers and broadcasters received from foundations at that time. Most foundations had no appreciation of media's potential and lacked expertise to work with them; they saw media grants as costly, risky ventures—particularly proposals that had a policy edge to them. This video laid out a case for the support of media projects as an essential tool for foundations attempting to create social change. A decade ago, many foundations ignored several facts about the broadcast media. Although foundations might recognize that the media are pervasive and might concede that they have an important educational potential, they were generally less willing to acknowledge that broadcast media were—and are—central to certain aspects of modern life:

- Setting the public and political agenda
- Describing the cultural context for decisions about the policy issues of the day

- Suggesting alternative visions for how some aspect of social and economic systems could work
- Giving an increasingly diverse society some common reference points (values, history, ideas)
- Serving as the primary source of news for large numbers of Americans
- Shaping people's perceptions of the "other" in society

In short, foundations didn't sufficiently recognize that the important decision making in various sectors of society increasingly takes place in a media-driven environment. For all the frustrations that working with the media entail, it is virtually impossible to think about changing public views on important issues without engaging the media. Because half of Americans today obtain most of their information from television, the term "mass media" often signifies one medium and one medium only—TV. "Most large foundations now recognize that they must be in that marketplace if they want their ideas and their grantees' ideas to be seen," says Karen Menichelli, associate director of the Benton Foundation, a Washington, D.C.–based organization concerned with the public-interest use of communications.

Although The Robert Wood Johnson Foundation made only a few media grants in its first fifteen years, in her view it was an early exception to the we-don't-fund-media rule, in that it was an early foundation funder of National Public Radio for programming related to health care. The Foundation made these grants for strategic reasons: funding NPR was seen as an opportunity to reach a relatively small but influential audience. The Foundation's rationale for NPR support, as stated at that time, applies equally well to its approach to broadcasting grants today: "Public consensus is increasingly essential for progress to occur. The soundness of any such consensus, in turn, is dependent on a public informed about all sides of the issue."

With its broadcasting grants, the Foundation has a secondary agenda, too: it derives a public relations benefit from its association with well-regarded programs and organizations. According to Menichelli, its issue-oriented support of NPR has become "almost a branding," given our tagline that associates the Foundation's name with "making grants to improve the health and health care of all Americans."

BROADCASTING PROJECTS THE FOUNDATION FUNDS: OVERVIEW

With few exceptions, The Robert Wood Johnson Foundation considers only those media grant proposals that directly relate to its access, substance-abuse, and chronic-care program goals. In the 1987–1997 period, the Foundation made more than $56 million in grants to broadcasters. This funding has been divided into several major categories in the accompanying Exhibit 10.1. Listed first in the exhibit are projects that support the continuing news gathering and analysis functions of a broadcast organization. This kind of funding has enabled radio and television networks to expand their news coverage of health care issues. The second category (Grants for Specific Productions) funds producers of specific programming—usually one-time specials. Some of these grants include funding for outreach, promotion, and other corollary activities. Grants devoted solely to these corollary activities are the third category.

The dollar figures noted in Exhibit 10.1 for the specials do not necessarily reflect the total cost of the programs, merely the Foundation's investments. Sometimes a project has multiple funders. Sometimes the Foundation's grant covers more than just production costs (including, for example, outreach, promotion, marketing, distribution, training, additional products, web sites, and research). As an example, the $4.38 million grant to Public Affairs Television for an addiction series includes the production of a four-part broadcast program featuring Bill Moyers, the cost of a community and educational outreach campaign, minigrants to stations for community activities, preview screenings of the series in Washington, D.C., and state capitals, print materials, a national video conference, and a state-of-the-art on-line project. Other times, such corollary activities are funded separately.

The two main categories in Exhibit 10.1 arise from different motivations:

• Grants to *news organizations* for "hard news" —ongoing reporting, over a period of years, via short news pieces on a wide variety of timely health care topics; the information is useful for audiences interested in breadth and staying current; much of the value of the grant depends on the credibility of the news organization; these grantees treat the funder like any other news source; the goal is to keep the public generally informed.

• Grants to *producers* for specific productions—specials—are one-shot or for only a few feature programs, usually on a very well-defined topic; the value depends in part on the ultimate venue in which the project airs; specials appeal to people who want depth; these grantees are more open to the funder's ideas, at least in a project's formative stages; the goal is to convey a complex subject in a dramatic, compelling way.

A CLOSER LOOK AT SELECTED GRANTEES

A few of the Foundation's larger grants to broadcasters illustrate the range of projects and suggest some lessons.

Grants for News Coverage

WGBH. The Robert Wood Johnson Foundation had limited experience with grants to television until a series first funded in 1988, called *The AIDS Quarterly,* out of Boston public television station WGBH. At that time, the Foundation was heavily invested in two major AIDS programs—one a demonstration program of the "San Francisco model" of AIDS care in eleven communities and the other a group of fifty-four innovative, independent community projects. The call for proposals for this latter program elicited more than a thousand replies. Public concern about AIDS was rising, yet serious shortcomings existed in HIV and AIDS treatment. The prevention of HIV infection—through significant, long-term behavior changes—was the only apparent solution, but how to achieve such changes was unclear.

High-quality, thoughtful television appeared to be a promising way to explore these issues for the broadest possible audience. The characteristics of AIDS itself helped justify this choice of medium, because the actions that would have an impact on the epidemic were far beyond the control of the health care sector. This award-winning magazine-format program, hosted by Peter Jennings, attracted around eight million viewers per airing. And the segments that aired stimulated additional print news coverage.

After a few seasons, *The AIDS Quarterly* metamorphosed into *The Health Quarterly.* This program employed a similar format and looked at issues in health care generally. Decreasing public anxiety about AIDS and a stronger care system response supported this shift to new topics. An early segment of *The Health Quarterly* examined the plight of America's uninsured work force and the competing interests trying to affect American health policy, for example.

The project had a dramatic finale in late 1993, midway through a $10 million renewal grant. Long-standing friction between Foundation staff members and the show's producers reached a critical point, and the Foundation canceled its funding. Foundation staff members believed that long delays between programs—it was never truly quarterly—undercut the potential value of having a regular media presence. They also thought that the outreach was minimal, and the show's costs were high. Moreover, they were frustrated by the producer's lack of responsiveness to topics they suggested—and to the choice of topics made instead. This type of friction, which can occur in any media grant, reflected a basic unresolved difference of opinion: the WGBH producers thought of their project as a hard news endeavor—in which case the Foundation's role normally would be hands-off—whereas Foundation staff members viewed the project more as feature programming, which to them meant working more closely with the producer. This quarrel eventually came to public light in a June 1997 *Boston Globe* series by Daniel Golden. He saw the principal quarrel in stark terms: the Foundation concerned about project management, high overhead, and productivity, WGBH concerned about "interference with editorial decisions." As a result, in subsequent negotiations with potential broadcasting grantees, Foundation staff members have worked before the grant is awarded to clarify the kind and amount of input they will have.

NATIONAL PUBLIC RADIO. NPR and other radio news networks have received grants to establish continuing coverage of health news. Foundation communications staff members who want to pitch a story about a particular grantee or issue to these outlets approach their reporters and editors just as they would approach any other news organization. Sometimes they succeed, and sometimes they don't. The potential awkwardness of this situation—the Foundation's being both news source and funder—has been overcome by scrupulous separation of the business, or grant, aspects of its relationship from the media relations aspects. The grant is handled by the NPR development office, news items by the news and information staff.

Support for NPR's coverage of health care for the last thirteen years is widely viewed within the Foundation as a success, contributing in a very real way to its goal of having a more informed public on health care matters. Much good reporting and much public understanding would have been lost over the years without the special expertise NPR's several full-time journalists and skilled stringers have developed. For example, they broke the story on the Food and Drug Administration's move to assert regulatory control over tobacco and won a prestigious Peabody Award for this coverage.

The Foundation also funds National Public Radio because of the audience it reaches—12.4 million listeners every week, 56 percent of whom hold college degrees. NPR reaches educated, activated listeners, and the Foundation believes that this audience needs to be well informed about health issues, particularly at a time when the health care system is changing so profoundly.

At the height of the national health care reform debate, NPR approached the Foundation regarding separate support to enable small grants for local public radio coverage and outreach projects around health reform. The Foundation funded this project jointly with the Henry J. Kaiser Family Foundation and the Commonwealth Fund. Under it, NPR assembled a panel of experts and reviewed stations' proposals, ultimately awarding thirty-three grants for a variety of community activities and enhanced coverage. NPR provided programming and outreach materials to aid them. Called *Critical Decision,* this project enabled public radio stations in many locales to become actively involved in helping citizens discuss and understand problems in the health care system and the potential impact of changes. The local stations produced lively, award-winning coverage that engaged a wide cross-section of their communities. The success of *Critical Decision* prompted the Foundation to develop its own grant program for local public radio, Sound Partners for Community Health.

SOUND PARTNERS FOR COMMUNITY HEALTH. This program, announced in the late spring of 1997, offers competitive national grants for local public radio stations. It is administered for The Robert Wood Johnson Foundation by the Benton Foundation. Grants of $15,000 to $35,000 are awarded to stations to increase public awareness of one of four key health issues and to facilitate citizens' involvement in making decisions affecting health care.

There will be two rounds of grant making, totaling $2 million altogether. As of this writing, grants have been awarded for the first round of funding. Of the 408 stations eligible to apply, 104 did, and 35 ultimately received grants. Their projects cover the four topic areas as follows:

- The impact of welfare reform on access to health care
  (ten stations)
- Providing health care for young children (nine)
- New approaches to curtailing youth substance abuse (nine)
- Health care decision making at the end of life (seven)

Some forty-two million Americans live within the primary signal area of the thirty-five grantee stations. They serve areas as diverse as Charleston, West Virginia; Elkhart, Indiana; San Francisco; and New York City.

In the short term, the Foundation believes that the Sound Partners program will permit local stations to devote the resources necessary for good, in-depth coverage of important health issues in their community—a luxury that tight budgets often do not permit. It also will help them to establish strong partnerships with local organizations as they work on the project together. Each party in the effort can gain from these relationships. The Foundation expects the grants to increase the impact of the stations' reporting and to bring more community residents into contact with public radio. In the long run, the outreach skills developed under the program and the involvement of new audiences may help stations in their quest for sustainability.

Grants for Community Radio

The Foundation's grants to community radio over the past five years have supported several activities: reporting on health issues, call-in programs, marketing, and training. The community radio grantees—Radio Bilingüe, National Native News, and High Plains News Service—are all networks or news services that provide programming to subscribing stations in many states. They perform an invaluable service for niche audiences (Spanish speakers, Native Americans, and rural residents) very different from NPR's "elites."

Radio is a particularly effective way to reach people isolated by culture, geography, or language, many of whom do not have newspapers available to them, and some of whom cannot read. Radio listenership among these groups tends to be higher than average, and radio programming that is sensitive to their culture—and, in the case of Hispanics, in their own language—is particularly valued. These three news services combined reach some 2.5 million people weekly, and all three consider health topics a strong area of listener interest. Community radio networks cover more than hard news; they also have a commitment to improving the health of their listeners and will run stories about, for example, the importance of mammograms or preventing substance abuse.

- Radio Bilingüe used its first two-year grant to establish a national health desk for its nationwide Spanish-language radio news programs. In early 1995, Radio Bilingüe introduced the first national Spanish-language daily talk show, *Linea Abierta* ("Open Line"). Radio Bilingüe also produces public service announcements and radio *novelas* about health topics. Such community-service programming led to Radio Bilingüe receiving an award for excellence in community health promotion from the Secretary of Health and Human Services in 1994.

- High Plains News Service, a radio network created by the Western Organization of Resource Councils, established a rural news and multicultural information program for public and community radio stations in 1989. It serves mainly the North Great Plains and Rocky Mountain West areas, but has station subscribers in twenty states, from Alaska to Arkansas and Kentucky to California.

- At National Native News, the first national news service for Native Americans, the health reporting unit established with Robert Wood Johnson Foundation funding has produced stories affecting Native Americans throughout the country and has guided more than a hundred correspondents in their coverage of Native health issues. NNN's public affairs call-in program, *Native America Calling,* for the first time gives Native Americans the chance to engage in a direct dialog with health care leaders. A measure of NNN's significance is the Smithsonian Institution's decision to preserve its broadcasts in an archive at the new National Museum of the American Indian.

The three community radio grantees face common problems. One is the lack of skilled reporters. In part to compensate, all three networks use advisory committees or other experts, sometimes people they have encountered through their Foundation connection, to provide story leads and interview ideas and to help monitor the quality of their health coverage. They also engage in training programs.

Their other large problem is financial viability. They have differing organizational structures, but all face cutbacks from the Corporation for Public Broadcasting. They must increase both the number of stations subscribing to their service and the number of listeners to their programs. Many subscribing stations are small and cannot afford high programming fees or promotion, but the networks have survived by changing from providing services free to developing a fee structure. Radio Bilingüe developed an innovative marketing approach, requesting funding for satellite equipment that it could give to seventeen small stations in return for carrying the programming. Health programming is very popular with listeners, so it helps build the station's audience. Increasing the subscriber base also makes the programs more attractive to national underwriters, and the networks need to improve their fundraising capacity, too. This involves obtaining grants and underwriting, not on-air fundraisers such as individual stations conduct.

Recognizing that these three networks had limited resources, in 1993 the Foundation funded a radio technical assistance project to help address such issues as editorial content, technical quality, marketing, and fundraising. Under the direction of an experienced radio consultant, a Media Resource Committee was established, involving representatives from the three grantee networks, their radio reporters and editors, and other Foundation grantees and consultants involved in health care policy, rural health, and minority issues. Four semiannual meetings were held, offering a variety of program ideas and resources. The radio grantees met a wide variety of other Foundation grantees in Denver, Albuquerque, Minneapolis, and Phoenix, enriching their pool of resources. A by-product of the regular interaction among the radio grantees is a heightened sharing of their human resources and increased cooperative training.

American News Service

A relatively recent trend in the news media, which some foundations have supported, is the development of "public journalism" or "civic journalism." These terms are defined variously, but, according to one of the movement's leaders, Jan Schaffer of the Pew Center for Civic Journalism, civic journalism can be distinguished from "everyday good journalism" both by its attitude and by the tools it employs.

"The attitude is an affirmation that journalists have an obligation—a constitutionally protected obligation—to give readers and viewers the news and information they need to make decisions in a self-governing society," she writes in a description of the program. That is, "simply raising an alarm or spotlighting an injustice, which is traditional journalism, is not enough." People need to see that they can "play a role, have a voice, or make a difference" in improving society. The Foundation's grant to the American News Service, or ANS, in Brattleboro, Vermont, is just such a project. ANS's goal is to cover initiatives in various communities that tackle such thorny problems as race relations, education, crime, poverty, health care, and the environment.

"Millions of people across America are engaged in constructive, solution-oriented activities that directly address the key issues confronting society," the ANS project director, Frances Moore Lappé, says. Yet many news media rarely cover them or the positive steps individual citizens and projects are taking. The more typical "if it bleeds, it leads," approach to journalism contributes to "growing despair, cynicism, and feelings of powerlessness," Lappé says. Ironically, "today's problems can be successfully addressed only with the active engagement of millions more Americans."

In its pilot phase, the American News Service produced stories used by the nation's top newspapers and broadcast media outlets—1,700 media outlets overall, as of summer 1997. Examples of the kinds of stories covered in the health area include these:

- *Elderly Avoid Nursing Homes, With Community Support.* Concerned about the unmet needs of the elderly and an unusually high proportion of elderly people moving into nursing homes, some neighbors in the Twin Cities took action. They created the Living at Home/Block Nurse Program, which saves money and allows the elderly to remain in their homes longer. It thrives on neighborly support and is becoming a national model.

- *"Doulas" Help New Moms When Family Support Is Missing.* As professional women move away from their extended families and poor women, too, often lack family support, a new term has entered the American childbirth scene. "Doula," a Greek word, refers to experienced women who help, encourage, and accompany women during pregnancy and labor and after birth. Having gained a certain cachet among highly mobile professionals, new doula programs are arising to meet the needs of more vulnerable women. Their benefits are many, advocates say.

• *Unique Approach Fights Teen Drug Epidemic With Treatment for Every Child.* Little Rock, Arkansas, has embarked on a unique program giving every youngster in the city access to drug-abuse treatment. Called Insure the Children, it provides services for all youths from the ages of seven to eighteen. It is free to those not covered by private insurance or Medicaid. Citing early signs of effectiveness, sponsors hope it will become a national model.

• *Peers Teach Abstinence—Plus a Whole Lot More.* In the often-contentious arena of teenage pregnancy prevention, slogans range from "just say no" to "safe sex." Some new programs are dramatically reducing teenage pregnancy rates with a new "abstinence-plus" message: don't have sex, but know what you're getting into if you do. A new nonprofit initiative called the National Campaign to Prevent Teen Pregnancy also says that a mixture of strategies is most effective.

Some early responses suggest that ANS stories have stimulated greater citizen involvement and replication of good ideas across communities. Some journalists and editors have become more interested in this type of story, too.

Grants for Specific Productions

Most of the grants in the second group in Exhibit 10.1 are for broadcast projects brought to the Foundation by producers—usually video producers. In general, the Foundation has an opportunity to have an impact at the beginning of these projects, providing background and suggesting ideas and sources. But good producers conduct many such interviews, and ultimately the decisions—which issues are covered in the program, who is interviewed, what the bottom line is—are theirs. Occasionally, as research on a project unfolds, the producers return for additional ideas, clarification, or sources, or to test their conclusions. This happened several times in the production of the Fred Friendly special *Before I Die.* Sometimes producers have nearly completed a project before they even request funding, in which case the content decisions are already made.

When a documentary is being produced in a field where the Foundation has been working, staff members may hope and expect that the show will highlight some of the Foundation's work, but they do recognize that the piece is not a promotional vehicle for Foundation programs, and, in fact, would be weakened if it appeared to be so. Still, the Foundation and its grantees often can use these video productions in multiple ways after they are broadcast. In at least one case, the producer made a separate, short video for each Foundation site where he taped, which the grantees then used for community education, training, and fundraising.

Another type of project in this category is the development of pilot programs that the producers hope will be picked up by either public or commercial broadcasters. So far, the Foundation has made only two such grants, and these quite recently. Both are for pilots aimed at children and have education and entertainment goals.

The kinds of nonbroadcast support activities funded under this category are enormously varied. They can include activities like the elaborate community meetings and outreach built around the April 1997 Public Broadcasting Service airing of *Before I Die* or the Bill Moyers addiction series broadcast in March 1998. What follows are some examples of the variety of special programming.

ROCK THE VOTE. This grant took advantage of the highly visible policy debate about health reform to educate young people (ages sixteen to twenty-four) about the health care system, various health reform proposals, and behaviorally linked health problems that disproportionately affect young people. A pamphlet, *Rock The System: A Guide to Health Care Reform for Young Americans,* was published and promoted through video public service announcements. It included an overview of the problem of health care costs and why that problem motivated health reform efforts; sections on problems of young people in which prevention could avoid costs later (substance abuse, pregnancy, HIV/AIDS, violence, and sexually transmitted diseases); a section on then-current legislative alternatives; and a report on the Rock the Vote 1994 survey of young people. More than a million copies were distributed through requests to an 800 telephone number and in places frequented by young people, and the brochure was promoted in youth-oriented publications. As the issue of health care reform faded from daily headlines in the fall of 1994, the project shifted gears to produce videos on health issues of concern to young people. The videos were collectively called *Out of Order*. They were aired on MTV on three consecutive nights in May 1995 to an audience of 200,000 to 300,000. A significant increase in calls to the 800 number resulted. MTV also distributed ten thousand copies of the *Out of Order Resource Guide*, which listed national and state organizations involved in the health issues addressed by the specials.

THE NBC HEALTH CARE REFORM SPECIAL. At the time of the national health care reform debate, Foundation staff members were frustrated by the lack of public engagement in the process and the lack of solid, helpful information available to the public. For good policy to emerge, it seemed essential that the public understand what was at stake and what some of the choices were. Yet the viewpoints being heard were almost solely those of the special interests—people with a financial stake in the outcome of the debate.

What should be the venue for such a public education effort? Public television's reach was too small, and the Foundation had decided against a costly paid advertising campaign supporting expanded health insurance coverage. It instead turned to a commercial broadcaster, NBC News, with a request for a two-hour television event to inform Americans about the upcoming choices for the nation's health care system. NBC News promised its best production and on-air talent and, according to the network's president, Andrew Lack, "a highly visible, serious, and creative exploration of a topic that is vital to the well being of everyone in the country."

A front-page story on this unprecedented partnership in the *New York Times* on May 4, 1994, began, "A leading foundation active in health care has bought a two-hour block of prime time on NBC television and has asked the network's news division to fill the slot with an ambitious examination of health care reform." Of the $3.5 million budget, $2.5 million was for air time and $1 million for promotion. The program was broadcast by the network commercial-free; local affiliates were asked not to accept advertising relevant to health care reform during station breaks.

Clearly, this would be the Foundation's most highly visible—and highly watched—television foray. Staff members were concerned about both objectivity and depth. Although the NBC team was willing to listen to the Foundation's ideas up front, just as it would solicit the ideas of many others, the Foundation would not have any say over the ultimate content. The Foundation had to rely completely on the professionalism and reputation of NBC News. The broadcast, on June 21, was watched by thirty million American adults.

The impact of this special was evaluated by two separate surveys—one by Kathleen Hall Jamieson, dean of The Annenberg School of Public Communication of the University of Pennsylvania, and one by Robert Blendon, professor of health policy and political analysis at Harvard University's School of Public Health. Using different designs, the two studies came to different conclusions. Both evaluations concluded that viewers saw the program as balanced and thought they learned something, but the Penn survey concluded that viewers actually did learn something and were less cynical as a result of the program, whereas the Harvard survey measured no actual learning and no change in cynicism. These results show how difficult assessing media impact can be.

ANALYSIS OF HEALTH REFORM COVERAGE. The way the media covered health care reform itself became a topic of national interest. The Foundation wanted to learn from this experience, so it funded a special PBS program to look at the way health reform had been presented to the American people. Aired in October 1994, it featured Bill Moyers and Kathleen Hall Jamieson, dean of the Annenberg School for Communication at the University of Pennsylvania, who under another grant had been assessing media coverage of reform in both news reporting and advertising. In this broadcast, the commentators made several principal critiques:

- The debate had been conducted in language not accessible to many people.
- Although TV, radio, and print media dedicated significant time and space to the reform debate, their reporters focused on political strategy, not on the content or pros and cons of the various health reform proposals.
- Reporters focused so heavily on the fortunes of the President's health care plan that other proposals were virtually invisible and, consequently, unlikely to succeed.
- The public's lack of exposure to multiple ideas meant that polls necessarily narrowed their queries to a thumbs-up or thumbs-down on "the Clinton plan."

• The majority of ads from all sides were designed to stimulate
fear, not provide facts, and engaged in attack, not advocacy.

Dean Jamicson's project had followed the news articles, analyses,
editorials, op-eds, and cartoons in ten newspapers, as well as coverage
of health reform on the morning and evening news shows on the
major broadcast networks, CNN, *The MacNeil/Lehrer News Hour,* and
others. This study ran from mid-January 1994 through early October,
when it became clear that Congress was not going to act on the issue.
Subsequently, the Annenberg project published a report, provided
videotapes of the Jamieson/Moyers special, and conducted a sympo-
sium on "The Role of Communication in the Reform Debate." This
set of materials, called *Media in the Middle,* showed serious shortcomings in journalism's ability to cover such a complex issue. Sets
were distributed nationally to schools of journalism and of public policy studies.

Moreover, journalists were unable in this instance to easily assess
or counter the other highly promoted stream of media information—
advertising. More than 120 organizations of many viewpoints spent
at least $68 million on advertisements both for and against health care
reform. The project's analysis suggests that broadcast advertising was
particularly misleading—nearly 60 percent of broadcast ads were
judged unfair, compared to only 28 percent of print ads.

The result, the report concluded, was coverage "unprecedented in
cost, intensity, and confusion." It drew five key lessons for future programming around complex topics:

• In policy debates, journalists can play a useful role by clarifying
the language and jargon being used.

• When many different pieces of legislation are being considered
in Congress, it would be helpful to adopt a common, consistent
description of the various proposals.

• Polls can be used to reveal how the public sees the problem
and its responses to various specific aspects of proposed legislation—instead of using polls as a measure of winning and losing.
When public opinion is clearly uninformed, it shouldn't be
treated as important news.

• Assess the fairness and accuracy of policy-oriented ads, including who sponsors them, what issues are raised, and what the
agenda of the sponsor might be.

• Assume that public policy deliberations are a serious business that needs to be responsibly and fully reported and that not all of those involved are cynically promoting their own gain.

CHILDREN'S TELEVISION PILOTS. The Children's Television Act of 1990 mandated that starting September 1, 1997, every commercial broadcast television station in the United States broadcast at least three hours a week of educational and information programs designed specifically for children ages two to sixteen. Such a requirement was long sought by parents and children's advocates, but its implementation remains in doubt because of the paucity of high-quality children's programming.

The problems associated with children's television—particularly heavy viewing—often overshadow the medium's potential to enrich children's lives. Television can and does inspire and educate the developing mind, influence behavior and health habits, and provide positive role models. Programs geared to preschool children, such as *Sesame Street,* are popular with parents and children alike and have helped children become more academically successful than their nonviewing peers. But once children reach school age, good programs are few and far between. Although children ages six to eleven are still enamored with television, the shows available to them are entertainment-driven, action-oriented, and superhero-dominated. There are significant economic barriers to producing and broadcasting high-quality educational programming for this age group and little understanding of which programs will succeed.

The Foundation's goal for grant making in this area reflects a long-range approach to promoting health and well-being in the next generation. If the resulting programs become popular, they will help children lay a solid foundation for good decision making on health-related matters. By the time they are in their teenage years and faced with choices about smoking, drug use, and sexual activity—choices that could adversely affect their health throughout life—it may be too late to reach them.

The Robert Wood Johnson Foundation has funded two projects to develop pilot children's programs: one through a competitive project, administered by the Annenberg School for Communication at the University of Pennsylvania, to develop a series called *Young Heroes,* and one by the Judge Baker Children's Center in Boston. (The former grant also includes an effort to improve the measurement of young audiences. Experts believe many children are not counted with traditional audience rating methods. This makes the programs they watch less attractive to advertisers and, consequently, less financially viable.) The latter program, *Willoughby's Wonders,* which premiered as a half-hour pilot on WGBH in Boston, features the players on an urban kids' soccer team. It won two New England area Emmy Awards for "Outstanding Children's Special" and "Outstanding Individual Achievement in Directing." The Foundation now has awarded a second grant to the Judge Baker Children's Center for the development of a plan to extend *Willoughby's Wonders* to a thirteen-week series for PBS. It's too soon to predict whether either of these programs will achieve financial viability—and viewership.

COROLLARY PROJECTS. Exhibit 10.1 lists a number of corollary projects to the Foundation's broadcasting grants—a list that illustrates the growing complexity of the communications field. Funding a stand-alone broadcast program probably isn't a good investment. Over time, Foundation staff have learned that such a program may require a number of supporting activities. For one, it probably needs to have a strong promotion component in order to draw a large and interested audience. It may warrant accompanying print materials, so it can become a teaching tool in communities and schools. It may require outreach efforts to let communities discuss how the problems and approaches discussed play out locally. It probably needs a plan for additional, postbroadcast distribution to stakeholders, so its full value is reaped. And today, it may need a web site too.

A recent example of this full-court press is the program *Before I Die,* produced by the Fred Friendly organization as a Socratic-style dialog on issues of decision making near the end of life; it was broadcast in April and September 1997 in seventy-four cities. Because the program was intended to help promote a dialogue about what can be done at the community level to improve care of dying people, pre-broadcast meetings were held in some forty markets. These outreach meetings involved hospice professionals, other service providers, consumer advocates, emergency medical personnel, and interested citizens, who discussed the program and its local implications. The meetings also were intended to encourage the attending organizations' members and participants' colleagues to watch the program when it was broadcast, some three weeks later. In addition, advertisements for the program were run in major markets to encourage

viewing by the general public. A viewer's guide was widely distributed. Subsequently, PBS and the Foundation distributed video copies
of the program, along with a "tool kit" of activities that local chapters of consumer organizations, religious congregations, and professional groups could use. WNET established an interesting web site
rich with information and personal stories for *Before I Die*—a site
that enabled an unprecedented level of interactivity with program
audiences.

In most cases, the Foundation funds corollary projects for productions that have already received money; occasionally, it supports
these activities for an existing program, such as the Western Public
Radio grants for distribution of a series on alcohol abuse to colleges
and schools.

CONCLUSION

Virtually all philanthropic funding in the broadcast media goes to
public broadcasting—itself a creature of philanthropy, originating
from a seminal report by the Carnegie Commission in 1967. The experience is mixed. The programs are expensive and reach a small—but
presumably influential—audience. There are the almost inevitable tensions between journalistic independence and funders' interests. Sometimes documentaries take a glacially slow time to produce. Worse, as
the industry increasingly recognizes, public television stations do not
act like a network; just because PBS is feeding a program at a particular time, local stations across the country may not air it then, or ever.
Cost-effectively promoting the program nationwide is next to impossible. Guaranteed air time is elusive, except for the most notable series
and hosts. In short, public television really does not offer a news funding opportunity analogous to National Public Radio. But public radio
does not offer the prime-time special.

The alternative to working with public broadcasting is working
with commercial broadcasters. This has problems, too. It's costly, for
one. In the case of the NBC special on health care reform that The
Robert Wood Johnson Foundation funded, the Foundation worried
about its minimal input. Would a commercial network, with its different incentive structure and operating in real time, take shortcuts,
rely on analytic clichés, skim the surface? Would the show attract a big
enough audience to justify the Foundation's investment, and, if it did,
would it be worth watching?

Although grants for television and radio are a small percentage of the Foundation's total grant portfolio, in terms of what people see and hear that they associate with the Foundation and the issues it cares about, they are an important component. Including radio and television in the mixture of media funding is now an accepted way for the Foundation to do business. At the same time, the politics of health care have made its issues more interesting to producers and networks. The Foundation now receives more grant applications from producers, even though its funding is targeted to a relatively narrow range of health areas. Because of the media's importance in shaping issues, the Foundation continues to look for good funding opportunities, including some in cable television and other distribution systems. These hold the potential for reaching both new and very specific audiences. Despite the tensions that are inherent in the broadcaster-funder relationship, most of the Foundation's experience has reflected a healthy balance of interests.

Note

1. Not covered in this chapter are routine Foundation media relations activities, grants for nonbroadcast audio and video productions, and print media. Also not addressed in detail, but important to note, is another tack we have used in our grant making: trying to improve journalists' understanding of health care issues. More knowledgeable reporters and editors presumably will produce better stories. Our grants to community radio have included training sessions for stringers (freelance reporters) and seminars for grantees; the new local public radio grant program, *Sound Partners for Community Health,* includes grantee workshops on content and outreach; grants to the Radio and Television News Directors Foundation have attempted to improve local broadcast coverage of the changing health care system and end-of-life issues; and, finally, a new joint Peabody and Foundation broadcast media awards program will recognize good health care coverage and encourage additional reporting on health issues.

Ten Tips for Making Broadcasting Grants

1. Keep the lines of communication clear. Arrange for grant management issues to be addressed by, say, the development officers, news issues by the journalists.

2. Smaller media grantees will need proportionally more funding than large grantees to expand their news operations.

3. Help news outlets expand their reach by funding activities and public information campaigns that they see as part of a community mission.

4. Funding public television is comfortable for foundations, but it reaches only a small audience. Secondary distribution may increase the impact.

5. Production budgets that are augmented by promotion, advertising, print materials, outreach, secondary distribution, and evaluation are costly and need to be weighed against the number of viewers or listeners and the Foundation's programmatic goals.

6. A broad array of creative outreach activities and partnerships between broadcasters and community groups can increase the potential impact of broadcast investments. These relationships may not take a lot of money to nurture, but will require time.

7. Foundations like commitments to broadcast a program up front, but PBS resists.

8. Even supporting the most independent-minded producer does not insulate the funder from criticism in a highly politicized environment.

9. Radio is much less expensive than television, is particularly suited for certain audiences, and provides name recognition through constant repetition of underwriting announcements.

10. Useful measures of impact remain elusive—anecdotal and too particular to be generalizable or Nielsonian and too broad to be meaningful.

ৡৢৣ

Exhibit 10.1: RWJF Broadcasting Grants, 1987–1997.

	Original Grant Amount	Original Grant Period
Grants for News Coverage		
Television		
1 WGBH Educational Foundation[1]	$15,928,917	9/88–12/93
2 Rutgers University	93,105	2/92– 1/95
3 Foundation for New Jersey Public Broadcasting	100,000	1/94– 7/97
Radio		
4 National Public Radio[2]	4,571,163	1/87–10/99
5 Alaska Public Radio Network/Koahnic Broadcasting (National Native News)	674,154	5/91– 7/98
6 Radio Bilingüe	923,521	9/92– 8/98
7 Western Organization of Resource Councils (High Plains News Service)	210,000	5/93– 7/98
8 National Public Radio (health care reform project–Critical Choice)	236,396	9/94– 3/95
9 American Communications Foundation	224,452	2/95– 3/97
10 Radio Bilingüe—Coverage of flood emergency	6,000	4/95– 6/95
11 National Multiple Sclerosis Society (disability news service)	355,703	11/96–10/98
12 Sound Partners for Community Health	2,000,000	8/97– 7/02
Both Television and Radio		
13 Institute for the Arts of Democracy (American News Service)	351,228	1/97–12/98
Grants for Specific Productions		
Television		
14 RLP Incorporated (film on youth substance abuse)	426,788	5/91–10/01
15 Physicians' Association for AIDS Care	15,000	11/91–4/92
16 University of Wisconsin-Madison (town meeting on access to health care)	50,000	10/92–11/92
17 Appalshop (AIDS documentary)	25,660	11/92–12/92
18 American Re-Education Corporation (children's mental health documentary)	376,160	3/93–10/94
19 Educational Broadcasting Corp. (health system documentary)	150,000	5/93–10/93
20 Rock the Vote (health care reform specials for youth)	2,894,600	2/94– 1/95

✐

Exhibit 10.1. RWJF Broadcasting Grants, 1987–1997, *continued.*

	Original Grant Amount	Original Grant Period
Grants for Specific Productions		
Television (*continued*)		
21 National Broadcasting Co. (health reform special)	3,500,000	5/94– 4/95
22 Home Box Office (substance abuse television specials)	3,307,626	5/94– 4/95
23 Educational Broadcasting Corp. (health reform documentary)	400,000	8/94– 7/95
24 Educational Broadcasting Corp. (managed care documentary)	424,852	6/95–10/95
25 Caucus Educational Corp. (substance abuse-NJ youth series)	60,000	1/96–12/96
26 Judge Baker Children's Center (children's series pilot)	50,000	6/96– 5/97
27 Educational Broadcasting Corp. (end-of-life special)	639,705	8/96– 7/97
28 Public Affairs Television (addiction series)	4,380,107	11/96–5/98
29 University of Pennsylvania (children's series pilot)	169,000	1/97–12/97
30 Judge Baker Children's Center (planning for 3-part series)	99,733	11/97–2/98
Radio		
31 Kathy McAnally (rural health radio special)	38,750	5/94–11/94
32 Kathy McAnally (health care changes radio specials)	112,319	8/95– 7/97
Corollary Projects		
33 Hill & Knowlton, Inc. (advertising, placement of feature stories, and assessment for the *AIDS Quarterly*)	313,628	8/88– 9/89
34 Western Public Radio, Inc. (distribution of a series on alcohol abuse to college radio stations)	148,068	11/91–7/92
35 Public Agenda Foundation (local media campaigns re health care reform linked with a public television program)	250,000	3/92– 3/93
36 WETA (studio discussion of youth substance abuse program, promotion)	85,500	4/92– 9/93

JP

Exhibit 10.1. RWJF Broadcasting Grants, 1987–1997, *continued.*

	Original Grant Amount	Original Grant Period
Grants for Specific Productions		
Corollary Projects *(continued)*		
37 Continental Cablevision (distribution of public forums on health care reform)	18,000	6/93– 8/93
38 Western Public Radio, Inc. (nationwide public radio broadcast of program on preventing youth substance abuse and distribution of audio tapes to schools)	44,361	10/93–3/94
39 Western Public Radio, Inc. (additional distribution of substance abuse tapes to schools, based on strong response)	50,000	5/94– 7/94
40 U. of Pennsylvania-Annenberg School for Communications (health care reform media tracking project)	55,959	3/95– 7/95
41 Educational Broadcasting Corporation (expansion of WNET's world wide web site to support managed care documentary)	10,981	9/95–11/95
42 Educational Broadcasting Corporation (paid advertising for WNET's managed care documentary)	49,881	9/95–11/95
43 Hedrick Smith Productions, Inc. (educational outreach and promotion for programs on the tobacco lobby and health care policy)	150,000	7/96– 2/97
44 Barksdale Ballard & Co. (outreach to grassroots organizations around end-of-life special, *Before I Die*)	181,000	8/96– 7/97
45 Boston University School of Public Health (outreach to community coalitions around HBO substance abuse specials)	138,404	12/96–6/97
46 Cine Information, Inc. (print advertising for *Before I Die*)	491,758	4/97– 5/97
Total	**$44,782,479**	

[1]This project was terminated at the midway point of its final grant.
[2]Funding prior to 1987 totaled $171,388.

A Look Back

CHAPTER ELEVEN

⟿ Support of Nurse Practitioners and Physician Assistants

Terrance Keenan

Editors' Introduction

Since the Foundation began as a national philanthropy in 1972, it has given high priority to increasing access to medical care. Survey research in the 1970s revealed that Americans felt that having access to a physician was one of their most serious health needs. In its earliest programs, the Foundation tried to address this problem. Its very first grants were medical school scholarships for minorities, women, and students from rural areas—on the grounds that these people were likely to provide services to those with the least access. In succeeding years, the Foundation supported rural health initiatives, programs designed to bring services to inner cities, training of generalist physicians, and a host of other efforts designed to make physicians more accessible to patients.

The Foundation also recognized that increasing the availability of physicians, although important, was not the only answer to solving the problem of lack of access. Other health care professionals needed to be trained—particularly those thought to be more likely to work in underserved locations such as inner cities and rural areas.

Among those professionals were physician assistants and nurse practitioners. In the seventies, these professions were just becoming established, and federal funding for training was not yet available. In fact, there was some opposition from both the medical and the nursing communities to establishing a new category of health professional. The Foundation entered at a very opportune time and was able to boost the development of a new breed of health professionals. In time, nurse practitioners and physician assistants became recognized health care professionals, but when the Foundation initiated its support, both groups were in their infancy and it was not at all certain they would survive to maturity.

Terrance Keenan, who joined the Foundation in 1972 as a vice president, played a key role in shaping the development of programs that developed the fields of nurse practitioners and physician assistants. Now serving as a senior fellow with the Foundation, he tells the story of the early days of nurse practitioners and physician assistants.

Unlike the other chapters in this book, this chapter takes a look back. It offers the chance to reflect upon grant making done largely in the relatively distant past and to consider the lessons to be drawn from more than a quarter-century's experience.

From its inception as a national philanthropy in 1972, The Robert Wood Johnson Foundation has endeavored to establish nurse practitioners and physician assistants as part of the nation's professional workforce in patient care. The Foundation has pursued this goal with persistence, and staked both its hopes and money on a positive outcome. Why did the Foundation make this commitment? Why has this goal remained important to it for so long? A brief account of the Foundation's grant making record concerning nurse practitioners and physician assistants may provide some answers.

Sometimes referred to as "new health professionals" or "mid-level practitioners," members of these two professions have much in common. Working in concert with physicians, practitioners in both domains are qualified to take a complete patient history and give a physical exam; perform or order standard laboratory tests; recognize and interpret abnormal clinical findings; diagnose and treat common illnesses; and give appropriate emergency care. Although both can and do see patients without the presence of a physician (at rural and inner-city satellite clinics, for example), they must have formal arrangements for dependable physician backup and referral. Finally, both nurse practitioners and physician assistants are institutionally based. They are employees of hospitals, health centers, HMOs, and solo and group medical practices. These institutions charge for their services, but both nurse practitioners and physician assistants are salaried staff.

As for the differences between the two professions, physician assistants function within the context, the rules, and the norms of medical practice, whereas nurse practitioners define themselves as an integral part of the nursing profession. Physician assistants are licensed by state boards of medical examiners, and they practice under the auspices of physicians as members of a medical provider team. Nurse practitioners are equipped to assume advanced responsibilities analogous to the roles performed by certified nurse midwives, nurse anesthetists, and such clinical nurse specialties as critical care and neonatal intensive care. The scope of practice of nurse practitioners and, usually, their education and certification are defined by state boards of nursing. In some states, however, statutes call for joint regulation by both medical and nursing boards.

Although the differences between nurse practitioners and physician assistants may seem subtle, they have meant that two professions with similar functions could not emerge within a single structural framework but instead required separate and parallel structures and policies for their advancement—a fact that compounded the challenge to The Robert Wood Johnson Foundation in its effort to establish the professions.

The Foundation's emergence as a national philanthropy in the early 1970s occurred at a time when communities across America were losing their general practitioners to retirement and the demand for new doctors in primary care far exceeded the supply. One major Foundation response was a series of initiatives to rebuild the educational and practice infrastructure of primary care medical practice, particularly general internal medicine, pediatrics, and family medicine.

In a corresponding set of initiatives, the Foundation targeted the education and deployment of nurse practitioners and physician assistants. Evidence that nurse practitioners and physician assistants could perform, with equal competence, perhaps 80 percent of the tasks confronting physicians in office practice was a compelling factor in this decision. In addition, they could be prepared for practice in much less time and at a much lower cost than physicians—eighteen months to two years of formal professional training against at least six years for primary care physicians. Moreover, it seemed likely that nurse practitioners and physician assistants, in general, would find greater satisfaction than physicians for their work in underserved communities. Finally, the services rendered by these new providers were more affordable than the services of primary care physicians. In combination, these factors became powerful incentives for a commitment to establishing nurse practitioners and physician assistants as a cardinal feature of patient care in the United States.

MAKING A BEGINNING

The concept of nurse practitioner originated in the early 1960s, when a few physicians began to expand the clinical skills of their nurses and accept them as full partners in practice coverage. Formal training of nurse practitioners began in 1965 at the University of Colorado Health Sciences Center under a doctor-nurse team in pediatrics—Henry Silver and Loretta Ford. Supported principally by the Commonwealth

Fund, this program helped to define the nurse practitioner's functions, relationships with physicians, and the essentials of effective education.

The role of physician assistant had roots in part in the medical corpsmen of the military, many of whom subsequently trained for civilian service in the Medex programs established by such eminent academic health sciences centers as the University of Washington, Seattle. However, the acknowledged pioneer in thinking of physician assistants as a key primary care profession—and in providing educational and practice leadership for its emergence—was the late Dr. Eugene Stead of Duke University. This program, brought to fruition by Dr. Harvey Estes of Duke's Department of Family Practice, has served from its outset as a model of excellence nationwide.

By 1972, when The Robert Wood Johnson Foundation became a national philanthropy, the viability of nurse practitioners and physician assistants as recognized health professionals had thus been tested to some degree. Even so, what was known about these two fields, however promising they seemed, was hardly sufficient to justify the Foundation's vision for their future. There was widespread opposition, from within both organized medicine and the professional nursing establishment. Medical education (as opposed to organized medicine itself) was relatively accepting, and even supportive, of the idea, but nursing education was not. Indeed, the great majority of America's nursing deans were outraged. The issues were largely ideological, and therefore quite volatile and difficult to contest. To many physicians, the concept of the new professionals meant authorizing unprepared and unlicensed medical practice. To many nurses, the concept meant that the nurses would become "physician extenders," and that the profession would lose ground in its struggle to escape subordination to medicine.

Professional resistance to the introduction of the new health professions foreclosed engagement by the federal government and the states. This did not change until the advent of the 1980s.

It might have seemed reasonable to expect that the Foundation, as a new national philanthropy, would be circumspect about addressing controversial issues. But in this case two things argued against that sort of caution. First, the logic of using the two professional fields to expand primary care was intrinsically convincing. Second, several of the staff members had come from funding or service institutions— the Carnegie Corporation, the Commonwealth Fund, Yale—that had participated in the birth of the new professions, and in the face of considerable odds had nurtured them through their infancy. The Robert Wood Johnson Foundation, they believed, could be instrumental in helping the new professions develop into thriving fields. They did not realize at first how difficult this journey would be, or how long it would take.

FROM EXPERIMENTS TO REALITY

The Foundation's first major thrust consisted of a series of regional demonstrations focused on the in-service training and deployment of nurse practitioners. (The physician assistant profession did not lend itself to in-service training and, early in its history, adopted a quite different and more formal educational strategy.) These five multisite networks, devoted to building physician-nurse practitioner teams, were intended to move these fields from an experimental, single-site stage to patient-care networks covering many sites.

University of California, Davis

This university provided an environment for demonstrating how a new type of professional could help rural America prevent the decline of its patient care. First, Davis was a land-grant institution that embodied the tradition of community service. Second, the University was the home of a new medical school specifically established to attract and train physicians for practice in rural Northern and Central California. Third, to serve as the prime mover of this mission, Dr. Len Hughes Andrus was recruited from private practice to head the school's Department of Family Practice. Andrus had the trust of the physician community and a sure understanding of the potential of office nurses in sharing the burdens of rural practice.

Together with two nurses—Mary O'Hara-Devereaux and Leona Judson—Andrus quickly organized a training program for family nurse practitioners as an integral component of the department. Over the next several years, this group established a network of primary care practices made up of nurse-physician teams that served locations ranging from small coastal fishing villages to remote mountain valleys. The nurse practitioners were recruited directly from practice, and received instruction at regional hospitals under the direction of circuit-riding faculty from Davis. They then completed their clinical education under physicians in their home towns (often their employers) whom Davis trained and qualified as preceptors.

Davis expanded further by collaborating with an established physician assistant program at Stanford University. Stanford—perhaps the epitome of research-based academic health science centers—had organized a medical residency in family practice in affiliation with several Central California community hospitals. Using this base, Stanford also formed an alliance with a number of California community colleges to establish a physician assistant program. The ingenuity of these measures matched those of the Davis initiative, and the two faculties in family practice came together in the nation's only program to train nurse practitioners and physician assistants as colleagues.

Utah Valley Hospital, Provo

In the annals of American philanthropy, the Utah Valley Hospital—at Provo, just south of Salt Lake City—has landmark significance. It was one of a dozen or so model community hospitals established by the Commonwealth Fund in the 1930s. The governance, the administration, and the staffing of these institutions became the blueprint for the Hill-Burton legislation enacted by Congress in 1948.

For the small towns scattered across Utah, however, the Hospital's standing as an exemplary community institution had no special meaning. These remote towns—many founded by Mormon pioneers—had no doctors, no nurses, and no ready access to health care. The residents were poor but by no means impoverished. Their land was arable, and was kept productive by irrigation. The men were good hunters and tracked game in the desert hills. People were self-sufficient. They survived by thrift, hard work, and a disciplined love for their families and for one another. With the nearest doctor as distant as two hundred miles, there was no way to manage a medical crisis. For generations, these communities had endured a heavy burden of suffering from illness and injury.

This began to change for the better during the 1970s, when the Utah Valley Hospital administration and medical staff organized a network of rural clinics. Based in the hospital's emergency department, the system consisted of local facilities built by the communities and staffed by family nurse practitioners recruited, trained, and deployed by the department. The nurses were experienced professionals who were eager to assume a new level of responsibility for patient care. Around-the-clock backup support was provided by emergency department physicians. Twice weekly, and sometimes at considerable risk, physicians piloted their own planes to the sites to see patients who, in the nurses' judgment, required their attention.

Tuskegee Institute

Founded by Booker T. Washington, the Tuskegee Institute in Tuskegee, Alabama, offers young African-Americans across the rural South an opportunity for higher education. The town is also the home of a Veterans Administration hospital, which for many years enabled Tuskegee to attract a physician staff of sufficient size to operate a small community hospital—the John A. Andrew Memorial Hospital.

Under the leadership of Dr. Cornelius Hopper, this community institution became the base for a three-county rural health system employing state-of-the-art communications technology. Local citizens who were trusted and respected throughout their neighborhoods were recruited and trained by Tuskegee to serve as health aides. Stationed in churches and other local institutions, the aides identified people who needed care and scheduled them for visits by a provider team from the Tuskegee-based hospital.

The team traveled to the sites in a specially designed mobile van staffed by a Tuskegee-trained nurse practitioner and a laboratory technician, who doubled as a van driver. The van was outfitted as a mobile medical office, and was linked to its Tuskegee base by phone and fax. This enabled the nurses to communicate readily with Tuskegee physicians, who could fax signed prescriptions and medical information immediately to the vans.

This project died after reductions in federal health spending that began in the 1980s, but it stands as a prototype for the delivery of rural health services that has great potential, especially in the light of the advances that have been made in electronic communications.

Frontier Nursing Service, Hyden, Kentucky

In 1925, deep in the mountainous terrain of East Kentucky, Mary Breckenridge founded this country's first training and service program in nurse midwifery. Headquartered in Wendover, where she made her home, and using a primitive community hospital in nearby Hyden, the program became renowned as the Frontier Nursing Service, or FNS. The FNS was dedicated to the needs of women and families trapped in a culture of social isolation, and it emerged as a cause among women leaders nationwide. Those who came to the FNS school for training and service were characterized not only by their idealism but also by their stamina and courage. The FNS nurses, stationed in a far-flung network of clinics, visited their patients on horseback—summoned at all hours, braving any weather. Their impact is beyond dispute. The calamitous infant mortality rates of the remote area they served fell dramatically, and in time, the statistics were among the best in the country.

Although FNS nurses had long provided care for all age groups in the families they visited, their training was focused largely on maternity and newborn care. With the advent of the nurse practitioner movement, the FNS decided that it would be advantageous for its staff and students to have dual training as family nurse practitioners. The Robert Wood Johnson Foundation provided funding to the FNS to develop a curriculum, which was used to train family nurse practitioners. FNS nurses are still stationed in a dispersed clinic network, but the use of jeeps and telephone and radio communications has made their work easier. Also, the FNS now has a new and modern hospital, which has increased the availability of physicians to back up the nurses.

University of Tennessee Medical Center, Memphis

The Department of Community Medicine, at the University of Tennessee College of Medicine, in Memphis, has a demonstrated ability to attract and hold top clinical faculty. It was built by a visionary chairman, Dr. John Runyon, who believed that the department should function as a community-based clinical service. Not only did the department set out to define community health problems such as hypertension, it also set out to solve them. Concern over these problems prompted Runyon and his colleagues to help initiate a large network of primary care clinics that targeted the city's large African-American community.

This system was a collaborative venture among the medical school, the Memphis City Hospital, and the Memphis-Shelby County Health Department. It consisted of a strategically placed set of comprehensive community health centers, each responsible for a cluster of satellite neighborhood clinics staffed by carefully trained nurse practitioners. The system was coordinated through a central command post based at the hospital. For example, nurses at the satellite posts promptly reported referral requests that had come into their area centers to the central command center. If the referral was not completed in a timely way, corrective action was taken. Managerial steps of this kind assured that this complex urban provider network would remain responsive to the needs of the front-line nurses.

IMPACT ON THE FOUNDATION'S PROGRAMMING

The Foundation's experience in the 1970s with these five nurse-based community health networks affirmed its confidence that nurse practitioners could play a vital role in the nation's health care, and the Foundation proceeded to promote this role in two areas of special need—emergency services and school health services.

In the first area, the Foundation recognized that emergency department nurses, especially in small rural hospitals, confronted a relentless load of nonemergency health problems. People with all manner of complaints came to emergency rooms. Doctors were rarely there, as they were usually local practitioners on rotating coverage. Thus, nurses had to solve the problems that patients presented.

To equip rural emergency nurses more fully for this responsibility, at the close of the 1980s the Foundation established a multisite program to give them training in primary care. The program was headed by Mildred Fink, nursing director of Allegheny General Hospital in Pittsburgh, which became a regional training site for the area's rural hospitals. Other sites included Herman Hospital in Houston; Maricopa General Hospital in Phoenix; Good Samaritan Hospital in Portland, Oregon; Nebraska Methodist Hospital in Omaha; and the University of Alabama Medical Center in Birmingham.

Each site developed a rigorous curriculum in the basic sciences as well as in clinical reasoning and procedure. Students were enthusiastic about the opportunity for professional growth and learning, but the program failed to find a niche in the health care labor market. It was a casualty not only of hospital cost cutting but also of the hostility of academic nursing, which had no interest in its success.

In school nursing in the early 1980s, the Foundation initiated a training program to enable nurses in elementary schools to provide on-site primary care. The program encompassed thirty-six school districts enrolling 37,000 children in four states—Colorado, New York, North Dakota, and Utah. The program was directed by Catherine DeAngelis, a pediatrician with a prior career in nursing. This program was successful as an experiment, but it, too, was a market failure. Costs were higher than school districts were willing to pay, and (with the sole exception of the University of Colorado) the innovation was shunned by academic nursing. In the mid-1980s and into the nineties, the Foundation resumed its investment in nursing in the public schools—this time targeting adolescents.

CONFRONTING ACADEMIC NURSING

In part because of the apparent success of the regional training and demonstration programs for nurse practitioners, the Foundation was slow to think strategically about how to promote the concept over the long run. The failure of its efforts in emergency care and school health were disappointments that prompted the staff to reconsider the strategy it was pursuing.

What was missing was an authentic educational infrastructure. The Foundation's initial approach was to retrain the existing registered nurse workforce for expanded clinical roles through the engagement and support of physicians. The approach worked, but only in part. It did not enlist the educational and intellectual base of nursing—did not call upon the scientific and scholarly leadership of the profession. The nurse practitioner field, in fact, had no professional home— nowhere to grow a faculty of its own. If it had a future, that future was most uncertain.

When the Foundation made this discovery, it shifted its strategy from in-service training and continuing education to an effort to build clinical primary care nursing into the heart of advanced graduate education in the profession. The change required that the Foundation enlist the participation of academic nursing—especially of nursing deans. Most of them responded negatively.

Yet a handful of leaders on graduate nursing faculties envisioned primary care as an important new scholarly and practice discipline of nursing; they had been trained as nurse practitioners and were emerging as thinkers in this evolving area. They espoused the Foundation's cause and became its allies within academic nursing. This group included, among others, Claire Fagin at the University of Pennsylvania, Ingeborg Mauksch at the University of Missouri at Columbia, Loretta Ford, who had moved from Colorado to Rochester University, and Rheba de Tornyay at the University of Washington (who in 1990 became the Foundation's first female trustee). With their counsel and that of their colleagues, the Foundation made a series of grants to establish new master's-level programs in several primary care domains (adult nursing, pediatric nursing, family nursing) at a number of universities. The recipients included the universities of Indiana, Pace, Pennsylvania, Rochester, Seton Hall, and Washington.

Although these graduate programs did become thriving enterprises that helped win acceptance of the nurse practitioner concept among the profession's academic élite, the Foundation soon realized that the concept could not establish an educational base without qualified faculty members. Recognition of this need led the Foundation to establish the Nurse Faculty Fellowships in Primary Care. The program proved to be a timely initiative that had first-rate leadership. Ingeborg Mauksch served as program director, and Loretta Ford was chairwoman of the program advisory committee. The fellows received their training at one of four university nursing schools—Colorado, Indiana, Maryland, and Rochester. Over five years—1977–82—ninety-nine outstanding young faculty members completed the fellowships, and as a group they made a decisive difference in the ability of nursing education to secure the future of the nurse practitioner field.

Despite its satisfaction with the program and its pride in the fellows, in the final years of the initiative the Foundation's vision for nurse practitioners began to wane. Almost out of nowhere, questions surfaced about the projected demand for nurse practitioners in the health care marketplace. A wave of doubt caused the Foundation to falter, and the fellowships were not continued beyond 1982. No one at the Foundation could predict that in a few years, nurse practitioners would be serving as the cornerstone for a system of adolescent health care based in the public schools. Nor was it foreseen that in the mid-1990s the Foundation would be fostering programs for the joint training of nurse practitioners and physician assistants from defined geographic regions—initiatives similar to the Davis-Stanford project it had funded twenty years before.

PHYSICIAN ASSISTANTS:
BLUEPRINT FOR A NEW PROFESSION

The physician assistant profession emerged more clearly than did the nurse practitioner field. In its early days, its membership established a group to assure professional standards and accountability—the American Academy of Physician Assistants. Similarly, training facilities formed the Association of Physician Assistant Programs as a national accrediting body to guarantee consistency of curricula and educational performance. In addition, a national certification examination was established under the auspices of the National Board of Medical Examiners to establish a level of competence for entry into the profession.

The Robert Wood Johnson Foundation provided startup funding for these efforts. However, although they helped define performance and training standards of the profession, the physician assistant field still faced contention and challenges. State and local medical societies feared the advent of the physician assistant concept, and for years blocked the new profession in several states through their control of state licensing laws. Nevertheless, the profession has prevailed in every state except Mississippi. This is in no small measure due to the fact that a number of preeminent academic medical centers—notably Duke, Stanford, and Yale—took part in the formation of the field.

Although a significant proportion of current training programs—about a fourth of them—are offered at the master's level, physician assistant education has emerged largely as an undergraduate professional major. In the mid-1970s, the Foundation helped to create two early models for this development. The first—which had been funded initially by the Commonwealth Fund—was based at Alderson-Broadus College in Phillipi, West Virginia. The college had a number of features that made it a logical place to undertake this innovation. First, it was the site of a community hospital, so the program had a clinical home. Second, the hospital's key staff was made up of physicians from a multispecialty group practice, the Myers Clinic, in Phillipi. Finally, Hu Myers, chief of the clinic, was a person of exceptional standing and vision. His commitment to physician assistants as first-line providers facilitated the acceptance of the concept by the state and local medical community.

Lake Erie College, in Painesville, Ohio—site of the second program to create an undergraduate professional major with Foundation assistance—had attributes comparable to those of Alderson-Broadus. A small institution for women, it forged a professional training base in health by joining with the nearby Cleveland Clinic. Although the clinic was an acclaimed specialty referral center, it was assuming increasing responsibility for primary care in its community. Physician assistants were seen as a way of helping the clinic fulfill this role. In partnership with Lake Erie College, it initiated a superb program.

Two other model projects funded by the Foundation were intended to train first-line practitioners capable of assuming an expanded level of physician delegation. One project, as noted earlier, was initiated by Henry Silver at the University of Colorado, who (with Loretta Ford) had established the country's first formal nurse practitioner training program. Known as Child Health Advocates, graduates of this new program were especially well equipped for practice in medically underserved areas, which included much of the American hinterland. The program remained small, however, and was not replicated by other universities.

The second advanced-level program financed by the Foundation was designed to train a group known as physician associates. The project was initiated by Johns Hopkins University, which established the School of Health Services as a new academic entity for this purpose. A talented faculty was recruited to launch the school. Leadership included Malcolm Peterson and Archie Golden, members of a young physician team engaging the university in service innovations. On the strength of the apparent commitment from Johns Hopkins, the Foundation invested heavily in this enterprise, but when economic adversity confronted the university its commitment collapsed, and soon after so did the school.

Clearly, the Foundation could have renewed its support and assured the school's survival for a further period. However, it faced the decision that sooner or later confronts every source of venture capital—to continue its funding or not. It elected to cut its losses.

As is evident in the Foundation's history of investing in the development of nurse practitioners and physician assistants, the two fields have simply coexisted and done almost nothing to help each other succeed. True, this observation does not apply to most individual practice sites, where collegiality has a palpable and necessary presence. But it is a characteristic of professional education where there is an immense distance between the faculty of the two fields—and thus no strategic activity to bring them together as a united force working to expand access to patient care services.

To help the professions surmount this structural impasse, the Foundation undertook a six-year program, Partnerships for Training, in 1995. The idea was to build collaborative regional networks among providers and develop training programs that would build a strong areawide workforce in primary care. Twelve planning grants and as many as eight implementation grants were authorized. By the end of 1997, three implementation grants had been made—to the University of Colorado, University of Minnesota, and University of Wisconsin. The networks include certified nurse midwives as well as nurse practitioners and physician assistants. Students are to be recruited locally, and that should help ensure their long-term retention as regional providers. The program is administered by the Association of Academic Health Centers under the direction of Jean Johnson-Paulson, an accomplished nurse clinician who is associate dean of the George Washington University School of Medicine.

REMAINING CHALLENGES

Over the twenty-five years of its investment in the potential of nurse practitioners and physician assistants, the Foundation has done much to help bring about the progress these fields have made. With the exception of Mississippi, which still does not authorize physician assistants, these new professionals are licensed by all states. Rapid headway is also being made among the states on breaching such remaining barriers as permission to write prescriptions.

Some 24,000 nurse practitioners are now at work, and 28,000 physician assistants have been trained and deployed. Further, an educational infrastructure of two hundred nurse practitioner programs and sixty programs for physician assistants is in place.

Although only about half of each group works in primary care settings, this is still a combined workforce of 25,000 new professionals— a resource equivalent to 12.5 percent of the 200,000 physicians in primary care fields.

The Foundation's early interventions helped to make it safe for the federal government and the states to encourage and fund the nurse practitioner and physician assistance professions. The United States Bureau of Health Professions has played a pivotal role in financing the educational infrastructure these fields have developed.

After twenty-five years of engagement, what lessons have been learned?

First, medical specialities and in-patient practice compete with primary care for the services of nurse practitioners and physician assistants. Surgical specialties attract many of them and hospitals also seek to substitute them for resident physicians.

Second, the geographic distribution of these new professions is governed by their employment base. Inner-city and rural areas have limited health care resources and few jobs for health care professionals. Notwithstanding these limitations, nurse practitioners and physician assistants offer an important resource for undertaking health service initiatives targeted on underserved and at-risk populations. That is the purpose of the regional care networks being instituted under the Foundation's Partnerships in Training Program authorized in 1995.

At-risk population groups in the United States, including the elderly and working poor, are growing. Issues of financing, including health insurance, are dominating the emerging public policy debate surrounding this phenomenon. Ultimately, however, the challenge will be to develop and bring to scale an effective and economical system for assuring health and medical services for these groups. Nurse practitioners and physician assistants are a key to building the workforce called for by this challenge.

⎯ᴧᴧᴧ⎯ The Editors

Stephen L. Isaacs, J.D., is the president of the Center for Health and Social Policy in San Francisco, California. A former professor of public health at Columbia University and founding director of its Development Law and Policy Program, Isaacs has written extensively for professional and popular audiences. His book *The Consumer's Legal Guide to Today's Health Care* was reviewed as "the single best guide to the health care system in print today"; his articles have been widely syndicated and have appeared in law reviews and health policy journals. He also provides technical assistance internationally on health law, civil society, and social policy. A graduate of Columbia Law School and Brown University, Isaacs served as vice president of International Planned Parenthood's Latin American division, practiced health law, and spent four years in Thailand as a program officer for the U.S. Agency for International Development. He serves on the Advisory Council of the National Institute of Child Health and Human Development, the Advisory Board of Women's Rights Project of Human Rights Watch, and the board of trustees of the Royce mutual funds.

James R. Knickman, Ph.D., is vice president for research and evaluation at The Robert Wood Johnson Foundation. Prior to joining the Foundation in October 1992, he was a professor of health administration at New York University's Robert Wagner Graduate School of Public Service. He has published extensively on a range of health care issues and done research on insurance markets and health care reimbursement systems, with particular attention to long-term care services. He also has written about methods for improving health services for urban, vulnerable populations such as the homeless, the frail elderly, and individuals with HIV illness. Knickman has served on a range of state government, local government, and health care sector advisory committees and has offered consultation to numerous health sector organizations. Currently, he serves on the board of trustees of

231

the Robert Wood Johnson University Hospital. He received his doctorate in public policy analysis from the University of Pennsylvania and did undergraduate work at Fordham University.

~~~ The Contributors

David G. Altman, Ph.D., is a professor of public health sciences at the Wake Forest University School of Medicine. He currently serves as national program director of the Substance Abuse Policy Research Program and is past president of Stop Teenage Addiction to Tobacco (STAT). Over the years, he has conducted a variety of studies in community health promotion. He is a fellow of the American Psychological Association and the Society of Behavioral Medicine; in 1997 he was selected as a Fellow of the W. K. Kellogg Foundation National Leadership Program. Altman is also a member of the American Public Health Association, the Council on Epidemiology and Prevention of the American Heart Association, and the Society of Public Health Education. Before arriving at Wake Forest University in 1994, he spent ten years at the Stanford Center for Research in Disease Prevention, Stanford University School of Medicine.

Terri Gibbs Appel, M.P.H., is a former program officer at The Robert Wood Johnson Foundation. Before joining the Foundation, she served as the director of the managed care program at St. Vincent's Hospital and Medical Center, the director of corporate and regulatory affairs for the Metropolitan Health Plan/HMO, and as a senior management consultant in Ambulatory Care Services at the New York City Health and Hospitals Corporation. She has provided volunteer services in a number of arenas, including religious education, teen health education, and AIDS service. Her volunteer activities have continued in Asia, where she is currently living, through a teen health counseling program. Appel received a B.A. from Dartmouth College and an M.P.H. in health policy and management from Columbia University.

Theodore P. Cross, Ph.D., is a senior research associate at the Family and Children's Policy Center, Heller School, Brandeis University, and an adjunct professor in the department of psychology at Brandeis. He was the coprincipal investigator of the evaluation of The Robert Wood Johnson Foundation's Mental Health Services Program for Youth. His research interests include the development of children's mental health services and the institutional response to child abuse. Trained as a clinical psychologist, Cross also consults on program evaluation and maintains a small private practice in child therapy.

Marjorie A. Gutman, Ph.D., is the director of prevention research at the Treatment Research Institute at the University of Pennsylvania. In addition, she is the codirector of the Substance Abuse Policy Research Program and, as a special consultant to The Robert Wood Johnson Foundation, assists with the oversight of two other national programs on substance abuse prevention. Gutman's research and grant making has been devoted to health promotion and disease prevention, particularly with adolescents and high-risk behaviors. She was a senior program officer at the Foundation for nine years. Before coming to the Foundation in 1988, Gutman was a consultant on evaluation to the New Jersey Health Department and spent seven years conducting prevention research at the State University of New York Health Services Center in Brooklyn. She serves on the editorial advisory board for a newsletter on substance abuse produced by the Association for Health Services Research, and is a member of the United Way Task Force on Outcomes, the American Public Health Association, and the Association for Health Services Research.

Jonathan Howland, Ph.D., is a professor at the Boston University School of Public Health. He is currently conducting clinical trials on an intervention to reduce fear of falling among the elderly; an interactive-video intervention to reduce new infections among patients in an inner-city clinic for sexually transmitted diseases; and a study on the effects of low-level alcohol exposure and hangovers on commercial ship handling. His research interests include injury epidemiology and the development and evaluation of behavioral interventions for public health problems. Howland is the director of the Health and Housing Fellows programs, a project that places returned Peace Corps volunteers at public housing developments where they live and work while they matriculate through the School of Public Health.

Robert G. Hughes, Ph.D., is a vice president of The Robert Wood Johnson Foundation. His interests are in the areas of health policy research, philanthropy and social change, and children's health insurance coverage. His responsibilities within the Foundation have included the Tobacco Policy Research and Evaluation Program, the Investigator Awards in Health Policy Research Program, the Substance Abuse Policy Research Program, and the Health Tracking Initiative. Between 1991 and 1994, he was the convener of the "substance abuse working group," the staff committee charged with developing and reviewing substance abuse programs. Hughes came to the Foundation from Arizona State University where he was an assistant professor in the School of Health Administration and Policy. He received his Ph.D. from the Department of Behavioral Sciences, Johns Hopkins School of Hygiene and Public Health, and was a Pew postdoctoral fellow at the University of California, San Francisco.

Paul Jellinek, Ph.D., is a vice president at The Robert Wood Johnson Foundation. Since joining the Foundation staff in 1983, he has been involved in developing and managing programs to improve access to health care, reduce the harm from substance abuse, and improve the organization and delivery of chronic care services. He has a particular interest in developing programs to strengthen community capacity and volunteerism, including the Faith in Action program. A former fellow at the Bush Institute for Child and Family Policy in North Carolina, his articles have appeared in the *New England Journal of Medicine, American Journal of Public Health,* and *Issues in Science and Technology.* Jellinek received a Ph.D. in health economics and a master's degree in health administration from the School of Public Health at the University of North Carolina at Chapel Hill. He is a graduate of the University of Pennsylvania and the University of South Florida.

Terrance Keenan is a senior program consultant at The Robert Wood Johnson Foundation, where he joined the staff in 1972 as one of the founding Foundation vice presidents. He was a senior program associate at the Commonwealth Fund between 1965 and 1972. Before that, he was a writer for the Ford Foundation and head of its office of reports. Prior to his career in health philanthropy, he worked at Merrill Lynch in New York City writing the biography of its founder, the late Charles E. Merrill, and taught secondary school in St. Louis. He is a graduate of Yale University.

Leonard Koppett has been a sports journalist for fifty-five years, and has been named to the writers' wing of both the Baseball and Basketball Halls of Fame. He has worked for numerous newspapers, including the *Herald Tribune, The New York Post, The New York Times,* and *The Sporting News* as a contributing writer, columnist, and an editor. Koppett has taught journalism-related courses at Stanford University and San Jose State University. The author of twelve books, most of them about baseball, his most popular include *A Thinking Man's Guide to Baseball, 24 Seconds to Shoot (An Informal History of the National Basketball Association),* and *Sports Illusion, Sports Reality;* his most recent is *Koppett's Concise History of Major League Baseball.*

Marianne Lee, M.P.A., is a consultant with the JSI Research and Training Institute. She has been the project manager for a series of alcohol studies at the Harvard School of Public Health, including the worksite alcohol study and the college alcohol study, funded by The Robert Wood Johnson Foundation and the National Institute for Alcoholism and Alcohol Abuse. Previously she was the executive director for the Massachusetts Governor's Alliance Against Drugs, a statewide alcohol and drug prevention education program for school-aged children. Lee is a graduate of the Kennedy School of Government at Harvard.

Lisa Lopez is a health care writer and an editorial consultant. As a journalist for twelve years, she has covered a broad range of health care issues, including primary and preventive health care, the elderly and chronically ill, community health, and Latino health care issues. While an editor with *Business & Health* magazine in the 1980s, she expanded the publication's coverage to include emerging concerns such as health care access and maternal and child care. A former managing editor of *HMO Magazine* (now *Healthplan*), Lopez coauthored the book *Managed Care Strategies 1997: An Annual Report on the Latest Practices and Policies in the New Managed Care Environment.* She is a graduate of the Ohio University School of Journalism.

Thomas W. Mangione, Ph.D., is a senior research scientist at JSI Research and Training Institute, Inc. He is currently directing a comparative study of behavioral and lifestyle risk factors of two areas within the city of Newton, Massachusetts, with dramatically different breast cancer rates. Mangione has previously directed studies relating to alcohol and drug treatment outcomes, AIDS risk behaviors, and domestic violence, and has provided technical assistance to studies focusing on managed care systems, community health needs assessments, alcohol use, and AIDS needs assessments. In addition to his research efforts, he currently teaches a course in survey research methodology at both the Boston University and Harvard University Schools of Public Health. He was a senior research fellow at the University of Massachusetts Center for Survey Research, and has authored several articles and two books on survey research methodology. Mangione obtained his Ph.D. in organizational psychology from the University of Michigan in 1973.

Barbara Norrish, M.S.N., is a student in the doctoral program in health services and policy analysis at the University of California, Berkeley, and is a part-time faculty member in the graduate nursing program at California State University, Dominguez Hills. She has a particular interest in the impact of hospital restructuring on the work of registered nurses, the subject of her dissertation. Norrish is a former assistant director of nursing in Michigan and California, with over ten years of experience in clinical practice, including five years as a specialist in cardiovascular nursing. She received a Master's of Science in Nursing from Wayne State University.

Robert L. Rabin, J.D., Ph.D., is the A. Calder Mackay Professor of Law at Stanford Law School. He was program director of the Tobacco Policy Research and Evaluation Program, and is currently a senior program consultant to the Foundation's Substance Abuse Policy Research Program. Rabin served as reporter for the ABA Action Commission to Improve the Tort System and as associate reporter of the American Law Institute study, Enterprise Liability for Personal Injury. He has published many books and articles in the areas of tort law and regulatory policy, including the coauthored work *Smoking Policy: Law, Politics and Culture.*

Richard Reynolds, M.D., is Courtesy Professor of Medicine at the University of Florida College of Medicine. In his previous role as executive vice president at The Robert Wood Johnson Foundation, he participated in the development and oversight of several programs in medical education. He is a former dean of The Robert Wood Johnson Medical School and a senior vice president for academic affairs at the University of Medicine and Dentistry at New Jersey. Previously, while a faculty member at the University of Florida, he helped to initiate a program in general internal medicine and became the founding Chairman of the Department of Community Health and Family Medicine. He has coedited two books, *Health of a Rural County* and *On Doctoring.* Trained as an internist, he first practiced in a small city in western Maryland.

Thomas G. Rundall, Ph.D., is professor of health policy and management in the School of Public Health, the director of the graduate program in health services management, and the founding director of the Center for Health Management Studies at the University of California, Berkeley. Before joining the Berkeley faculty in 1980, he taught for four years in the Sloan program in health services administration at Cornell University. Rundall is a nationally recognized scholar in health services research. An elected fellow of the Association for Health Services Research, he has been a Robert Wood Johnson Foundation Health Policy Fellow. He served as editor of *Medical Care Review,* a leading journal in the field of health services research. Rundall received his Ph.D. in sociology from Stanford University.

Lewis G. Sandy, M.D., is the executive vice president of The Robert Wood Johnson Foundation, where he oversees the activities of program staff and is responsible for strategic planning and administrative operations. Between 1991 and 1996, Sandy was a vice president of the Foundation. Sandy has been active in the Foundation's workforce initiatives, its efforts to track the changing health care system, its programs to improve services for chronically ill people, and its programs to improve managed care. An internist and former health center medical director at the Harvard Community Health Plan in Boston, Massachusetts, Sandy received his B.S. and M.D. degrees from the University of Michigan and an M.B.A. degree from Stanford University. A former Robert Wood Johnson Foundation Clinical Scholar and Clinical Fellow in Medicine at the University of California, San Francisco, Sandy served his internship and residency at the Beth Israel Hospital in Boston. He continues to practice and teach at the University of Medicine and Dentistry of New Jersey/Robert Wood Johnson Medical School where he is an associate clinical professor of medicine.

Leonard Saxe, Ph.D., is a professor of psychology at the Graduate School and University Center of the City University of New York and an adjunct professor of social welfare at the Heller School of Brandeis University. A social psychologist whose work focuses on human behavior and social policy, Saxe's research has included studies of drug, alcohol, and mental health treatment for adults and children, as well as the evaluation of community prevention programs. He served as a Congressional Science Fellow at the Office of Technology Assessment (OTA) and has authored several OTA studies, including *The Effectiveness and Costs of Alcoholism Treatment* and *Children's Mental Health.* He has written or edited more than one hundred publications. Saxe is a recipient of the American Psychological Association's prize for Distinguished Contributions to Psychology in the Public Interest, Early Career.

Steven A. Schroeder, M.D., is president of The Robert Wood Johnson Foundation. A graduate of Stanford University and Harvard Medical School, Schroeder trained in internal medicine at the Harvard Medical Service of the Boston City Hospital, in epidemiology as a member of the Epidemic Intelligence Service of the Communicable Diseases Center, and in public health at the Harvard Center for Community Health and Medical Care. He served as an instructor in medicine at Harvard, assistant and associate professor of medicine and health care sciences at George Washington University, and associate professor and professor of medicine at the University of California, San Francisco (UCSF). At both George Washington and UCSF he was founding medical director of a university-sponsored health maintenance organization, and at UCSF he founded its Division of General Internal Medicine. Schroeder continues to practice general internal medicine on a part-time basis at The Robert Wood Johnson Medical School. He has more than two hundred publications to his credit and has served on a number of editorial boards, including—at present—the *New England Journal of Medicine.* He received honorary doctorates from Rush University, Boston University, and the University of Massachusetts.

David B. Starkweather, Dr.P.H., is professor emeritus of health services management at the School of Public Health at the University of California, Berkeley. In 1995, he received the Berkeley Citation, the highest award granted a university professor for teaching, research, and professional contributions. Starkweather has had a long-standing interest in patient-centered hospital reorganization. For eight years, he was in the administration of the Stanford University Hospital, eventually serving as the hospital's director. He joined the faculty at the University of California, Berkeley, in 1968 and, subsequently, founded the graduate program in health services management, the first joint M.B.A./M.P.H. curriculum in the country. Starkweather served as chairman of the Accrediting Commission for Education in Health Services Administration, and for twelve years was a hospital trustee and director of a multihospital system in northern California.

Victoria D. Weisfeld, B.A., M.P.H., is a senior communications officer at The Robert Wood Johnson Foundation. Weisfeld is responsible for a wide range of communications activities, including dissemination of the findings of SUPPORT (the Study to Understand Prognosis and Preferences for Outcomes and Risks of Treatment) and development of the Foundation's gopher and World Wide Web site. She served three terms on the Communications Committee of the Council on Foundations and is past president of the Communications Network in Philanthropy. Before coming to the Foundation, Weisfeld was a senior associate with the Institute of Medicine, Division of Health Promotion and Disease Prevention, at the National Academy of Sciences in Washington, D.C. She has written numerous articles on health care and edited a quarterly health services research newsletter for The Robert Wood Johnson Foundation. She graduated from the University of Michigan with a Bachelor of Arts degree and from the University of Pittsburgh with a Master's degree in Public Health.

～～ Author Index

⚬⚬⚬ Subject Index

~~~ **Table of Contents**
To Improve Health and Health Care
1997